Damien Lewis is a number on  books have been translated into wide. For decades he worked as a war and conflict reporter for the world's major broadcasters, reporting from across Africa, South America, the Middle and Far East and winning numerous awards. His books include the World War Two classics *Churchill's Secret Warriors*, *SAS Nazi Hunters*, *Hunting the Nazi Bomb* and *SAS Ghost Patrol*. A dozen of his books have been made, or are being made, into movies or TV drama series and several have been adapted as plays for the stage. He has raised tens of thousands of pounds for charitable concerns connected with his writings.

Damien Lewis

SAS
ITALIAN JOB

THE SECRET MISSION TO STORM
A FORBIDDEN NAZI FORTRESS.

Quercus

First published in Great Britain in 2018 by Quercus.
This paperback edition published in 2019 by

Quercus Editions Ltd
Carmelite House
50 Victoria Embankment
London EC4Y 0DZ

An Hachette UK company

A CIP catalogue record for this book is available
from the British Library

PB ISBN 978 1 78747 516 8
Ebook ISBN 978 1 78747 514 4

PICTURE CREDITS

1. Credit/©: Imperial War Museum 2. Credit/©: National Archives and Records Administration.
3. Credit/©: James Selby Bennett 4. Credit/©: http://wio.ru/galgrnd/podryvnk.htm
5. Credit/©: UK Government 6. Credit/©: UK Government 7. Credit/©: Wikimedia 8. Credit/©: Imperial War
Museum 9. Credit/©: Don North, from *Inappropriate Conduct* 10. Credit/©: Don North, from *Inappropriate
Conduct* 11. Credit/©: Don North, from *Inappropriate Conduct* 12. Credit/©: Don North, from *Inappropriate
Conduct* 13. Credit/©: German Federal Archive. 14. Credit/©: Imperial War Museum. 15. Credit/©: Imperial
War Museum 16. Credit/©: German Federal Archive 17. Credit/©: Nikki Cartlidge 18. Credit/©: WWII SAS
veteran families 19. Credit/©: Lees family 20. Credit/©: National Defence Library and Archives Canada
21. Credit/©: Lees family 22. Credit/©: WWII SAS veteran families. 23. Credit/©: WWII SAS veteran families.
24. Credit/©: Wikimedia 25. Credit/©: Luke Griffiths 26. Credit/©: Lees family 27. Credit/©: Imperial War
Museum 28. Credit/©: Imperial War Museum 29. Credit/©: Wikimedia 30. Credit/©: Tara Mulvey
31. Credit/©: US Army 32. Credit/©: WWII SAS veteran families. 33. Credit/©: WWII SAS veteran families.
34. Credit/©: Imperial War Museum 35. Credit/©: Jack Mann 36. Credit/©: Blind Veterans UK

10 9 8 7 6 5 4 3

Typeset by CC Book Production
Printed and bound in Great Britain by Clays Ltd, Elcograf S.p.A.

For the fallen of the SAS and SOE as depicted in these pages

Major Neville 'Temple' Darewski DSO, SOE
Major Ross Littlejohn MC, SAS
Lieutenant James Riccomini MBE MC, SAS
Serjeant Sidney Guscott, SAS
Corporal Sammy Bolden MM, SAS
Corporal Joseph Crowley, SAS
Lance Corporal Robert Bruce (Balerdi), SAS

And for Michael Lees, SOE, who was
denied a Military Cross at war's end.

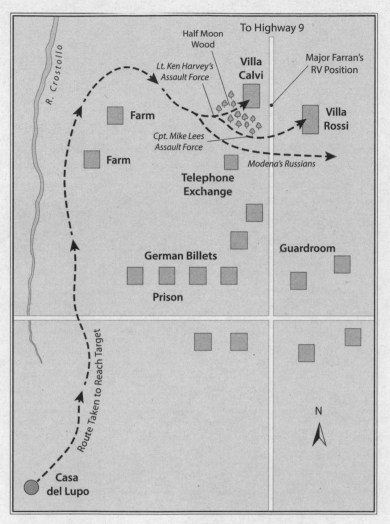

Attack on the German 14 Army Villa Headquarters
(*Adapted from Major Farran's official report on Operation Tombola*)

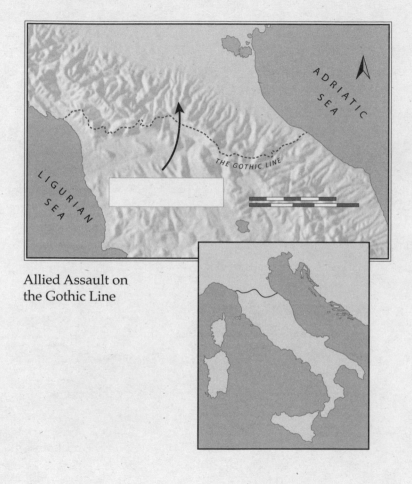

Allied Assault on
the Gothic Line

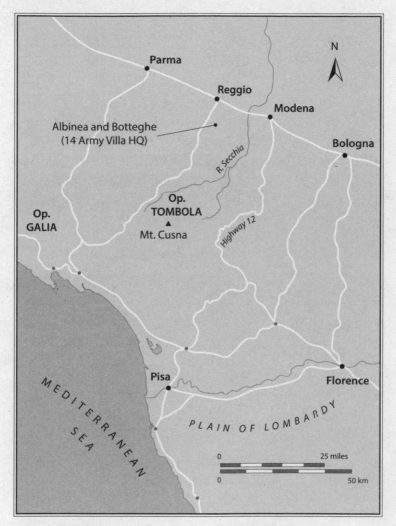

Operations Galia and Tombola – Area of Operations

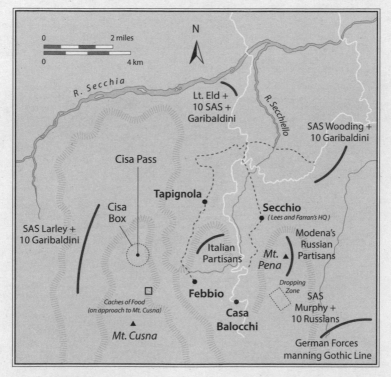

SAS and Partisans' Defence of 'Tombola Valley'

Author's Note

There are sadly few survivors from the Second World War operations depicted in these pages. Throughout the period of researching and writing this book I have endeavoured to be in contact with as many as possible, plus surviving family members of those who have passed away. If there are further witnesses to the stories told here who are inclined to come forward, please do get in touch, as I will attempt to include further recollections of the operations portrayed in this book in future editions.

The time spent by Allied servicemen and women as Special Forces volunteers was often traumatic and wreathed in layers of secrecy, and many chose to take their stories to their graves. Memories tend to differ and apparently none more so than those concerning operations behind enemy lines. The written accounts that do exist also tend to differ in their detail and timescale, and locations and chronologies are often contradictory. That being said, I have endeavoured to provide a proper sense of place, timescale and narrative to the story as depicted in these pages.

Where various accounts of a mission appear to be particularly confused, the methodology I have used to reconstruct where, when and how events took place is the 'most likely' scenario. If two or more testimonies or sources point to a particular time or place or sequence of events, I have opted to use that account as most likely. Very occasionally, I have re-created small sections of dialogue to aid the story's flow.

The above notwithstanding, any mistakes herein are entirely of my own making, and I would be happy to correct any in future editions. Likewise, while I have endeavoured to locate the copyright holders of the photos, sketches and other images and material used in this book, this has not always been straightforward or easy. Again, I would be happy to correct any mistakes in future editions.

Chapter 1

The Italian admiral was a proud man and justifiably so. Before joining the resistance he'd commanded a good proportion of the Italian fleet. Too old to operate like a partisan any more, fighting against an occupying force, his role now was to observe Allied airstrikes from this mountaintop fastness positioned well behind enemy lines, and to radio through battle damage reports to Allied headquarters.

Entirely military-like in his attitude, he had an eye for detail and for range and bearing that made him ideally suited to his task. But on this late-September evening in 1944 he'd put away his binoculars, turning his mind to entirely different and more urgent matters.

Captain Michael Lees felt the admiral's firm grip shaking him awake. He'd been drifting into sleep, hoping for a rare night uninterrupted by enemy ambushes, shellfire or raids. It was remarkable how comfortable a rickety old hayloft could prove, after so many weeks living rough behind enemy lines. It made a passable billet for himself, assorted Brits and other nationalities who'd come here to assist the Italian partisans, striking with lightning speed from the mountains.

'There's a message from Major Temple,' the admiral hissed. 'You're to get to his headquarters immediately.'

Lees fumbled for his boots, hurrying to pull them on in the

chill night air, the admiral's tone reflecting the import of the major's summons. In Major Darewski – 'Temple' was his operational cover name – Lees had discovered a fellow adventurer who hungered for action. After parachuting into the unknown and executing a tortuous and perilous route to get here, Lees was keen to lead the kind of guerrilla operations for which Major Temple was famed.

Lacing up his boots and pulling on a jacket, he set off at a run. The path ahead glistened blue-white in the moonlight, the night beautifully starlit and crystal clear. As his feet pounded upon the rough, stony ground, Lees felt the excitement rising within him. He wondered what might lie behind the major's summons. It was either a juicy sabotage mission, or perhaps the Germans were launching a sweep through the valley, in an attempt to encircle the partisans, in which case they would need to act swiftly to organise their defences.

Such efforts as this – to raise, train and arm the Italian partisans for war – were largely at the behest of Winston Churchill. The Allied invasion of Italy in the summer of 1943 had been at Churchill's urging, designed to drive a dagger into the 'soft underbelly of Europe'. By doing so, Britain's wartime leader intended to strike at Nazi Germany via Italy, so splitting the enemy's defences in the run-up to the D-Day landings. Initially the proposal had met with fierce opposition, especially from the Americans. By way of response Churchill had sketched out a picture of a crocodile, pointing out how it was just as good to strike at the belly as the snout.

Eventually the Americans had been convinced that hitting Europe's 'soft underbelly' was the right thing to do. Yet despite early successes in southern Italy, the Italian campaign had proven anything but 'soft'. Hitler had little intention of leaving the back door to Europe open. He'd rushed reinforcements into the country, the Germans fighting a series of die-hard battles, first under the command of General Erwin Rommel, and then under another of Hitler's favourites, Field Marshal Albert Kesselring.

Come the approach of winter, the Allied advance had stalled on the Gothic Line, a string of formidable defences – thousands of machine-gun bunkers, concrete gun emplacements, deep tunnels, minefields and razor wire – stretching from coast to coast across northern Italy's Apennine mountains. The forces manning the Gothic Line were some of Germany's finest. They included the 1st and 4th Parachute Divisions, arguably some of the best troops in the Reich, plus two *Panzergrenadier* – mechanised infantry – divisions equipped with heavy armour.

All of Italy south of the Gothic Line had been seized in fearsome fighting by the Allies. But territory to the north of the line remained in enemy hands, excepting pockets of remote, mountainous territory held by the Italian resistance – Major Temple's mission being one such example. At Churchill's urging, the partisans were being armed and trained to rise up in the enemy's rear, to help achieve a decisive breakthrough. Lees and Temple's operation, headquartered towards the western end of the Apennines and just to the rear of the Gothic Line, was intended to strike hard at enemy lines of supply and communications.

Whatever tonight's mission, Lees felt an immense sense of respect and camaraderie for Major Temple, who'd already won a DSO (Distinguished Service Order) in the war. Formerly an officer with airborne forces, but now serving as an agent with the Special Operations Executive (SOE) – Churchill's shadowy 'Ministry for Ungentlemanly Warfare' – Lees was second-in-command here, and in Major Temple he believed he had found a real kindred spirit.

On his earliest operations with the SOE, Lees had earned the nickname 'Mickey Mouse'. It was Yugoslav guerrillas who had coined the name, Mickey Mouse being the only 'Michael' they had ever heard of. But there had been nothing Mickey Mouse about the long months Lees had spent soldiering with them: he'd led dozens of dramatic raids on enemy railway tracks, blowing trains laden with war materiel to smithereens.

When told to cease offensive operations with the Yugoslav guerrillas, Lees had decided to interpret his orders rather literally: he'd stopped working with the resistance, launching a string of solo sabotage missions instead, ones of breathtaking – some might argue suicidal – daring. In doing so he'd earned a somewhat more apposite nickname – Michael 'Wild Man' Lees. His linking up with Major Temple promised fireworks and heroics in equal measure.

With delicious irony, Temple's mission had been codenamed Operation Flap. In truth, no one was inclined to 'get a flap on' with Temple – or Lees – in command. At thirty years of age, Major Neville Lawrence Darewski was comparatively old for an SOE operative. (By contrast, Lees was still in his early twenties.) The son of Polish-born Herman Darewski, a famous music hall musician of the time, and the English actress Madge Temple, it was from her that Darewski had coined his *nom de guerre*.

Major Temple had been operating behind the lines for months now. He'd parachuted in to link up with the partisans prior to Italy's signing the 3 September 1943 Armistice of Cassibile, in which the Italian people had renounced their deal with the devil – the alliance with Nazi Germany and Japan, forming the Axis Powers – surrendering to the Allies.

The signing of the Armistice was a watershed moment, as far as Temple was concerned. Prior to that, he'd reported to SOE headquarters on what a perilous existence he'd been forced to lead with the partisans. It was a 'cloak-and-dagger affair, only moving at night . . . minimum of smoke from fires, kit always ready for immediate move . . . I covered some one thousand miles on foot carrying my kit and arms . . . We had to cross rivers, roads and railways all held by the Germans . . . in small, very mobile parties . . .'

Come the Armistice, all that had changed. Temple had urged his partisans to seize the moment and embrace the spirit of resistance. Taking advantage of the ensuing confusion, he'd led his band of fighters to strike at a major airbase lying just to the rear of the Gothic Line, in a daring mission that had proven spectacularly successful.

'We surrounded the airfield and held it for long enough to destroy eighty-nine Italian planes on the ground, and all the hangars and buildings,' Temple had reported. Then with characteristic flair: 'We flew away one CR.42 to start the Partisan Air Force . . .'

In destroying those dozens of enemy warplanes, Temple's operation was on a par with some of the most successful raids of the war. The lone CR.42 *Falco* – Falcon – that his force had liberated was a biplane fighter widely used by the Italian air force. Despite its seemingly archaic design, it had scored an enviable kill ratio on many fronts due to its robustness and manoeuvrability.

In the aftermath of the raid, Temple's forces had been hunted remorselessly by the German military using armour, artillery and dive bombers. The lone CR.42 *Falco* that they'd 'liberated' was blown up by a tank. Temple responded in textbook fashion: 'We withdrew from direct offensive tactics and went back to guerrilla warfare.' While the enemy held the main population centres, his bands of partisans began to tighten their grip on the remoter villages and hills.

'Outside the perimeter of the towns the Germans put up notices: BEWARE, YOU ARE NOW ENTERING BANDIT TER-RITORY,' Temple reported of the time. He sent out his men at night to turn the signs around, so that 'BANDIT TERRITORY' became the German-held towns. 'The Hun got very annoyed and threatened the direst of penalties to anyone caught doing this,' Temple pointed out, which only served to encourage him.

By late September 1944, Major Temple was master of all that he surveyed. Set at an altitude of some 3,000 feet, his headquarters lay in a mountain hut nicknamed 'The Farm'. It boasted views across the plains to Turin – once Italy's capital, and a major business hub – and the Alps beyond. On a clear day the glistening peaks of Mont Blanc and the Matterhorn were visible. On a flat patch of ground several thousand feet higher Temple had established his dropping zone (DZ), into which the Allies were flying loads of kit, explosives and weaponry.

From their Apennine valley fortress Temple's 500-strong band of partisans launched daring raids, using captured vehicles to execute fast hit-and-run strikes. As Mike Lees was about to learn, Temple's night-time summons was the result of one such recent mission.

After thirty minutes dashing through the moonlit landscape, Lees arrived at The Farm. Typically, he was in standard British battledress. By contrast, Major Temple cut a very different kind of a figure. A big part of Temple's remit here was intelligence-gathering, and he'd just paid a clandestine visit to Turin disguised as a local. Such derring-do was all part of a normal day's work as far as Temple was concerned. With his dark looks plus his tanned and weather-beaten features, he could easily pass as a local.

'Dressed as he was,' Lees remarked of Temple that evening, 'he could never have been recognised as an Englishman.'

At well over six foot and with a broad, rugby-player's physique, Lees towered over most of his contemporaries. Blessed with no-nonsense, honest looks, he was a man born and bred for plain-speaking action, as opposed to subterfuge. Hailing from a family with a long history of soldiering, he had cousins and even a sister serving with elite forces in various theatres of the war.

Temple and Lees had operated together for little more than three weeks here, and for much of that time Temple had been away in Turin on clandestine business. It was precious little time to really get to know each other. Temple viewed Lees as a hard and a tough operator, but what he was about to propose would test any man's resolve. It would be the measure of Lees as to whether he accepted the mission. No man could be ordered to do as Temple intended, especially as all in SOE were volunteers.

'Sorry to drag you out at this time of night,' Temple began, 'but we've got an important decision to make.'

As he spoke, he gestured at the two – presumably Italian – civilians who were with him. Lees had never laid eyes on either of them. They were older, better dressed and somehow more distinguished looking than your average partisan. Lees closed the door firmly behind him, sensing that tonight's business was especially sensitive. Temple introduced the two strangers, using their war names only.

'Salvi' and 'Piva' hailed from Turin, he explained, and they were senior members of the Italian resistance. They had crucial intelligence that they somehow needed to get into Allied commanders' hands. 'This information from Turin is red hot . . . they also know a lot about enemy dispositions and weaknesses . . . They've volunteered to go to southern Italy if we can get them out.'

'How d'you intend to do that?' Lees queried. 'By air?'

The partisans were busy building an airstrip so Allied cargo planes could land with supplies, but Lees didn't think it was going to be ready for some time.

Temple waved a hand dismissively. 'We can't wait for that . . . They'll have to walk out through the lines.' He paused. 'Salvi and Piva are damned important, and I don't want them falling by the wayside. It's going to prove a tricky journey, especially as there are no guides who've been through before, and the front is always changing.' Temple gazed at Lees, searchingly. 'I need someone who knows the ropes to command the party.'

By now Lees realised what was afoot. 'Would you like me to go?' he ventured.

Someone had to say it, even though it would mean attempting to cross the formidable defences of the Gothic Line. It had never occurred to him that this might be the kind of mission he would be offered. Indeed, he had been looking forward to waging war with the partisans, making life a living hell for the enemy until all of Italy was liberated from Nazi control.

As if sensing what was on Lees' mind, Temple began outlining exactly what he intended, stressing just how quickly Lees could return. 'You get the party through to France – if you're with them they won't get held up by security. Beg a plane to take you all to southern Italy, report on everything we've been doing to the chaps at base and chivvy them up to send more supplies. Then come back again, dropping with the first sortie.'

That was more like it, as far as Lees was concerned. 'All right, I think it's an excellent idea,' he agreed, his spirits brightening.

He had another, personal reason for accepting the mission. Shortly before deploying Lees had married Gwendoline Johnson, who was serving with the First Aid Nursing Yeomanry – the FANYs – in Italy. To a large degree the FANYs provided cover for women who were serving as SOE agents. He and 'Gwen' had met during a time when Lees had been agitating to join Temple's mission and refusing to take the leave to which he was entitled, post-Yugoslavia. That had only served to fuel his 'wild man' reputation, but Gwen hadn't seemed to mind.

Indeed, as she was serving as an assistant to one of SOE's key planners in Italy, she began quietly lobbying for her sweetheart to land a mission with Temple, despite the fact that it would take him behind the lines once more. If he took up Temple's present proposal, Lees figured he could catch a few days in his wife's delightful company, before flying back to rejoin the partisans.

'Just make sure you come back as soon as you can,' Temple reminded him.

'Don't worry,' Lees replied, 'I want to be in at the kill. So, when do we start?'

'How does tomorrow morning sound?'

All being well, Lees would set out to cross the lines on 28 September 1944.

For Temple, Lees was the only man able to execute such a hazardous mission. In addition to the two Italian resistance leaders, he would be leading a group of fourteen, including escaped prisoners of war and downed US airmen. Brits, Americans, Australians, French and Italians, his was a distinctly motley escape party, many of whom had little military training of the type required to sneak through enemy territory. It would take superlative leadership skills, immense daring and real single-minded tenacity to shepherd such a disparate party to safety.

Fortunately, Lees had such attributes in abundance. Following the long months that he'd spent in Yugoslavia, none other than Major General Colin McVean Gubbins – known simply as 'M' and the head of SOE – had poured lavish praise on the young Lees, then only twenty-one years of age. 'An enthusiastic and reliable officer. Had a difficult area in southern Serbia and did all he could to carry out operations there against the Axis . . . most successfully maintained good relations between the Mission and Jugoslav forces . . . has plenty of go and initiative.'

Scion of a titled, landed family hailing from Lytchett Minster, a village in deepest rural Dorset, Lees' means of recruitment into the SOE had been highly unconventional. In 1943 he'd been kicking his heels in Cairo, lamenting the lack of action he seemed to be getting with regular forces, when he'd ended up in Shepherd's Bar, one of the city's more popular drinking dens. He'd got talking to an intriguing individual who'd let slip that he served with 'the Tweed Cap Boys'. Upon learning that this mysterious force was sending in lone operators to Europe charged to wage war no-holds-barred, Lees desperately wanted in.

He'd never for one moment imagined there might be scope for himself to operate deep inside enemy-occupied Europe. It was a tantalising proposition. He proceeded to get that 'Tweed Cap Boy' as drunk as possible, all the while pumping him for information. It turned out that the route into the SOE was somewhat convoluted. It was hardly possible to advertise for volunteers to join a secret service that was not supposed to exist: you could only be recruited at the personal behest of someone already in.

As Lees wasn't personally known to any of this exclusive club, he decided to manufacture a 'recommendation' from his new Shepherd's Bar acquaintance. Learning that he was just about to take several weeks' leave, a day or so later Lees brazenly walked into the SOE'S Cairo office, claiming to be there at the personal behest of a 'schoolboy chum' – in truth, the man he'd met in the Cairo bar. He even had a freshly-forged letter to back up his claims.

To those charged to investigate Lees' story, it appeared to have merit. He hailed from the right kind of background. He'd been educated at Ampleforth – the Roman Catholic boarding school known as the 'Catholic Eton', of which David Stirling, the founder of the SAS, was a fellow alumnus – plus the Lees family was steeped in military tradition. Grandson of Sir Elliott Lees, the First Baronet of Lytchett Minster, Michael's father, Bernard Percy Turnbull Lees, had served with distinction in the Queen's Own Dorset Yeomanry during the First World War, winning a Military Cross (MC).

Bernard Lees had died in a shooting accident when Michael was just two years old, so he had never got to know his father. After the tragic loss, Michael had grown very close to his cousin James Lees – direct heir to the baronetcy – hunting, fishing and riding together in the Dorset countryside. They'd become inseparable, to the extent that James's father had become an honorary guardian to Michael. Bereft of a father and brought up by his widowed mother and elder sister, Dolores, Lees was effectively the man of the house and felt fiercely protective over all. When he was just twelve, he caught an older boy trying to kiss his sister. He stepped forward and punched the boy firmly on the chin.

Lees hungered for more male and martial company, which was largely why at age seventeen he'd joined the Queen's Own Dorset Yeomanry, the regiment that his father and grandfather had served in, before volunteering for airborne forces at the outbreak of war and being posted to India and Egypt.

Michael's sister Dolores would serve as a nurse with both the French Army and later the French resistance (the Maquis), with whom she would earn the Croix de Guerre twice – once for walking into a minefield to rescue a wounded comrade. Michael Lees' cousin, James, was also about to start serving on special operations. At the very moment that Michael was trying to blag his way into the SOE in Cairo, James was volunteering for the Special Boat Service (SBS), the sister regiment to the SAS, which specialised in daring seaborne sorties.

The Lees family pile, the grand edifice of South Lytchett Manor, had been turned over to war use, the grounds harbouring American tanks and the house itself becoming war offices. Likewise, during the First World War the Manor had served the war effort, being transformed into a hospital for those evacuated from the battlefields of France. In short, the Lees family was steeped in the kind of special duty warfare of which Churchill would be proud, but that didn't earn anyone an automatic right to join an outfit like the Tweed Cap Boys.

With Lees' 'sponsor' away on leave, he performed a sterling act at the SOE's Cairo office. After several robust cross examinations, he'd bluffed his way in. His SOE recruitment file listed Lees' 'Hobbies and Sporting Interests: Riding, shooting, running, rugby football, fishing, skiing, driving, sailing.' His subsequent SOE training courses included: 'April '43, Para Military. May '43, "Cloak & Dagger". July '44, Lysander – Above Average.' (The

Westland Lysander – nicknamed the 'Lissie' – was a light aircraft used for inserting lone SOE agents into enemy-occupied lands.)

At grand country mansions scattered across Britain the SOE had established their Special Training Schools – teaching the dark arts of killing, sabotage, espionage, deception and more. In what became known as their 'school for mayhem and murder', at the apparently genteel Ashdon Manor, in Hertfordshire, recruits were trained to fight 'without a tremor of apprehension, to hurt, maul, injure or kill with ease.' Instructors taught killing by silent strangulation, how to disable with a powerful blow by boot or fist to key organs, and how to wield a pistol fast and deadly, shooting from the hip. In a pistol duel, the first on the draw was almost always the winner, and by firing from the hip the shooter was very likely to get the drop on his or her opponent.

One such school, in Borehamwood, was devoted entirely to the arts of camouflage and subterfuge in all its forms. Part of its remit was to furnish agents with proper clothing, documents and accoutrements, before they were dropped into occupied Europe. Whenever the genuine article wasn't available, the SOE's forgery factory would rustle up a convincing copy. At MD1, an SOE facility nicknamed 'Churchill's Toyshop', boffins and inventors worked on perfecting the most secretive and innovative forms of weaponry. These included booby-trapped rats and animal droppings, plus exploding 'coal' – the latter to be slipped into the fuel supply of an enemy train, so blowing up the steam engines.

After passing through various such training schools, Lees was ready to pursue Churchill's 1940 edict – issued during Britain's darkest hour, following Dunkirk and the surrender of France – 'to set Europe ablaze'. The formation of the SOE – after the Army, Navy and Air Force, the 'fourth armed service' – was in response to such calls. Gubbins defined the SOE's early remit as being 'paramilitary and irregular warfare, the sabotaging and subversion of our enemies by every possible means . . . a free-for-all . . . with no holds barred. Germany was engaged in total war . . . and total war is a very cruel business indeed.'

The SOE was a secret service whose very existence was deniable. The normal rules of war would not apply. In the SOE's version of total war, the unethical and illegal were to be commonplace. Agents were expected to lie, deceive, bribe, blackmail, and where necessary, assassinate and kill. If captured, an agent would be disowned by his or her government, and torture and execution would doubtless follow. Before deploying on his first mission, Lees, like all agents, had been given 'communion' – a suicide pill that he could take if he feared he was about to break under torture.

The SOE recruited from a broad church. Its early volunteers included actors, professional burglars, peers of the realm, a rubber-goods salesman, several baronets, a pimp, prostitutes, jockeys, art experts and bankers. They shared certain traits in common: robust independence of mind and contempt for regular hierarchies.

Gubbins exhorted those early recruits to execute 'sabotage, ambushes behind enemy lines, and calling out secret armies into open warfare'. By the autumn of 1944, the SOE'S Italian operations had become deeply personal for 'M'. In the spring of that year, his son Michael had been killed in Italy on SOE business. On 6 February he was hit by a German shell while operating behind the lines. Gubbins had received the news of his son's death via telegram, with its 'killed in action' message, and a hand-scribbled expression of 'deepest sympathy'. He had been consumed by grief and remorse.

All the more important, therefore, that the SOE's Italian operations were to succeed, and to be *seen* to succeed. One of the SOE's most secretive remits had become the spreading of 'black' and 'white' propaganda. The latter involved placing positive stories about the fortunes of the Allies in the press, and negative ones about the Axis powers, while the former spread disinformation among enemy ranks. There was another top-secret priority behind Michael Lees' Italian mission: it was to further the SOE's 'white propaganda' role.

When Lees had parachuted in to join Temple, in August 1944, he'd brought with him two highly unusual individuals: South African war artist Geoffrey Long, and Canadian war reporter Paul Morton. Of the two, Morton, a globetrotting newspaper man, was perhaps the more controversial. He was the first reporter ever embedded with a behind-the-lines SOE mission, and few would follow.

That summer, Churchill had decided that the Italian partisans deserved a far higher profile, both to encourage them in their operations and to spur Allied forces to train and arm them properly. A former war reporter himself, Churchill believed wholeheartedly in the need to win the 'information war'. Borrowing a phrase from Stalin, he believed that 'in wartime, the truth is so precious she should be attended by a bodyguard of lies.'

The Political Warfare Executive (PWE) was the arm of the SOE established to ensure that the information war would be won. In the summer of 1944, Paul Morton had been based in Italy, fearing the real war was passing him by. Desperate for a scoop, when the Political Warfare Executive approached him with their offer – that he should join Captain Lees to report from behind the lines – Morton jumped at the chance.

Morton's bona fides were exhaustively checked. Dated 4 July, his SOE 'Trace and Card' – his vetting form – recorded that he'd spent 'Ten Years with the Toronto Daily Star', and was a 'War Correspondent accredited to Canadian forces'. It noted that his brother, David Morton, was 'possibly in enemy hands (reported missing two months ago over North Sea)'. Morton had personal reasons to hate the enemy, and he was a seasoned reporter with one of Canada's most respected publications. On paper, he was the ideal recruit.

By 6 July Morton had been signed up as an 'attached corre-spondent' with 'Maryland', the codename for the SOE in Italy. Shortly thereafter he was issued with his SOE 'Operational Instruction'. It read: 'To provide the Press an account of patriot activities and sabotage exploits . . . You will be dropped to [Oper-ation] FLAP . . . in the September moon period . . . On arrival you will ask for Major TEMPLE and will put yourself under his command.'

Morton was given the honorary rank of Captain, armed and expected to fight if the need arose. His reporting was to be syndi-cated – distributed – to all Allied press outlets, promising a series of global scoops. It was heady stuff. Six weeks after parachuting in with Lees, Morton had prepared a series of scintillating articles, describing in vivid tones the heroic exploits of the partisans – including one episode in which they'd surrounded enemy forces holed up in a church, and wiped them out to the last man.

He'd given his first article the dramatic headline, 'I LIVE WITH PATRIOTS IN NAZI LINES – MORTON'. In short, Morton was poised to fire a propaganda broadside, showcasing the daring and panache of the Italian resistance. Geoffrey Long, the war artist, had drawn a series of brilliant sketches to illustrate, including one of the partisans scavenging boots and explosives from the enemy dead, and portraits of the key Allied players – Morton, Temple and Lees included.

But Morton and Long's stories and images – their white propaganda – would only get to hit the press if Lees managed to shepherd them through the lines, for they were to join his escape party.

It was dawn on 29 September when the group formed up. They'd been delayed for twenty-four hours by the late arrival of some. As Lees surveyed his men, he was assailed by doubts as to whether they really could complete such an unproven route passing through such formidable defences. Temple sought to calm his fears. If it reached the stage where Lees felt it necessary, he was to drop all but the essential members.

Even so, Lees decided that he really did need a trusted pair of hands to share the load. Glaswegian William McClelland was six-foot-six tall and about as broad in the shoulder, dwarfing even Lees. His craggy, bearded features, snaggle-toothed grin and dress – shorts, ski boots, faded battledress tunic adorned with the Scots Guards insignia, and slung Sten gun – lent him a decidedly piratical air. It was absolutely fitting.

Captured by Rommel's Afrika Korps when serving in North Africa, Private McClelland had escaped from an Italian prisoner of war (POW) camp and fled into the mountains, linking up with the partisans. Over the past year he'd hijacked vehicles, kidnapped their occupants and raided Nazi cellars. His favourite occupation was ambushing German staff cars, finishing off the officers, then rifling the pockets of the dead. When one partisan band had run short of funds, he'd done the obvious thing and organised a bank robbery.

In short, McClelland was a freelance raider who owed no particular allegiance to any one partisan unit. He and Lees had hit it off immediately. 'He was a bandit, not a partisan,' Lees remarked of McClelland. 'Whatever his intentions, he was doing far more for the war effort than he could have done serving as an ordinary private . . . One William in the mountains was an incomparable asset, but thirty Williams in barracks would provide a problem with which I should hate to be faced . . .'

The other redoubtable operator Lees would have liked to join his party was Corporal Albert 'Bert' Farrimond, a dour Lancashire coal miner in civilian life, who'd proved as constant and unyielding as the moors in recent weeks. Hailing from Standish, near Wigan, Farrimond was a keen poacher who loved the wild freedom of the mountains. He and Lees had formed a special bond, but as Farrimond was Major Temple's radio operator – his vital link to SOE's Maryland headquarters – he was one man that was unable to join Lees.

His party thus assembled, it only left to bid farewell.

Temple offered a hand. 'Goodbye, old cock, and good luck. We'll expect you back in a couple of weeks.'

Little did Lees realise this was the last time he would ever see the man alive.

Lees turned away, taking a well-trodden bridleway that climbed into the hills. He'd opted to travel light, urging his party to do likewise. He was carrying only his trusty Sten gun, with the detachable wooden pistol-grip that he favoured, plus ammunition and a rolled blanket. The days were still relatively hot, so he wore shorts and a khaki shirt. The skies above were a cloudless blue and they'd rely on good weather to see them through.

At the head of the valley they paused by a goat herd, to refresh themselves with milk. Before them the path rose to a steep ridge several miles away. They were making for a pass set at some 6,000 feet, after which they'd descend to a mountain village on the far side. But as Lees gazed at the heights, they appeared to be wreathed in swirling cloud. It looked ominous: he knew how quickly the weather could turn in the mountains. He urged everyone on.

As they climbed towards the pass the sky overhead took on a dull grey hue and the first snow began to fall. The wind picked up, whipping icy flakes against Lees' bare legs, forming stiff little icicles. He cursed the fact that they had set out so ill-prepared and chiefly at his urging. It wasn't long before they had their first casualty. Long, the war artist, took a fall on the icy ground, bruising his spine. His pack and weaponry had to be passed to one of the guides, for he was in some pain.

Lees closed the column up, so they would not lose sight of each other in the gathering storm. But Long was soon at the very back, finding it difficult to keep moving. They reached a perilous section of terrain that required the use of both hands and feet to scale it. Lees had scrambled halfway up, when he heard the shrill blast of a whistle from behind, which normally signalled that someone was in trouble.

Holding onto a rocky outcrop, he craned his neck to see through the swirling snow. He counted heads: four were missing. Among their number were Long and Morton, the two press men.

Telling the guides to climb to a ledge one hundred feet above, Lees doubled back. It wasn't long before he found the errant four. They were slumped on a rock beside the path, smoking.

'What the devil are you doing here?' he demanded. 'No halt has been called.'

'Geoffrey's hurt,' Morton countered. 'I gave the order to stop.'

'I know,' Lees fired back, 'but you'll keep going 'til I order otherwise.'

Morton bristled. 'I'm an honorary captain, and as such I will not place myself under your command.'

Lees drew himself to his full height. 'I don't give a damn who you are or what you write. While you're with my party you'll do as you're told. So make your mind up: d'you want to continue, or go back to Temple?'

Morton glared at Lees, but the other three had already capitulated. Long and his two companions began to struggle onwards. Lees was deadly serious. On a mission such as this, he needed absolute clarity of command. If he and Morton were to pull in opposite directions, one or other party might get lost in the snows or blunder into enemy positions. Muttering darkly, Morton levered himself to his feet, before turning into the storm's icy blast. Lees felt a flood of relief. As he well knew, time was set against them now.

If they didn't reach the pass before the snow began to drift they were as good as finished.

Chapter 2

Major Roy Farran was already a legend within SAS circles, but even by his own standards this morning's mission was something of a stretch. During August and September 1944 he'd led a column of jeeps – the SAS's C Squadron – in a mission code-named Operation Wallace, breaking out from the bulge of terrain seized in the D-Day landings and pushing two hundred miles behind enemy lines.

His orders were simplicity itself: he and his men were to cause chaos and havoc behind the German front in north-eastern France, to give the impression that Allied forces had broken through and spreading panic through the enemy ranks. Hence today's daring assault on the German garrison headquarters, situated in the ancient town of Châtillon-sur-Seine, lying 250 kilometres east of Paris, a town graced with Roman-era cobbled streets and buildings.

The plans for the dawn assault had been hatched with Colonel Claude, the leader of the local Maquis – the French resistance – the previous evening, over a sumptuous dinner complemented by several bottles of fine wine. Late into the proceedings and partly inspired by Dutch courage, Farran had proposed they hit Châtillon in an all-out attack, Maquis and SAS united, and while the change of garrison was in full swing.

One hundred and fifty enemy troops were based at the

centuries-old Château du Maréchal Marmont, situated on a low hill surrounded by fine parkland. Built in the 1700s by the French General Auguste Frédéric Louis Viesse de Marmont, a native of the town, the chateau had been burned to the ground and rebuilt some seventy years earlier. Farran sensed that now was the time to have another go at wrecking the place, or at least killing its occupants.

Equipped with twenty army trucks, the German garrison housed at the chateau was about to be relieved by a unit of *Panzergrenadiers*, a mechanised infantry force riding in specialist combat vehicles, including *Sonderkraftfahrzeug* 251 half-track troop carriers. The previous day Farran and Captain Grant Hibbert – his second-in-command – had carried out a recce. After driving into town in their SAS jeep, Farran had covered Hibbert as he'd vaulted over the chateau's perimeter wall and checked out the trucks in the courtyard.

The alarm having been raised, the two SAS commanders had high tailed it out of there, but not before the recce had served its purpose. The intelligence they'd been given had proved correct: the column of trucks was laden with equipment for a garrison poised to move. One German unit was about to be replaced by another at the chateau, and amid the confusion of that change-over Farran sensed they could seize the advantage.

Colonel Claude had expressed suitable enthusiasm for Farran's plan, and toasts had been drunk long into the night. The colonel had pledged to provide five hundred local fighters, to match Farran's sixty SAS spread across a dozen-odd jeeps. The vehicles' raw firepower helped compensate for the SAS's paucity in numbers. Each Willys Jeep boasted two pivot-mounted weapons, often a heavier Browning machine gun matched with the rapid-firing Vickers K, invariably mounted in pairs. As such, they could put down a devastating field of fire.

Farran's intention was to keep it simple for this morning's attack. His men would seize the main junction on the outskirts of town, on the road leading south to the city of Dijon. Leaving some jeeps to hold that vital position – through which the German vehicles carrying the incoming garrison would have to pass – Farran would lead a party further into town, armed with mortars and Bren light machine guns. They would sneak up to the chateau on foot, the first round fired by the mortar signalling the all-out assault.

Setting out at 0630 hours from their deep woodland hideout, the column of SAS jeeps nosed through scenery typical of the region – small green fields, thick hedges and red-tiled cottages, set amid gently rolling, wooded hills. Farran kept the convoy's speed at a steady crawl. The roads were dry and earthy from the long summer months, and he needed to avoid throwing up a tell-tale dust cloud, which might reveal their position to any watching enemy.

The Châtillon road junction was taken without a shot being fired. Farran left Lieutenant 'Big' Jim Mackie – his long-standing right-hand man, who commanded his lead 'scout' vehicle – in charge of the roadblock, while he led the main force of forty men riding in nine jeeps further into town. Ominously, there was still no sign of Colonel Claude's Maquis, but Farran put that down to a delayed start due to the previous night's carousing.

At each road junction he left a jeep and a handful of men, so securing their route of retreat. They reached the main square seemingly without having been detected, cutting telephone lines as they went. Up ahead lay the chateau. It was the obvious place to billet a garrison: grandiose and thick-walled, boasting turrets, spires and parapets, it was a veritable fortress.

Of course, the beautiful grounds and approach would be guarded by enemy sentries, but that was where the mortar would come into its own. Farran intended to strike from a distance and by utter surprise, lobbing in as many rounds as possible to spread chaos among a garrison who would be in the midst of loading up in preparation for the move.

At seven sharp the mortar barrage began. By now Farran's men were experts in quick-fire shoot-n'-scoot tactics. Within minutes several dozen of the 3-inch shells had pounded into the chateau's courtyard, their high-explosive charges sending a swathe of razor-sharp shrapnel tearing through the air and ripping into the column of trucks. Hit by utter surprise, this was some awakening for the garrison. Chaos ensued as Farran ordered his Bren-gunners to open fire, raking the chateau's defenders with savage bursts.

The narrow, twisting streets of the town echoed with the deafening noise of battle – the rattle of the Brens, the rasp of the Vickers, the howl of rounds ricocheting off walls, and behind it all the deeper bass thud of the mortars, as one-by-one the high explosive shells hammered into the chateau's grounds. Towards his rear, Farran sensed the grunt of powerful diesel engines. Sure enough and bang on cue, the column of thirty vehicles was approaching from the south, bearing the *Panzergrenadier* relief column.

At this moment, Farran's sixty-strong force was outnumbered some five-to-one by the enemy, and it was high time that Colonel Claude's Maquis put in an appearance. But still there was no sign of them. Taking his jeep, Farran raced back towards the crossroads, where he'd left the redoubtable Big Jim Mackie in control. It was vital to stop that *Panzergrenadier* column from linking up with the forces presently under siege at the chateau.

As Farran neared the junction, he sensed there was little need for worry: typically, Lieutenant Mackie had it all under control. He'd positioned his own jeep to form the core of the roadblock, with a second set to one side. Those manning the guns allowed the enemy column to approach to within twenty yards, before opening up with an utterly devastating broadside. Within seconds, a whirlwind of fire had torn into the leading vehicles, two of which happened to be laden with stores. Moments later fuel and ammunition detonated in a sea of flame, exploding rounds tearing into the vehicles further along the column.

With the telephone lines cut, the *Panzergrenadiers* had been taken by total surprise. They'd driven into town unawares, presuming the SAS jeeps had to constitute some kind of a friendly checkpoint. It was an easy-enough mistake to have made: who would ever have expected to encounter an enemy roadblock this far behind their own front line?

'The first five trucks, two of which were loaded with ammunition, were brewed up and caused a great firework display,' was how the SAS operational report described the ambush. The jeeps hammered in fire, raking the column from either side. 'Those added to the fire, which the Germans returned, and for some time the fierce engagement continued . . . Fierce street fighting developed . . .'

Farran grabbed a Bren and, balancing it on a convenient wall, he began to hose down the trucks to the rear of the *Panzergrenadier* column. He watched as a German motorcycle-and-sidecar combination veered across the road and toppled over a bridge, plummeting into the river below. As Farran pumped in bursts of tracer rounds – following the red streak of the bullets to their targets – he saw figures bailing out of vehicles at the rear of the stalled column.

Machine guns opened up from the direction of the besieged convoy and mortars crashed down onto the streets. One of Farran's men collapsed, felled by a shot to the head. A brave French civilian dashed out and dragged his bloodied form into the shelter of a doorway. A pretty, dark-haired woman wearing a dashing red dress leaned out of an upper floor window, defiantly giving the 'V' for Victory sign. To Farran, that woman's smile and her poise offered the perfect riposte to the bursts of fire now tearing down the streets.

A runner approached from the direction of the chateau. He brought word that a force of Germans had broken out of the grounds and were fighting their way towards Farran's position. One SAS jeep had been hit, in a situation that was fast-moving and confused. The enemy had even begun to mortar their own side, mistaking the fire from the chateau as being that of the mystery Allied attack force.

Even so, Farran's men were going to be hard-pressed to defend their positions. He sent a jeep to reinforce those at the chateau, with orders that they should hold firm. His priority was to decimate what was left of the *Panzergrenadier* column, and to do that they had to stop the two forces uniting. At the same time his chief concern was becoming the absent Maquis. Where on earth was Colonel Claude and the five hundred fighters that he had promised?

As the battle intensified, Farran sensed his SAS squadron was in danger of becoming trapped – sandwiched between the Germans advancing from the chateau, and the *Panzergrenadiers* now mustering fierce resistance. He and his men had been embroiled in fierce combat for approaching two hours, and the Maquis were nowhere to be seen. Accordingly, he decided it was time for the 'scoot' period of the assault to be enacted.

With a gallant wave to the girl in the red frock – Farran was very much a charmer and a ladies' man – he strode into the centre of the road and fired two flares from a Very pistol. They looped a fiery arc through the sky, scorching a fierce scarlet across the battle-torn town – two red flares being the signal to withdraw.

As Farran and Captain Hibbert led the force in a helter-skelter retreat they finally ran into the vanguard of the Maquis, mustering on the outskirts of town. Two hours late and less than an eighth of the number that Colonel Claude had promised, at least they were here. The Maquis seemed desperate for a slice of that morning's action, so Farran and Hibbert decided they would lead a second push into Châtillon.

This time their numbers would be swollen to one hundred and twenty fighters, but the element of surprise was entirely gone. Even so, Farran was banking on the enemy mistaking his larger force for the vanguard of General Patton's 3rd Army, those American troops and armour that had spearhead the thrust east through France. If that happened, the entire enemy force – those at the chateau and the *Panzergrenadiers* – might break and run.

It was an audacious gamble, but hardly the first by this veteran SAS commander. Already one of the most highly decorated soldiers of the war, Farran would earn a DSO, MC and two bars (three MCs) during the war, among many other decorations. Of Irish descent, he was known to all as Major Patrick McGinty, after an irreverent and somewhat ribald Irish ballad entitled 'Paddy McGinty's Goat'.

Like many a former prisoner of war – Farran had escaped German captivity in 1941 – he'd adopted a nom de guerre, knowing that the Germans kept detailed records of all POWs. Major Patrick McGinty had become Farran's official war name, and indeed his DSO was issued in that name. The ballad about the goat gives something of a sense of Farran's nature: colourful, distinctly Irish, rebellious, unconventional, contemptuous of mindless bureaucracy and decidedly merciless towards his enemies.

> *Mr Patrick McGinty, an Irishman of note,*
> *Fell into a fortune and brought himself a goat.*
> *Says he, 'Sure, of goat's milk I'm goin' to have me fill.'*
> *But when he bought the nanny home he found it was a bill.*

The goat goes on to woo several of the young beauties in the Irish village of Killaloe, before it got shipped off to France as a mascot for the Irish Guards regiment in the Great War, whereupon it decided to fight, the enemy ranks breaking before its charge:

> *The Germans retreated, hurriedly they fled.*
> *Holding their noses they tumbled over dead.*
> *'Ach,' says the Kaiser, 'There's poison gas afloat.'*
> *But it was only the effluvium from Paddy McGinty's goat.*

Just twenty-four years of age by the time of the Châtillon attack, Major McGinty – short, sandy-haired and blue-eyed – had been born into a devout Roman Catholic family in England, but educated in India, where his father had served in the military. He'd been sent to the Bishop Cotton School, in Shimla – a province of India – the oldest boarding school in Asia, renowned for turning out judges, politicians and senior military commanders.

The alumni of the school were known as 'Old Cottonians', and its motto was 'Overcome evil with good'. Arguably, it was one that Farran had applied to the war with single-minded rigour.

In 1941 Farran – then serving in the 3rd King's Own Hussars, an armoured (cavalry) regiment – had been injured in both legs and an arm, in what became known as the battle of Cemetery Hill, in Crete. Farran was taken captive and held as a POW, but only for as long as it took for him to recover enough to walk on crutches, after which he managed to crawl under the camp's wire. Linking up with fellow escapees, he'd made a daring bid for freedom in a caique – a traditional wooden fishing boat. After an epic voyage and being marooned at sea, Farran and his fellows had finally made it to British-held Egypt.

He would win his first MC for his heroic actions on Crete and a bar – a second – for this daring escape. 'Throughout the whole of the operations this officer had shown courage, resource and initiative,' read the citation for his first award. 'He has set a very fine example of determination and leadership to the men of his command.'

Farran's physical courage and his apparent recklessness would lead him back into enemy fire, and in July 1942 he was wounded in the first battle of El Alamein. This time, his injuries were so serious as to require his medical evacuation to Britain. But via a judicious pulling of strings he managed to convince an Army medical board that he was fit to serve in a front-line role.

Not only that, but in February 1943 he'd volunteered for the

SAS. Brought into the regiment by a mutual friend, Farran was hugely impressed. He delighted in the no-nonsense, freewheeling and aggressive nature of the unit, and felt he had found his true home. In the regiment's founders he recognised true kindred spirits.

'The Stirlings did not leap over red tape; they broke right through it,' Farran would declare of David and Bill Stirling. 'Although they made many enemies by slipping round smaller fry, they always got there in the end.'

By September 1943 Farran was in action again, this time in Italy, commanding an SAS patrol on daring sabotage missions on the Adriatic coast. Within weeks he'd won a second bar to his MC. 'The success of the detachment was due to the courage, tenacity and leadership of Capt. FARRAN,' read the October 1943 citation, 'ably backed by his men, whom he has trained himself.' Arguably, there was no one better to be leading the daring and audacious Châtillon raid.

It was mid-morning by the time the combined SAS and Maquis force advanced back into town. Farran's main priority was to launch some kind of decoy action, so as to draw the enemy away from Captain Hibbert and his force of Maquis, who were moving into the narrow streets on foot. Gathering the redoubtable Jim Mackie, with his jeep as a supporting gun-platform, he led a foot patrol in a thrust east towards the far side of town, hoping to convince the enemy that they were being hit from all sides, as if by the US 3rd Army's vanguard.

As Hibbert's force pushed into the western outskirts of Châtillon, they stumbled upon an armoured car with thirty enemy soldiers in support, forming a bicycle patrol. They opened fire, gunning down four of those in the armoured car as they tried to bail out, and hitting the bicycle patrol from both the front and the rear. Savage street fighting ensued and another SAS soldier was hit. Forced to take cover in a large garden, Hibbert and the Maquis fought for their very lives as fierce bursts of gunfire echoed through the bullet-pocked terrain.

Meanwhile, Farran's force stole ahead through streets that were eerily quiet, apart from the bursts of fire echoing across from Hibbert's direction. Crouched low, he led his men past a unit of Germans positioned in the cover of some beech trees. He pushed on, crossing a canal, where his small force flitted along the towpath. Farran spotted another unit of German soldiers standing guard at the hospital, but somehow they failed to notice the SAS men.

Finally, having pushed east across two miles of terrain, they reached the road leading north to the city of Troyes. Taking cover in a narrow side street, Farran chanced a peek around the corner of the nearest building. He almost choked at what he saw. Just a few yards away were a pair of German machine-gun posts, flanking the Troyes road and covering the direction from which Farran and his men had come. Dressed in greatcoats, the machine-gun crews had their backs to the SAS party, seemingly oblivious to their presence.

Farran sank back into cover, wondering how best to proceed. From a nearby house one of his men begged some wine, cheese and bread. As they deliberated on their next move, they wolfed down the food and drink. It was approaching midday and they'd been on the go in fierce combat for six hours or more. Farran felt gripped by a leaden fatigue and he sensed that many of his men were likewise shattered. Still, this was an opportunity too good to miss.

On his word, he and his men leaned around the corner and took careful aim, opening fire on the German machine-gunners, raking their unprotected rear. A soldier on a bicycle was hit, tumbling off his machine, but the enemy were swift to respond. As more bodies fell, all hell let loose. The narrow street in which Farran and his men were hiding became a death trap, as fire from the Germans' MP40 'Schmeisser' sub-machine guns ricocheted off the walls.

Farran could see only one route of escape: to bolt through the front door of the nearest house and dash out the rear, in the hope they could scramble down to the banks of the canal. With rounds cutting around their heads, he led his men in the mad charge through.

They made it safely to the canal bank, reached a lock, scuttled across and darted further eastwards on the tow path, hoping to extricate themselves from enemy clutches. Farran felt confident that Big Jim Mackie would be following their every move, as so often he and his jeep had got them out of seemingly impossible situations.

As he led his men towards the cover of a ridge top hedgerow, one of the enemy's machine-gunners must have spotted them. Within moments, a long burst of fire from an MG42 'Spandau' was tearing into the terrain to either side. As Farran dived for the sparse cover of the hedge, a second Spandau joined in the turkey shoot. It was hellish, especially as he hadn't even realised that he and his men were visible to the enemy.

The Spandau had earned a telling nickname among Allied troops – 'Hitler's Buzzsaw', referring to the incredibly high rate of fire of the weapon and the corresponding noise it made. Capable of putting down 1,200 rounds per minute, it had twice the firepower of the British Bren, if not quite the accuracy. In spite of the terrifying effect of being pinned down by two such machine guns, Farran told himself they had to move. If they stayed where they were they were dead, yet still the veteran SAS commander felt frozen.

By this stage of the war many of those serving with the regiment had begun to view Farran as some kind of a lucky genius – the kind of commander who seemed to lead a charmed life, and who could miraculously command his men on an assault of today's daring and still somehow pull it off. But in truth, Farran feared that after four long years at war and numerous brushes with death, he was getting 'windy'.

Pinned beneath that hedge, he felt gripped by – frozen by – fear. He had never felt so scared as he did now, or so incapable of leading his own men to safety. He'd been in similar scrapes before, and he'd always managed to get him and his fellows out alive. He felt paralysed by fearful inaction, and above everything he hoped that his men hadn't sensed how he was feeling.

Over the years Farran had proved himself blessed with the most vital of attributes for an SAS commander: the instinctive ability to assess the level of danger posed by any battlefield situation, and to deliver an instant and optimum response. His spirited leadership inspired a deep loyalty in his men, not to mention the resistance fighters with whom they often operated.

But right at this moment, Farran had led his followers into what was seemingly a death trap. For every moment they remained pinned down beneath that bullet-blasted hedge, he sensed the enemy closing in for the kill. Finally, he forced himself to move. Keeping to his belly and with bursts of fire kicking up dirt on every side, he led his men in a desperate crawl, sticking to the sparse cover of the deepest furrows that lay beyond the hedgerow. As he steeled himself to press on, he realised that he had never felt so tired or dispirited. In the long years of operations stretching from the North African deserts to the shores of Italy, and from the Greek Islands to the Aegean Sea, he had rarely felt so close to being finished.

If they didn't get out of the machine-gunner's line of fire they were done for, but he couldn't get himself to move any faster. Behind him, Sergeant Roberts, another of his C Squadron veterans, was hit in the leg. Despite the wound, the man seemed to belly-crawl ahead faster than Farran, as he dragged himself along a bloody furrow. They reached a small patch of dead ground, beyond which they would need to move back into the enemy's line of fire.

Farran tried to go to the aid of his wounded sergeant, but he was so utterly exhausted that he could barely help himself. Momentarily lifting his head from the dirt, he sensed the grunt of a distant engine. He fancied it had the distinctive sound of an SAS jeep. Could it be the cavalry riding to the rescue? Had Big Jim Mackie found where they had gone to ground? If so, Farran would need to dig deep for one last burst of energy, to lead a dash for Mackie's vehicle.

He and his men might die in the process, but they were surely dead if they remained where they were.

Chapter 3

If anything, Mike Lees' descent through the Italian mountains had been even more hair-raising than the snow-bound ascent. Sometime after cresting the high pass two-feet deep in wind-driven drifts, they had linked up with a reception party from the neighbouring band of partisans. They'd brought with them a battered truck, one recently captured off the enemy. It looked close to derelict, but at least it offered the promise of mobility and shelter.

Frozen stiff, Lees and his party had clambered aboard, looking forward to arriving in the partisan village in a degree of comfort and style. Instead, the onwards journey had turned into the wildest ride any of the men had ever known. Apparently, a German garrison based beyond Pigna – the partisan village to which they were heading – had learned that their force was on the move. The enemy had fanned out in an effort to catch them – hence the need to reach the village by the fastest means possible. The journey ahead was a race against time.

That appeared to be the explanation for what happened next: the driver of the truck gripped the wheel tightly, turned off the engine, took his feet off the pedals and down they went, free-wheeling all the way. The truck just seemed to keep gaining speed, as it swung crazily from side to side, careering around hairpin bends in a death-defying fashion. Fear gripped the minds of those riding in it, until their hearts were in their very throats. Men became sick with fear. Soon the truck bed was slick with vomit.

There was little point trying to voice any objections, or of urging the driver to a greater degree of caution: the speed and the noise were so all-consuming, all they could do was hang on for dear life and mouth their prayers. Finally, miraculously, the truck gave a last series of death-defying lurches, before grinding to an uncertain halt in the village square. The driver practically fell out of the cabin door and lay on the ground, staring at the heavens.

He glanced at his sickly, pallid passengers. 'No petrol.' He shrugged, then guffawed. 'No brakes!'

Whether the story about the German hunter force was true or not, or just a smoke screen to disguise the perilous nature of their conveyance, no one was entirely certain. But of one thing they could be sure: even now that they had reached Pigna village, there seemed little hope for their onwards journey. The leader of the partisans declared that any attempt to push further south towards the Gothic Line would be akin to suicide.

He had no contact with the Allied forces positioned on the far side, the commander explained, so no way to warn them that a friendly force was coming through. The front line kept shifting as the battle ebbed and flowed, making any close reconnaissance impossible. Moreover, the ground ahead was broken, impassable country, so Lees and his men would be forced to move on well-trodden paths and roads, all which would be closely guarded by the enemy.

Behind the front ran a main road, he warned, slicing through the mountains in a knife-cut cleft. It was heavily patrolled, and if Lees and his force tried to cross it they were bound to be seen.

After much heated discussion, Lees finally managed to secure the offer of a guide who would take his party south as far as that road. After that, they would be on their own.

As Lees was painfully aware, it would be suicide to press on with his full party. As far as he could ascertain, the enemy fortifications stretched for miles either side of the Gothic Line. All of that terrain would have to be crossed by stealth and ideally under cover of darkness. He would need to lead a small, fit, fighting patrol, one able to travel fast and silently and primed to avoid contact with the enemy, or to fight ferociously should the need arise.

It was better to slip a few good men through successfully, than to get them all killed. The two Italian resistance leaders were in excellent physical shape, so would stand the march well. But the war artist, Long, was unfit to move, at least until he'd recovered from his fall. Lees and the reporter, Morton, had had their differences high on the mountain, and he reckoned Morton was best left behind. If Lees could establish an escape route, all the more chance that the both of them might make it through with their stories.

Lees decided to take two others only. The first was an escaped British POW called Fred Dobson, a fit and capable soldier who was keen as mustard to press on. The other was an Italian called Secondo Balestri, who had been serving with Temple's partisans for some time. Balestri had one of the most incredible war stories that Lees had ever heard.

A former Italian Navy wireless operator turned partisan, he had been captured by the Germans. Under Gestapo torture he'd acted as if he had broken, professing his willingness to transmit false intelligence to the Allies. Instead, Balestri, who was gifted with an extraordinary mathematical memory, had altered a coded signal which read 'I am in good hands', to 'I am in German hands'. He'd also managed to insert further warnings into the radio messages the Gestapo forced him to send. Because he could do so 'live' – during the process of encoding the signal – the Gestapo had never suspected what he was up to.

Balestri had subsequently escaped from the enemy and made it back to partisan lines. He, like Fred Dobson, was keen to continue despite the dangers. That, Lees decided, would make up his escape party. He'd leave William McClelland, the Royal Scots private turned piratical raider, to shepherd the remaining men through – but only once they had received word from Lees of what was the best route, or, conversely, that he and his party had failed.

It was some twenty-four hours after reaching Pigna that Lees called his party together. Once he had outlined his intentions to split them into two groups, neither Morton nor Long appeared particularly upset. On the contrary, they could see the sense – not to mention the sheer courage – in Lees trying to forge a path for the rest to follow.

'He was twenty-one, tough, brave as the British are brave; born, as they say, to command,' Morton would write of Lees. In that there was perhaps a tacit admission that he had been wrong to rebel against Lees' orders, high on the snow-swept mountain. As for Lees, he'd realised by now that the Canadian press man had a certain grit and spirit: indeed, enough of each to place him in formal command of those left behind.

Lees eyed the reporter, searchingly. 'You, Morton, seem to think everything is a big joke ... You fraternise too easily with the Commos; with everyone for that matter.' By 'the Commos'

Lees meant the communists, for a good proportion of the Italian partisans professed to communist leanings. 'Still, I'm putting you in charge.'

Morton, amply assisted by McClelland, would lead the second escape party, Lees explained. 'You're loaded down with money. That's better than guns or brains in a situation like this. Use the money to get the rest of this crowd through to France . . . And Morton, that's an order.'

'He never called me Paul whenever he was giving orders,' Morton reflected wryly of Lees, 'and he seemed, mostly, to be giving orders.' Morton – like Lees – had parachuted in on the present mission carrying a slush-fund provided by the SOE: cash, with which to oil the wheels of guerrilla warfare. Now, he was to use that money to buy their way out again.

Lees shook hands with all, speaking a few last words to the Canadian reporter and the South African war artist. 'Well, goodbye. We'll tell the Americans you're coming through. Perhaps they'll polish their bayonets, so you give them a good write up.'

Morton snorted. 'That'll be the day. They might be a million miles away, for all the use they are at the moment.'

'You'll get through all right,' Lees reassured him.

'Well, thank God I'm not going today,' Morton confessed. 'I couldn't walk another step.'

'That's the worst of you correspondents,' Lees needled him. 'You don't do enough PT.'

Morton laughed. 'Oh, shut up and push off, you bloody thug.'

With those final words ringing in his ears, Lees and his fellows departed Pigna, mounting up the death trap of the partisan truck for the initial stage of the journey. It would take them as far as the first major obstacle, a road bridge that the partisans had blown up to prevent the Germans from raiding their valley stronghold, not far beyond which lay the first of the massive defences of the Gothic Line.

The *Gotenstellung* – the Gothic Line – was Nazi Germany's last line of defence in northern Italy, running coast to coast in essentially an east–west direction. Positioned on the slopes of the Apennine mountains, it consisted of a series of massive fortifications strung between the natural defences of the high ridges and snowbound peaks. Concerned about whether the *Gotenstellung* would hold, Hitler had ordered 15,000 slave labourers shipped in, to extend the defences in strength and depth. Working under the Todt Organisation – Nazi Germany's forced labour ministry – they consisted of prisoners of war, concentration camp internees, plus conscripted Italian civilians.

Those slave labourers had constructed hundreds of reinforced-concrete gun pits, deep trenches, 2,376 machine-gun nests boasting interlocking arcs of fire, 479 anti-tank, mortar and artillery positions, plus observation posts with interconnecting tunnels burrowed deep beneath the ground. Miles of anti-tank barriers had been dug, plus 130,000 yards of barbed wire strung between key positions. As a result, Field Marshal Kesselring had declared himself satisfied, contemplating any Allied assault on the *Gotenstellung* 'with a certain confidence'.

Sure enough, by the autumn of 1944 Allied forces had fought themselves to a standstill on the *Gotenstellung*. With combat losses mounting and the harsh winter weather setting in, General Harold Alexander, Kesselring's opposite number, had accepted that the Allied push through Italy had hit a major stumbling block. 'The last battles in Italy were just as fierce as any we had experienced . . .' General Alexander remarked. 'I was not faced with a broken and disintegrating Army . . .' No breakthrough was going to be possible, at least not before the spring.

The partisans' decrepit truck coughed and backfired spasmodically, but after an hour's tortuous drive it made it to that first obstacle. There, Lees and his four-man party dismounted and clambered across what remained of the demolished bridge. They pushed ahead on a road cut into the sheer side of the mountain, one that had been built to service the rearmost defences of the *Gotenstellung*.

The first massive bunkers hove into view. Lees was astounded at the sheer impregnability of those fortifications. The last line of defence, they looked to be deserted at present, but once manned by German troops they would constitute a veritable mountain fortress. As the partisan leader had warned, the only possible route ahead lay along a thin ribbon of road, and they were forced to pass below the giant, gaping, eyeless sockets of those concrete bunkers.

It was an eerie, shadowed place and Lees was hugely relieved to reach the ridge that lay on the far side. It was midday by now and their partisan guide pointed out the main road that cut through the valley below. Lees gazed upon that highway: what he saw was not encouraging. To either side of the twisting ribbon of black rose grey-walled mountains, slashed through by precipitous ravines. The terrain looked utterly daunting.

Here and there tiny white puffs of smoke revealed where Allied shells were bursting amid the hidden defences. The noise of battle drifted across to them, echoing confusingly around the rocky slopes.

'It's going to be difficult,' Salvi, one of the resistance leaders, ventured.

'Very,' Lees confirmed, grimly.

Salvi found a cleft in the rock-face via which he assured Lees they could descend. The Italians led the way, Lees and Dobson following. Big, heavy and ungainly at heights, Lees found the next hour or so hellish, as he clung to the rock with aching fingertips and with his Sten slung across his shoulders. Each glance down was rewarded by a fresh surge of nausea, and by the time he reached the bottom his legs were shaking uncontrollably.

From there, they followed a faint track that led to a small patch of woodland, lying just above the road. It was late afternoon by now, and Lees reckoned dusk was no more than two hours away. Already the highway was busy with trucks motoring to and fro. Come nightfall, it would become packed with traffic, for the enemy tended to use the cloak of darkness to shield their convoys from marauding Allied warplanes.

The guide from Pigna village was still with them, but he would go no further than the road. He was dressed like a local villager and carried ID papers, which meant that he should be able to pass freely through enemy positions. Lees persuaded him to press on to the nearest village, a small place called Fanghetto, which lay just before the road.

An hour later he was back. What he reported underscored the futility of trying to make it across anywhere hereabouts. The village was full of enemy troops whose job it was to patrol the road. Even if Lees and his men did sneak through undetected, on the far side lay a fierce mountain river. It was fast, deep and treacherous, and only one bridge spanned its breadth, which was under permanent guard. Beyond that lay a road snaking into the high-ground, but it was a heavily used supply route for German front-line troops.

In short, there was no way through.

With heavy hearts Lees and his men retraced their steps, arriving back at the cliff-face that they had descended earlier. Too exhausted to attempt the ascent, they found a deserted shepherd's hut in which to spend the night. At dawn the following morning, the climb up the sheer rock-face proved even more terrifying than the descent had done.

Once at the top, an exhausted Lees and Salvi took stock. They were all out of water and running low on food. They questioned the guide, but he had few viable suggestions. As Lees gazed out over the enemy-infested terrain, he felt utterly spent and close to beaten. His eyes drifted further south, to the beguiling shimmer of the Mediterranean. It was little more than a couple of miles away.

A British warship was steaming up the coast, shelling what had to be the *Gotenstellung*'s defences. A thought suddenly struck Lees: *the sea*. Why not use the sea? The sea was owned by the Allies, British warships keeping up a steady barrage of fire against the enemy. Surely, crossing the lines would be far easier if attempted by sea. In essence, if they rowed across they could outflank the enemy's defences. Surely, there lay the answer?

Lees turned to the guide. Did he know any fishermen, he demanded, ones who were friendly to the partisan cause? He did, the guide replied, but the Germans had confiscated all of their oars. Could any be found, Lees asked. The guide thought they could, with the right kind of incentive. A plan was hatched. The guide would get a letter through to his fisherman friend, offering a bundle of cash if he could get a boat ready and meet with Lees and his men that afternoon. The letter would have to be bicycled through to the fisherman, to make it into his hands in time.

'What if he fails to show or gives us away?' Salvi asked Lees.

Lees shrugged. 'We'll have to take our chances . . . If he fails to make it, we can't wait another night. We'll just have to risk trying to get across near the coast.'

The plan set, Lees felt a surge of renewed energy. They set off, keeping to the cover of woodland and descending by a gentler slope. By midday, they were in sight of the fisherman's village. With little food remaining, they gorged on bunches of juicy black grapes plucked from a nearby vineyard.

The meeting point was a small quarry, set in a patch of woodland about two miles from the beckoning sea. They approached it with caution. As luck would have it, the place was occupied. A gypsy family were using it as a site for making charcoal. Typically no friends to the enemy – along with the Jews, Slavic peoples, the disabled and others, gypsies were also classed as *Untermensch* (subhuman) by the Nazis – they proved decidedly welcoming, once they understood who Lees and his party were.

They offered food and wine, but Lees was more interested in what intelligence they might furnish. The elder of the family led Lees to a small knoll on the fringes of the woodland. He pointed out two steep-sided hills that lay before them, each like a mini-volcano and covered in dense scrub. Each was fortified by hidden German positions, he explained.

Beneath their vantage point the road was busy with horse-drawn carts, laden with artillery shells: to one side of the woodland lay a camouflaged gun battery. Every now and then Lees heard the whine of a passing shell, followed shortly by the crack of the gun firing. He realised then that some of the enemy artillery was positioned behind them, lobbing shells high into the air at the Allied lines. Somehow, unwittingly, Lees and his men must have slipped through the rearmost enemy defences that morning.

Lees sketched out all the positions the gypsy could identify. If they did make it across the lines this would constitute priceless intelligence for planning bombing raids with pinpoint accuracy. They returned to the quarry. By four o'clock there was still no sign of the fisherman, and Lees was getting worried. With the approach of dusk no one doubted that he wasn't coming. Something had gone wrong. Maybe the message hadn't even reached him.

Lees turned to the gypsy. Was he able to guide them at all, he demanded? The man said that he could, but only as far as the road. Beyond that, he knew little if anything of the terrain. Lees figured if they could reach the scrub that cloaked the first of the two fortified hillocks, from there they might spy a route ahead and try to sneak onwards in the gathering darkness.

'Our objective after that?' Salvi queried.

Good question. Lees eyed the distant wall of mountains. Somewhere among those towering peaks lay the Allied front line. Even via his binoculars, it was impossible to make out any obvious route through. Lees chose a particular peak, unmistakeable due to its pyramidal shape, and picked it out on the map.

'We'll make for Mount Grammondo. There's a full moon tonight, and we can't miss it.'

They'd set out as soon as it got dark, knowing they had to make safe territory by daybreak. Before departure, Lees penned a short letter to Morton. He outlined the route they planned to take, but advised the press man to explore the sea-borne option, if a suitable boat could be found. That done, he sent someone to carry the note back to Pigna village.

Lees and his men prepared for the off, checking kit and weaponry to ensure nothing was loose or clanked as they moved.

Apart from Lees' Sten, Salvi and Piva also carried sub-machine guns, and Balestri had a rifle, while Dobson hefted two grenades. It was scant weaponry if they ran into any trouble. Just then the gypsy man's wife emerged from their tent, pressing a hip flask of cognac into Lees' hands, with murmurs of good luck.

Lees thanked her, before turning to his men. 'No talk,' he warned them. 'We get through without a fight if possible. No one fires unless I give the order. Keep closed-up all the way. We are few enough to avoid being seen and we can't afford to get separated.'

They set out. The moon was not due to rise until nine, and Lees wanted to get as far as possible under the cloak of night. Below, he could just make out the phosphorescent shimmer of the river. Their gypsy-guide led them forwards until he dared go no further. Lees pressed a bundle of Lire gratefully into his hands. That done, they flitted onwards, hugging a hedge until the road melted out of the darkness.

Lees signalled a halt. From up ahead came the tread of boots on tarmac. Lees crept on a few paces, until he spied a sentry. He paced slowly past, so close that Lees could almost reach out and touch his boots. Fifty yards further on the sentry stopped to exchange a few words in German, before turning and pacing slowly back again. It looked as if there was a guard in place for every hundred yards or so.

From his right Lees heard a new noise, cutting the still night air. The thud of hooves and the rumble of wagons, bearing a heavy load. He signalled to his party. 'Dash across just as soon as the wagon column has passed,' he hissed.

The noise grew to a deafening roar, as the line of wooden carts thundered closer, the horses' manes flowing and their harnesses jingling rhythmically. Just as soon as the last was past, Lees dashed across, keeping as low as he could. Four figures flitted after him. They made the open field on the far side without any cries of alarm, and sprinted across it in pairs. Moments later they scrambled down the riverbank and were lost from view.

Just as Lees had intended, the column of passing carts had masked any noise that they had made. The river was wide but mercifully shallow. They waded across one at a time and pressed onwards into a maize field. To their right the clank of steel on steel revealed the location of an artillery position. Moments later, the roar of a gun firing split the night, the flash of the muzzle throwing all into momentary stark relief.

Monte Pozzo, the first of the wooded hillocks, was revealed in that harsh pulse of light, just a few hundred yards ahead. Keeping to the shadowed edge of the maize crop, Lees led his men on. Every now and then the guns fired a further salvo, and with each Monte Pozzo drew noticeably closer. Finally, Lees slipped in among the trees that fringed its lower slopes.

It seemed as if only a few scant minutes had passed, but in reality they'd been on the move for two hours. In another hour the moon would rise, and before them lay a second river that they had to cross. Lees hurried on. A road snaked this way and that up the side of Monte Pozzo. As Lees tried to steer a straight course, their route kept crossing it.

All of a sudden there was a clatter in the darkness. A pair of German soldiers had been freewheeling down the road on bicycles. Spotting Lees and his party, they'd jumped off, the bikes falling to the ground. As Lees dashed ahead shots rang out in the darkness. Thankfully, the German troopers were armed only with rifles, but those shots had doubtless raised the alarm. From behind, Lees heard the soldiers remount their bicycles to pedal frantically onwards.

Lees was hyper-alert for any watchers now. They reached a vantage point, looking outwards across the valley. Before them nestled the town of Torri, cradled at the foot of a steep ravine. That precipitous crevice offered the only obvious route via which to scale the mountains beyond. To reach it Lees would have to lead his men across the river, which lay just this side of the town, via a bridge. There was no other way.

As Lees scrutinised the road, he detected several glowing pin-pricks of light, rhythmically pulsing in the darkness: sentries enjoying a smoke. The moon rose, large and bright, bathing the river in its light. The main question in Lees' mind was whether Torri was occupied by the enemy. In the moonlight, it looked like a mass of shattered, shell-blasted ruins. It was just possible that the ferocity of Allied bombardments had caused the town to be evacuated.

Lees pulled his men in close. 'We've got to cross the bridge. If we try to wade the river they'll see us. We'll have to march openly, hoping they mistake us for one of their own patrols.'

There were silent nods in the darkness.

With Lees leading, five figures stole down the hillside, before stepping brazenly into the open. They formed up as a column, turned right and began to march towards the bridge. From behind Lees could hear figures talking and laughing in German. He tensed for a cry of challenge, but none came. After three minutes of utter spine-chilling tension, they made it across the bridge without a shot being fired or even a cry of alarm.

The war-blasted streets of Torri seemed utterly deserted. Once or twice a stray chicken or pig started at their presence, sending five pairs of hands to their weapons, but they reached the far side of the ghost town without facing a single challenge. Ahead rose the lower slopes of the mountain, terraced into vineyards like a gigantic ladder. They began to scramble up, scaling one terrace after another and tripping and stumbling over the wires which held up the vines. They were reluctant to seek out any paths in case they were mined.

Directly ahead lay the bulky form of Monte Grammondo, its peak grey and forbidding. A salvo of shells burst between them and the heights, setting a copse of pines ablaze. The fire scorched and crackled, throwing ghostly shadows across the dark heights. Now and again a machine gun rasped out a long burst of fire, but it was impossible to tell exactly who was shooting at whom, or if nervous German gunners were simply unleashing upon ghosts.

Finally, the vineyards came to an end. The slopes were more precipitous now, forcing Lees to take a path that snaked ever more steeply. It was around 0200 hours when Salvi tapped him on the shoulder. He sank to the path, doubled over and in pain.

'I can't go on,' the resistance leader murmured.

'What's wrong?' Lees hissed.

'My stomach. I have an ulcer. The walking must have aggravated it.'

Lees considered their predicament. He reckoned they had climbed about halfway to the heights, beyond which he figured lay the Allied front line. It would get light at six and they had to make it across by then. He allowed the resistance leader half an hour to rest, before telling him they had to press on.

Reluctantly, Salvi clambered to his feet. Lees dropped the pace a little, as they recommenced the climb. They entered a knife-cut ravine, following a faint path strewn with mule droppings. As

49

Lees led them through, Dobson, the escaped British POW, drew level with him.

'There's someone following us,' he whispered, hoarsely.

Lees turned and listened. Sure enough he could detect the faint murmur of voices from further down the narrow cleft. He had no option but to up their pace. If their mystery pursuers cornered Lees and his small party in that ravine, it would be the end of them.

A few minutes later, panting hard as he climbed, Lees stumbled over a wire strung along the track. It looked like a communications cable and it had to lead to a field telephone. As Lees stared at it, trying to catch his breath, Salvi pointed excitedly. 'That's no German wire! Theirs is always black.'

He was right: the strand of cable was a bright red. Still, Lees remained doubtful. 'The Americans can't be this far advanced,' he objected. 'We've only recently passed through the enemy's artillery. Ahead must lie their infantry.'

No matter how long they stared at that wire, glowing a faint red in the moonlight, there was no way of knowing. Lees ordered them on. The cable seemed to dog their every step. Twice they turned off the main path, only to run into that red strand of wire once more. Lees sensed they were about to stumble into trouble. They neared the crest of a ridge and crept into the cover of a small copse. The wire was there, running dead ahead. They followed it, rounded a bend and came upon a heap of equipment lying by the path.

Lees spied a pile of blankets, a distinctive metal helmet, a leather ammo belt and a Mauser rifle: *German stuff*. He bent to finger the nearest blanket: *still warm*. The enemy had to be close. As quietly as he could, Lees handed the ammo belt and rifle to

Dobson. They paused as he checked and readied the weapon. Fortuitous. One more of them was now a little better armed.

Lees signalled them on – five figures creeping silently as wraiths through the trees. They reached an area where the cover thinned out, and all five of them seemed to spy the enemy at the same instant. Barely ten paces ahead stood half a dozen German soldiers, gazing further across the mountainside. To one side knelt a signaller, speaking quietly into a field telephone. It was obviously some kind of forward observation position.

Lees and his men sank into cover. The standing figures stared ahead at shells bursting on a ridgeline some distance away. They were checking and correcting the artillerymen's fire, seemingly oblivious to the presence of Lees and his men. Their weapons and helmets lay beside them on the ground, their eyes fixed on the distant explosions.

Lees figured he'd seen enough. He stole to his feet, Sten levelled at the enemy. Four figures rose with him, their weapons likewise readied. As if warned by some sixth sense, one of the Germans turned towards them. Lees pressed his trigger. Half the figures fell in a matter of seconds, cut down by long bursts of fire unleashed at close range. As the survivors tried to flee, Dobson hurled a grenade in among them.

With the route ahead now clear Lees burst through, vaulting over the fallen enemy figures. The others followed. They tore out of the woodland, racing along a path snaking along the ground. The terrain here was open, the track leading to a final line of low, rocky cliffs, which delineated the high point.

As they sprinted for that escarpment, a machine gun opened up from behind. Bullets tore past, as Lees and his fellows slithered and dived into cover, then darted onwards. Salvi seemed to be fully recovered by now. A born mountaineer, he made a desperate dash for a crevice in the rock-face, one that seemed to offer a final route through. As they sprinted for its uncertain embrace, fierce bursts of machine-gun fire cut the night to all sides.

Salvi led the climb, shinning up the near-vertical cliff, with Lees and the others right behind. They were some fifty feet up when the first shell whistled out of the night and tore into the rocks below. Several more followed, splinters of steel cutting through the air on all sides. With zero shelter and a precipitous drop below, there was little option but to keep climbing.

The shells kept coming. Probing with his finger tips, Salvi steered them to the very top, before darting into the shelter of some rocks. Moments later, Lees had crawled in beside him, and shortly the others followed. They wormed their way further into cover, lying there in utter exhaustion. No one could believe that they had made it through thus far, and unscathed.

From behind, they could spy the baleful red flashes of the German artillery. Ahead, silhouetted against the moonlight glimmering off the sea, lay the ancient port town of Menton, which was held by the Allies. Lees reasoned it would be far safer to press on towards 'friendly' lines come daybreak. They rested for an hour, until the stars faded in the lightening sky.

All seemed eerily quiet as Lees led the small party off, moving cautiously through the dawn light. A path ran along the ridge, perpendicular to the way they needed to go. They crossed it, pushing due south, reaching a strand of wire running along the ground. Lees stepped towards it, mouthing silent prayers: if mines had been laid on this stretch of front, he figured the wire would delimit the borders of the safe ground.

He stepped gingerly across. No shattering explosion met his

footfall. They made one hundred, two hundred, then three hundred yards without mishap, when finally a burst of fire tore apart the silence. Directly ahead a machine-gunner had opened up, unleashing a burst of warning shots above their heads.

Lees threw himself flat on the earth. 'Don't shoot! Don't shoot! We're British!'

The voice that responded was the sweetest that he had ever heard.

'Put that gun down,' came a hard-edged, American-accented cry. 'Advance one and be recognised.'

Chapter 4

From the shelter of the rutted field beyond the bullet-torn hedgerow, Major Farran saw the distinctive form of an SAS jeep nose into view, with the redoubtable Big Jim Mackie at the wheel. It was the most welcome sight that he had ever seen. They now had its vehicle-mounted machine guns to counter the Germans' fire.

Under the cover of their smoking barrels, Farran and his men rushed the wounded Sergeant Roberts to the vehicle and bundled him aboard. Figures jumped on wherever there was space. The heavily laden jeep moved out, engine howling, its thick mud-eater tyres making short work of the ploughed field. Once they'd reached the nearby lane, the priority had to be to get as far away as possible from the hornet's nest that they had kicked – and kicked hard – in Châtillon, and to get Roberts some medical treatment.

They headed for the nearest friendly farmstead. There, Farran himself proceeded to dress Roberts' wounds, while he lay on the kitchen table and a bevy of farm-maids bustled about with hot water and towels. Once the SAS sergeant was stabilised, he was loaded aboard a vehicle and despatched to the nearest location where the Maquis were known to keep an operational field hospital. There, he'd be in good hands.

That done, Farran led his jeep column back through isolated

country to their remote, deep-woodland base. Reports filtered in from Châtillon of one hundred German dead and many more injured, plus scores of trucks, cars and motorcycle combinations destroyed. Almost of more importance, the entire German force occupying the town was said to be preparing to withdraw from what it believed was advancing US troops.

Farran had lost one SAS soldier killed and several wounded. By anyone's reckoning, the battle for Châtillon-sur-Seine had been a spectacular victory. The SAS's official report – marked 'SENSITIVE' – would declare that 'this must rank as one of the most successful sorties ever carried out by a small harassing force behind enemy lines.'

But Farran's greatest fear now was reprisals. The Gestapo and SS were bound to learn of the attack, and they were known to wreak terrible vengeance on the locals, as 'punishment' for the role the Maquis may have played. He decided to make himself scarce. If his entire force melted away, it would lessen any chance of any such savagery. If no SAS could be found, who was to say it wasn't forward elements of the US 3rd Army that had attacked the town?

He sent out a signal for his entire squadron to return to their woodland base: other elements had been out hitting a variety of targets. They gathered as one unit, boasting eighteen jeeps in all, before moving out to establish three separate bases, from where to plot further mischief and mayhem. They left behind them the one casualty, Parachutist Holland, who'd been killed in the initial stages of the battle. Unbeknown to Farran the enemy had found his body, which served to dissuade them from executing the fifty-odd locals they had taken hostage. As it was clearly a British-led raid, such reprisals against 'the Maquis' were deemed unjustified.

Farran led his patrol 150 kilometres east, to a patch of woodland not far from the town of Grandrupt-de-Bains. En route they reconnoitred key targets, radioing through coordinates for Allied airstrikes. 'Urgent. Recced today railway station at 14H/373305 ...' read one such message. 'Petrol train on track being used as refuelling point ... Impossible attack from ground as 200 enemy with heavy weapons dug in ... bomb whole area immediately to prevent escaping convoys from refuelling.' There were many such messages.

Grandrupt-de-Bains lay on the western border of the Vosges region of France, an area of thick woodland and rain-washed mountains that straddles the Franco-German border. Hitler had vowed that on the western wall of the Vosges his Panzer divisions and infantry would make a heroic last stand, hurling the Allies back into France and preventing them from marching into the Fatherland. It seemed a fitting area in which Farran and his SAS might cause trouble, but things weren't quite to turn out as he had planned.

It was the second week of September 1944 when Farran linked up with a new resistance group at Grandrupt. This one – somewhat implausibly – was based around a Boy Scout troop. The members of the Grandrupt Maquis struck Farran as being a little young to go to war, although those in command were seasoned resistance fighters. They'd set up base in a cluster of white canvas bell-tents pitched beside a mountain stream, and the whole scene struck Farran as being reminiscent of a scout camp in peacetime.

It was somehow so incongruous, yet their spirit to fight appeared to be unmatched. Farran delivered a stirring speech in his best schoolboy French and was mobbed by a crowd of young would-be warriors. He decided to arrange an air-drop of much-needed arms and supplies onto the boy scouts' drop zone, which if nothing else would give them some direct experience of a '*lancée*', as the Maquis tended to call such an event.

The DZ was a large flat field fringed by trees, so well screened from any watchers. There was a cold wind blowing, as September ushered in the autumn and winter storms so typical of the Vosges. Farran explained in detail the configuration of signal lights and fires that were required to guide the aircraft in, but he doubted if the scouts had completely grasped it. He was just giving up hope of any aircraft appearing, when, at around 0200 hours, the distant drone of a Handley Page Halifax's four Rolls-Royce Vulture engines cut the skies.

The Halifax was designed for use as a heavy bomber, but specialised versions had also been built for parachute and cargo operations. It had become the work-horse of special forces resupply missions. As the pair of aircraft homed in on the DZ, Farran figured they were making their approach at too high an altitude. Sure enough, when they released their loads the wind blew a good proportion of the parachutes off course, which plummeted into the trees.

By now, Farran and his men were shivering with the night's cold, but there was urgent work to be done. Three human parachutists had also dropped in, alongside the supplies. Lieutenant Hugh Gurney, Lance Corporal Challenor and Parachutist Fyffe had gone missing weeks earlier, shortly after Farran's column had crossed the lines. Somehow, they'd made it back to friendly forces and were now parachuting in to rejoin their unit. Unfortunately, the wind had driven Fyffe into a stand of tall pine trees. It was three long hours before Farran and his men finally got him safely to the ground.

The resupply containers were so widely scattered that by day-break several were still to be found. A somewhat disgruntled Farran took a break for some much-needed breakfast, leaving the boy-scout Maquis in charge. It was around 0900 hours when a youth of no more than ten came tearing over to Farran in something of a panic. He'd been sent with an urgent message: some 600 German soldiers, supported by armoured cars plus *Sonderkraft-fahrzeug* half-tracks – troop-carriers fitted with machine guns – were converging on the DZ.

There was, as Farran well knew, a crack SS battalion based at Grandrupt-de-Bains. They must have learned of the resupply drop and set out early intending to spoil Farran's day. Equipped as they were, the enemy were going to heavily outnumber his force, not to mention outgun it.

Farran ordered his men to mount up their jeeps. As he scanned their surroundings, searching for an escape route, the DZ seemed to be completely enclosed in thick, impenetrable woodland. There would be no slipping away via jeep through any of that. One rutted track led out of the clearing, but that was the direction in which the SS battalion were fast approaching.

Opting to stand and fight would be suicide. The half-tracks – known as 'Hanomags' to Allied troops – boasted half-inch-thick armour and pairs of pivot-mounted machine guns, and each could carry ten soldiers in full combat gear. Advising the boy-scout Maquis to disperse into the woodland, Farran set about trying to find some means for his jeep-borne force to escape. As if to underscore the dire nature of their predicament the first bursts of fire erupted from the eastern fringes of the DZ, from where the enemy were making their approach.

Farran led his column of jeeps in a desperate dash around the perimeter of the DZ, searching for an elusive means to make their getaway. Here and there expanses of white parachute silk still cloaked the odd tree top, if ever the enemy needed a marker to guide them to their prey. As they gunned the jeeps' engines, figures came charging out of the woodland – young Maquis, fleeing from the approaching convoy.

To the north of the DZ Farran spied a river cutting through the trees: it would be impossible to ford that in the jeeps. East lay only the enemy, and south and west rose dark walls of pine-woods. Giving up any hope of escape, Farran ordered his men to place their jeeps in the 'hull-down' position – so with their body-work sheltered behind a low ridge, but with the vehicle-mounted machine guns able to menace the line of approach of the enemy.

As they waited, Farran wondered whether they might be better off doing a Last Charge of the Light Brigade, as opposed to something more akin to the heroic stand of the 300 Spartans at Thermopylae. It was then that he noticed what appeared to be a small break in the wall of trees, in the far south-western corner. As the grunt of powerful engines rose to a crescendo to the east, Farran led his column in a mad dash for that tantalising promise of escape.

With bursts of fire chasing after them, the jeeps crashed through a wire fence and careered onwards through a copse of young sap-lings, mowing them down like a herd of crazed elephants put to flight in the jungle. Farran led the column across a small field, the jeeps bucking over the rough ground, before they made the better going of a small lane on the far side.

A mile or so later, they emerged onto a tarmacked road. Far-ran's thoughts now were all for the fate of the young Maquis. Facing an SS battalion was some baptism of fire. He ordered

Lieutenant Gurney, freshly parachuted into theatre, to take two jeeps to hit the enemy's rear, by motoring up the Grandrupt road. More jeeps were placed in ambush positions along the highway, intent on catching the SS as they withdrew from the DZ.

Lieutenant Gurney was the first to draw blood. Taking the enemy by complete surprise, he was able to strafe a group of officers positioned on a hillock, knocking out their command vehicle. Meanwhile, one of Farran's jeeps lying in ambush got lucky. Two staff cars were motoring for the DZ, intent on witnessing the success of the operation. Instead, they drove into a withering hail of fire.

Not a man riding in those vehicles was allowed to get out alive. As luck would have it, they were carrying the top commanders of the SS assault force – their colonel and his officers. While the SS had succeeded in seizing the drop-zone and some of the remnant supplies, Farran and his SAS had definitely cut the head off the snake. Having done so, his fear, once again, was of the reprisals.

He ordered his column to move out. They probed south, seeking a new patch of forest in which to hide. Over several days they covered just eighty kilometres, the enemy were so thick on the ground. Retreating from the advancing Allied forces, the Germans were converging on the western wall of the Vosges, being funnelled into the very area where Farran had chosen to operate. In short, at every turn the ground was thick with their forces.

Farran's patrols left more burning vehicles and dead Germans – as often as not, officers – in their wake. Their war diary gave the flavour of one such bloody confrontation. 'Two jeeps met an enemy six-wheeled car, which halted; two officers got out, one armed with a Schmeisser. Dvr. Beckett, expecting them to be Americans, walked towards them. One officer with a Luger pointed it . . . and said "Haende Hoch". Beckett pushed the gun away and fell into the ditch to escape the tracer fired from the jeep . . . The remaining officers in the car tried to get out. Two succeeded and attempted to climb over a wall, but were killed against it. The others perished in the car, which caught fire.'

But as the war diary reflected, the hue and cry was up for Farran's patrol. 'Truck loads of Germans had been inquiring at all villages to the south of the forest about British parachutists, and there were rumours that the maquis at Grandrupt had been betrayed by one of their own officers. The squadron felt a little uneasy.' To all sides the search intensified, and villages were put to the torch by a vengeful enemy.

Somewhere to the north of the town of Vesoul, Farran was forced to go to ground in a tiny patch of woodland no more than two miles square. It was mid-September by now and to all sides lay the enemy. It was last light by the time Farran had sorted his encampment, and he was gripped by a sense of unease. To left and right he could hear the sound of grunting engines – hostile forces on the move.

He ordered Lieutenant Gurney to take a jeep and push to the western fringe of the woods. Might it offer an avenue of escape, should there be trouble? Gurney was under firm orders not to 'brew up' any traffic on that side, but he'd been gone barely five minutes when the distinctive rasp of the jeep's Vickers machine-guns tore apart the dusk. As the war diary recorded, he'd 'brewed up a staff car containing five brass hats. The death of those senior officers, including a general, was confirmed . . .'

In short, the target had proved just too tempting. Farran had got his signaller to break out their wireless set, to send that evening's scheduled radio report to London, but he sensed that

Gurney's action spelled trouble. The lone jeep came charging back and Gurney had disturbing news. The vehicle he'd shot up was at the vanguard of a large enemy column, which had followed their jeep. As if to reinforce his warning, a sudden burst of fire tore through the woodland. 'The cover was thin . . .' the war diary recorded. 'More firing came through the trees, the bullets cutting the branches overhead.'

Any doubts that Farran had entertained vanished: the Germans knew the SAS were there and were coming in to get them. Worse still, with such a small patch of cover to hide in there would be little means to escape or evade the enemy. Farran yelled orders at his men to start up their engines and move out, as jeeps began to hammer out return fire, the smog of cordite fumes drifting thick beneath the trees.

The incoming fire intensified, as Farran kept yelling orders. It was then that he noticed Corporal Cunningham, his radio operator, calmly rolling up his W/T cable, a look of cool determination on his features: *just another night's work in the SAS.* Cunningham's steely calm was like a bucket of cold water in the SAS commander's face. As at Châtillon, when they'd been pinned under that hedge by ferocious machine-gun fire, it was time for Farran to get a grip.

He steeled himself to lead the column of jeeps onto the lone track that cut through the trees – the same one that the enemy were advancing along. He turned right, pushing ahead at top speed, the jeeps bucking over the rough ground as they raced away from the enemy. They reached the far end of the phalanx of woodland, turned right again onto a rutted farm track, finding their way into some thick bushes. Farran had just managed to steer them into cover, when the lead vehicles got bogged in deep mud. Now they were well and truly for it.

He ordered the engines cut. Frantically, desperately, men tore down branches and vegetation and threw it over the jeeps to camouflage them, while others hurried along the track to obliterate their tyre tracks, using the foldable spades that each of the vehicles carried. If they were discovered here they would fight, but there was little hope of getting mobile any time soon. There was nothing for it but to lie low and wait.

Noises drifted across to them. Cries in the night-dark woodland. The odd burst of gunfire. The sound of figures crashing about among the trees. The SAS men were afraid even to cough, let alone to drop a tin of food. One tell-tale sound might give them away. It began to rain – a cold, hard rain frosted by the high ground of the Vosges. There was no option but to sit in those jeeps mired in the mud, shivering, as the rain soaked everyone to the skin.

A long column of enemy vehicles began to move down the nearby road, less than a hundred yards away. They could hear a German military policeman directing the traffic, and yelling out warnings to each passing vehicle to be wary of 'terrorists'. It proved to be a night of knife-edge tension, deep discomfort and very little sleep and by first light the enemy half-tracks and trucks were still thundering past.

'It was the most unpleasant night ever spent,' Farran recorded in the war diary. 'The party was faced with a situation which almost seemed hopeless; if they were attacked at dawn as seemed probable, they would have lost their mobility, as three jeeps were completely stuck and the remainder behind in the bottle neck.'

But at eleven o'clock that morning the woods finally fell silent. Farran reckoned almost 2,000 vehicles had passed in the night, but now the highway was deserted. He ordered his men – sodden, fatigued and chilled to the bone – to wrestle the jeeps free of the mud. That done, they had to push them by hand down the track, as he dared not risk starting their engines. It was back-breaking work. Only when they had finally reached the road and could make a dash for uncertain safety, did he order his men to fire up the jeep's straight-four 'Go Devil' petrol engines.

The squadron took to the highway, racing further east, following the enemy's line of retreat. They'd motored for some thirty-five kilometres, when, on the approach to the town of Luxeuil-les-Bains, they encountered a sizeable patch of woodland. It appeared to be deserted, and Farran seized on it as their new base of operations. By luck, they managed to link up with a new band of Maquis, commanded by a surgeon called Docteur Topsent. With his help and guidance, Farran selected a slew of targets for the coming night's operations. He 'was determined to make the Germans pay for the miserable night he had just passed,' the war diary recorded.

Lieutenant Gurney was despatched to Velorcey village, about ten kilometres south of their hideout, where a column of enemy were said to be holed up. Gurney had one of Docteur Topsent's Maquis riding with him, as guide. Farran sent Lieutenant Burtwhistle, another officer newly arrived with the squadron, to Fontaine-lès-Luxeuil, ten kilometres in the opposite direction, where a German horse-drawn artillery column had recently set up camp. And Big Jim Mackie led an attack towards Luxeuil-les-Bains itself.

Gurney's team were the first into action, but they were dogged by bad luck. As fate would have it, their jeeps rounded a bend and came face-to-face with the enemy column at a range of no more than ten yards. Gurney got the drop on the enemy, but his initial burst of fire cut through a truck loaded with explosives. It detonated in an almighty explosion, both the enemy troops and the SAS jeeps being caught in the blast.

Both sides in the confrontation – SAS and Germans – were ripped to pieces. Gurney managed to extricate himself from the carnage, but he was cut down by a burst of fire as he dashed up the village street. 'Lieut. Gurney was hit in the back and fell; he died shortly afterwards,' the war diary recorded. 'The French . . . described how the Germans kicked the body of the "English terrorist", but eventually they were able to bury him in the village cemetery.'

Lieutenant Burtwhistle's patrol fared little better in Fontaine-lès-Luxeuil. Opening fire on the horse-drawn column, his guns tore into the enemy ranks and set a line of carts ablaze. But in the process, three of his men were wounded, and one jeep totally destroyed. They were lucky to make it out of there alive.

Typically, Jim Mackie's attack at Luxeuil-les-Bains went better, but after that night's losses Farran didn't doubt that luck was turning against them. By now, he could hear the thunder of American artillery somewhere to the west, and the roads were bumper-to-bumper with retreating enemy vehicles. There was little question of mounting any further offensive operations. Instead, they needed to shrink further into the depths of the forest and hide. 'The German resistance had stiffened,' the war diary recorded, 'and the situation . . . had become very precarious.'

No sooner had Farran's squadron camouflaged their vehicles, than a German artillery column drew into the cover of some nearby trees. It consisted of a unit of *Panzerabwehrkanone* 43 anti-tank guns, which had earned a fearsome reputation among

Allied troops. The 88mm cannon could penetrate the armour of any British, American or Russian tank and it was accurate up to a thousand yards. It would make mincemeat out of the SAS's unarmoured jeeps, especially as the nearest guns were no more than a hundred yards away.

For three days Farran and his men hunkered down, listening to the voices of the 88mm crews filtering through the trees. Other than sending out the odd patrol on foot, to try to make contact with US forces, there was little they could do but keep silent, hide and wait. In the war diary Farran described this time as 'absolute hell. No one dared talk above a whisper, and every time somebody dropped something they expected a German to appear.'

At one juncture a tin of bacon spontaneously exploded. It must have been damaged during a drop and the contents gone off, the pressure of the gas caused by decomposition building up inside the tin. It sent everyone into a panic, diving for their weapons. If the German gunners heard it, they didn't seem inclined to respond. US artillery was hurling forward a constant barrage of fire, so what was a tin of exploding bacon between enemies?

On the morning of their fourth day in hiding, the Maquis led a group of figures into Farran's position. Overnight, the 88mm gunners had collapsed their camp and melted away. Docteur Topsent had brought with him the crew of an American armoured car, who were riding at the vanguard of the advancing US forces. Farran and his men were so overjoyed at seeing them that they danced a highland jig on the spot.

During a month of such operations deep behind the lines, the SAS commander and his men had been under enormous nervous strain. It wasn't a moment too soon to have been relieved. So began the squadron's long drive back through liberated France, during which Farran was able to observe the burned-out skeletons of staff cars and trucks that they had destroyed, as they'd wrought carnage among the enemy across northern France.

Farran would be awarded a DSO for his actions, the citation for which speaks volumes: 'Confirmed damage, inflicted upon the enemy by the small force under Major Farran, amounted to approximately 500 killed or wounded, 23 staff cars destroyed, 6 motorcycles, and 36 vehicles including trucks, troop-carriers and a petrol wagon. In addition a dump of 100,000 gallons of petrol was destroyed, a goods train taken out, and . . . much essential information and bombing targets passed back by W/T.'

'W/T' stood for wireless transmission – reflecting the ability of Farran's signallers to radio back target coordinates.

Of the Châtillon attack in particular, Farran's citation stated: 'at least 100 Germans killed and a considerable number wounded, while SAS casualties were 1 killed and 2 wounded. This well-conceived and brilliantly-executed operation caused the enemy to mistake Major Farran's squadron for the advance elements of the US 3rd Army and therefore to withdraw from Châtillon sooner than necessary. His personal courage, initiative and tactical sense, enabled him to direct his small force with minimum loss.'

A week or so after linking up with those advance US troops, Farran and his men arrived back in the UK. They were looking forward to some much-needed leave, before the next behind-the-line mission, most likely northern Europe again – possibly the Netherlands or Norway.

But for Major Roy Farran an entirely different future beckoned, on a mission of untold sacrifice and daring.

Chapter 5

Unsurprisingly, Mike Lees emerged from his epic crossing-the-line mission to a hero's welcome. His verbal briefings and the sketches he carried of enemy positions electrified Allied high command, while the two Italian resistance leaders – Salvi and Piva – also yielded priceless intelligence. Lees' record from October 1944 reflected what a star performer he had become in the eyes of the SOE.

'He is energetic, courageous, fit and willing to undergo physical hardships, and has a good knowledge of Para Military activities for which he is ideally suited,' concluded Lt.Col. R. T. 'Dick' Hewitt, one of SOE Maryland's senior commanders. 'An excellent paramilitary officer,' added none other than Major General William Stawell, head of special operations across the Mediterranean region. 'He has a most attractive personality.'

Lees seemed destined for higher things. Hewitt and Stawell's Special Confidential Report on Lees was rushed to SOE's headquarters, in London. His record from autumn 1944 reflected the fact that Lees was being shaped for a new role – namely to join the Secret Intelligence Services (SIS, also known as MI6). MI5 – the UK's domestic intelligence agency – began running deep background checks on Lees, with a view to clearing such a role.

Oddly, MI5 picked up an issue of possible concern. 'During 1939 and 1940 a titled lady with identical surname, of Lytchett

Minster, Dorset, came to our notice as a pacifist propagandist. Her pacifism was based upon religious principles . . .' MI5 were referring to Lady Madeleine Lees, Michael Lees' aunt, known as 'Auntie Maddie' to all. Thankfully, the domestic intelligence agency was able to conclude there were 'no grounds for believing her activities intended to be subversive'.

That October a formal application for Lees to transfer to SIS was got underway. Lees duly signed the Official Secrets Act, declaring: 'I undertake not to divulge any official information gained by me as a result of my employment either in press or book form . . .'

Perhaps unsurprisingly, those at the helm of SOE were less than keen to let Lees go, or at the very least not until the war was won. SOE wrote to the Secret Intelligence Service, agreeing only to 'submit this officer's name and qualifications . . . at the termination of hostilities in Europe . . . His name will not be submitted now, as it is felt that his release from S.O.E. at this stage . . . is undesirable.' A few days later a reply on 54 Broadway headed paper – for two decades 54 Broadway was the central London headquarters of the Secret Intelligence Service – read: 'Let us leave it that when the time comes that you have no further employment for him, you will let us know.'

While the tug-of-war over Michael Lees was underway, what the man himself hungered for most was getting a flight over the Gothic Line to rejoin Major Temple and his Italian partisans. That autumn Lees found himself in the SOE's forward base in the city of Florence, which lay just to the south of the Gothic Line. Florence had recently been liberated and was fully under Allied control, and Lees was desperate to find a way to return to war.

His other chief concern, of course, was whether Morton, Long, McClelland and the rest of his original party would make it safely through the lines. The news, when it reached him, was most edifying. It came by telegram in November 1944: 'Morton and Long with four others arrived by boat at Mentone this morning.' Mentone was the same ancient port town that Lees and his party had first been taken to, after crossing the lines on foot.

War reporter Morton had commanded a reduced party of just six, including the giant piratical raider, McClelland, plus Sergeant Bob La Rouche, a USAAF air gunner who had been shot down on operations. Forced to leave Pigna village when it had come under enemy assault, they had disguised themselves as Italian country-folk, opting to follow Lees' advice and seek a sea-borne means of escape.

En route to the coast they'd stumbled upon a piece of priceless intelligence. A partisan leader had passed on captured German documents, including maps showing all the minefields for that section of the Gothic Line. Morton, Long and party had proceeded to sneak through German checkpoints carrying those documents, and disguised in the traditional dress for locals sheltering from the rain – potato sacks.

'We were able to wear sacks over our heads in the approved peasant fashion, which added to our disguise,' recorded Morton and Long in their post escape report, penned for the SOE. It was a real dash of ingenuity.

Thus disguised, they'd made it to a friendly fisherman's house, intending to row across the lines themselves. Instead, he'd offered the assistance of his two strapping sons – seasoned seafarers. Their addition made what had been a daunting voyage something of a pleasure cruise. 'Once out of mortar,

88mm and machine-gun range we turned broadside to the coast,' Morton recorded. 'I unlimbered the bottle of Cognac and passed it around. We started to sing patriotic songs. Fair stood our boat for France!'

Upon reaching Allied lines, Morton, Long and La Rouche personally briefed Colonel Blythe, of the American 7th Army, on their escape. La Rouche and Morton went on to report to Major General Curtis LeMay, a senior USAAF commander in Europe, on all that they had learned. LeMay was keenly interested in their accounts of operations with the resistance. He wanted to build airstrips across territory held by the partisans, to greatly increase the Allies' reach.

Subsequently Long and Morton appeared on *Italia Combatte* (Italy Fights), a radio station based in southern Italy, and operated by the Political Warfare Executive, transmitting direct to the Italian resistance. They had emerged from their daring sojourn with a huge respect for the partisans, and this was reflected in their *Italia Combatte* broadcasts.

In his official SOE report Lees made clear he shared their enthusiasm. 'The Partisans are always ready to take advice and grateful for encouragement or acknowledgement of their work . . . The morale of the Partisans is excellent. The Italians are particularly suited to this flamboyant type of work. They have great ingenuity and are very keen. They do not need encouragement to carry out demolitions.'

Lees urged greater 'propaganda' support for the partisans, and for the message of their successes to be more widely heard. 'The Partisans should be encouraged by broadcast to mine all roads and attack German convoys and troops on the move. There are tremendous possibilities in this type of work.' Such efforts to arm and support the partisans could significantly aid the breaking of the Gothic Line, he argued.

Long was interviewed on BBC radio, where he spoke in glowing terms about how the partisans 'make the Germans' life a hell. They snipe [at] them in the street. They ambush them wherever they move in small numbers . . . I don't suppose the partisans kill more than ten Germans a week. They make for a constant nerve-racking hell for thousands every day though.'

Tellingly, Long concluded: 'There is a faith in one thing, an indefinable fineness in human nature, a quality they believe will live again in this their country, given one condition – that not one man of the enemy's [forces] will remain.' Such a message must have been music to the partisans' ears.

Morton echoed Long's sentiments, speaking on CBC (Canadian Broadcasting Corporation) radio. 'Patriot guns are roaming all northern Italy. They are hitting the Germans and Fascists wherever they find them. They are controlling villages and towns, helping the poor and depressed, feeding the starving. And when the opposition against them grows too tough they creep back into their mountain strongholds, fighting as they go.'

In so speaking out, Morton and Long were fulfilling Churchill's edict to win the information war by lauding the achievements of the resistance. They were also fulfilling their SOE brief, to 'provide the Press an account of patriot activities and sabotage exploits'. Their daring escape and the intelligence – and white propaganda – they had furnished was another feather in Michael Lees' cap, or so it should have been.

But it was now that a shadow began to cast its malevolent presence over the SOE's Italian operations, one that would dog Mike Lees' return to behind-the-lines operations. As Morton set about preparing a series of scintillating newspaper reports – which the British Army censor declared to be the most exciting that he had ever read on the Italian campaign – the winds of fortune were rapidly turning against him.

By the time Morton had polished off his stories, which were to be syndicated worldwide, he was called to Rome, to appear before the senior commanders of Canadian Army Public Relations. Having led a daring escape across the lines, bringing with him priceless intelligence and an American airman, plus the 'white propaganda' that he and Long had prepared, Morton was more than a little surprised at the reception he received.

With little ceremony, he was told that due to 'inappropriate conduct' and other 'unspecified offences', his accreditation as a Canadian war correspondent was being revoked. Further disciplinary action was pending. On the night before deploying to the field it was SOE tradition – long-standing, irrevocable – that agents would have a few stiff drinks. Indeed, a redoubtable SOE veteran, one Sergeant Carter, ran a bar beside the flight line for just such purposes.

Likewise, Lees and his party had enjoyed a good booze-up before they deployed on Operation Flap. Someone had challenged Morton's martial credentials, for he was a reporter and no soldier. Morton had responded by pulling his pistol and shooting some holes in the bar. Fairly tame stuff, by the standards of SOE pre-departure high jinks. Supposedly, that was the 'inappropriate conduct' being cited as the reason for Morton's accreditation being cancelled.

Far worse was to follow. When Morton contacted his employer, the *Toronto Daily Star*, he learned that only one of his reports – the first, 'I live with patriots in Nazi lines' – was to be published.

It was too late to stop that. But all the rest – Morton's eight subsequent stories, all of which had been cleared by the British Army censor – were to be cancelled.

Stubborn, dogged, undeterred, Morton sought other outlets for his stories, but after initial enthusiastic reactions doors kept slamming in his face. In short, he could find no publisher for those further articles, and the original plans for worldwide syndication withered and died. That this should all be due to some drunken high spirits immediately prior to mission departure made little sense.

In truth, the dark machinations now being orchestrated against the hapless reporter went far deeper. Morton had earned a reputation among the SOE as being a brave and talented reporter and a capable leader of men, so who had slid in the proverbial knife? Why the stab in the back for a man who should have won fulsome praise?

That autumn, the Political Warfare Executive had been transferred to the Foreign Office, the arm of the British state overseeing foreign affairs. Subsequently, it had been amalgamated with the equivalent American body, the new organisation being renamed the Psychological Warfare Division (PWD). PWD was to specialise in many forms of psychological operations. One of its favourite tactics was scattering 'black propaganda' leaflets over enemy lines from the air, or assaulting the enemy ranks with loud-speaker-born propaganda.

In the autumn and winter of 1944 the message emanating from the PWD – the mouthpiece of the secret British and American states – began to change markedly over Italy. At first, there were intimations that the role of the resistance should be given a little less prominence. Suggestions were made that the partisans, many of whom had avowedly communist leanings, should no longer receive such widespread Allied support, with a view to the new war that was coming – the Cold War.

By November 1944 this had crystallised into a specific set of directives, by which the Foreign Office sought to redefine Allied objectives. They identified the first and overriding policy in Italy as being the need to halt the spread of communism. Second was the need to create a stable nation following liberation, which would look to the Allies – and not Soviet Russia – in the post-war world. The third – *and last* – priority was to mobilise the partisans to aid in the defeat of Nazi Germany.

'I am very much afraid that, if we are not careful, we shall be building up in northern Italy with arms and money a rival Italian government,' the Foreign Office (FO) warned. The FO criticised the eagerness of Allied commanders to 'make use of this Resistance Movement', worrying that communist partisans would seize control. In November PWD issued a clear directive ordering the 'playing down' of the role of the partisans by all concerned.

Those at the helm of SOE Maryland railed against this *volte face*. They lobbied for the support of the partisans to continue. Time and again they argued that the communist partisans would come peacefully into line once the war in Italy was won. That same month General Alexander himself – Allied commander-in-chief in Italy – issued his 'Winter Directive', in which he continued to laud the achievements of the Italian resistance, working hand in glove with the SOE.

'What do the partisans do?' he asked, rhetorically. 'The toll of bridges blown, locomotives derailed . . . small garrisons liquidated, factories demolished, mounts week by week, and the German nerves are so strained, their unenviable administrative situation taxed so much further, that large bodies of ... troops are constantly tied down ... Almost any frontline troops could tell stories of Partisan assistance ... Their fighting qualities and local knowledge are constantly proved invaluable.'

An increasingly bitter power struggle was in train over the fate of the Italian resistance. On one side was the military and the SOE; on the other, the Foreign Office and the PWD. It was no secret who wielded the darker power: the Psychological Warfare Division were past-masters. In the dying months of 1944 war reporter Paul Morton's message – that the Italian partisans, communists included, were embroiled in a noble and heroic struggle deserving full Allied support – ran contrary to what they intended.

There was a rift developing between those determined to further military support for the partisans, in order to help vanquish the enemy, and those who believed the need to combat communism should take priority. That fault line had sucked in an unwitting victim: Paul Morton. That was why he – and his stories – had to be disavowed and, if necessary, destroyed.

Of course, Michael Lees was privy to little if any of this. His reports made clear that he had few concerns regarding the partisans' political leanings. Pragmatically, he concluded: 'At present, the political situation is not dangerous. There is ill-feeling amongst the two main Parties, but as yet no action. With firm Allied control there is no reason why any dissention should arise ...'

Unaware that moves were afoot to sideline – betray – the Italian resistance, Lees continued to lobby for a return to 'his' partisans, as he saw it, rejoining Major Temple's mission. But in late November 1944 his hopes were to be utterly dashed. Lees received a shattering message: surrounded by enemy forces determined to finish off his partisan forces, Major Temple had been killed. News of his tragic loss had reached SOE headquarters via radio, from Bert Farrimond, Temple's dour Lancastrian coal miner turned W/T operator.

'The area was under considerable enemy mortar fire,' Farrimond telegraphed, 'and Major DAREWSKI decided we should leave on a truck loaded with stores . . . Before he was able to climb on the truck the driver let in the clutch and the truck seemed to skid and crush Major DAREWSKI against the wall. I was told that he had fractured both arms and probably his pelvis.'

Major Temple had been evacuating his headquarters, as the enemy executed a fierce sweep of the valley. Never one for hyperbole, Farrimond reported that 'everything went wrong, catastrophe overtook us, the Major receiving fatal injuries in the accident.' Within forty-eight hours Farrimond had been pulled out by air. 'With the Major gone the mission was finished, so to this end . . . I came out with eleven others in a bomber . . .'

Lees mourned the loss of such an iconic figure and good friend, not to mention the collapse of the entire Flap mission. A few days after being pulled out, Farrimond met up with him in Florence. They had much to discuss. In the days prior to his death Temple had taken his mission to new and unprecedented heights. Via the landing strip that they'd just finished constructing, he'd requested a drop of fifty million Lire, to fund ongoing partisan operations. He'd also asked for twenty-five cargo aircraft to fly in, with weaponry and arms.

Temple's 12 November shopping list reflected the scale of combat that he feared was coming: '25 81mm mortars (English), petrol 500 gallons, clothing and 3,000 blankets, 2,500 rifles and Stens and heavy automatic weapons. What about Breda 20mm or even 40mm [heavy cannons]. Is it possible to land? If so both the landing ground and the whole area could be held against all-comers.'

He reported on a recent raid by his partisans, one that had been so successful that Il Duce – Mussolini, the Italian Fascist dictator – himself had decreed that Temple's partisans were to be destroyed 'at all costs'. In response, some 3,000 German and Italian troops backed by armoured cars and tanks had thundered into the region, to wipe out Temple's 500-odd partisans.

It was mostly to resist this offensive that Temple had sent his 12 November shopping list of arms and equipment. Though its tone was somewhat desperate, little had reached him in terms of the supplies that he'd requested, and six days later Temple was dead, his surviving partisans scattered into the mountains. As for Farrimond, he'd got out by the skin of his teeth: he'd been lifted out from the airstrip just before enemy forces overran it.

Had Major Temple received the supplies that he'd requested, his forces might have held firm. The failure to provide them arguably cost him his life and signalled an end to the Flap mission. By the winter of 1944, supply flights to the partisans had dropped off to critically low levels. SOE agents in the field were complaining bitterly that they and their partisans were being thrown to the dogs.

Having lamented the loss of their dear friend, Lees turned to the other business that was foremost in his mind. He had a sense that an alternative mission was about to come his way, and he wanted to know if the long-experienced radio operator might join him. Married to local Lancashire girl Jane Glover, Farrimond was an utterly reliable salt-of-the-earth type. Now approaching his 34th birthday, he was a hugely-experienced pair of hands, hence Lees' hunger to recruit him.

At outbreak of war Farrimond had signed up to the 2nd Fife and Forfar Yeomanry, an armoured regiment more commonly known as the 'Knife and Forkers' – motto, 'For Hearth and Home'. But in August 1943 he'd been sought out by SOE. On paper Farrimond was an odd recruit: it was his wireless abilities that would draw him into the cloak-and-dagger world. In October 1943 he'd duly signed the Official Secrets Act, pledging to preserve 'any sketch, plan, model, article, note, document or information which relates to munitions of war,' or 'any secret official code word, or pass word . . .'

In November 1943 the former coal miner was posted to India, to complete a short course at SOE's Eastern Warfare School, before being sent for wireless training at their specialist radio school, codenamed ME9, situated near Meerut, a city in northern India near the foothills of the Himalayas. In a sense, there was no better training ground for behind-the-lines operations in the Italian mountains. For his subsequent services on Operation Flap, Farrimond was recommended for a Mention in Despatches. But the gritty former collier didn't much hanker after gongs: what he wanted most was to return to the mountains.

Lees asked what he had been up to since his evacuation. 'I'm just waiting around for orders,' Farrimond replied.

'D'you want to get back into North Italy?' Lees probed.

Farrimond paused before answering. 'It all depends on what I'd have to do.'

Lees had already been assigned a radio operator, but he'd far prefer to take a man of Farrimond's pedigree, one with whom he'd built up such a close rapport. 'Would you like to come in again with me, Bert?'

Farrimond was silent for a moment. 'I'd go with you, sir, if I went with anyone . . .' he ventured. 'When are you going?'

Lees replied that he didn't know for sure, but no sooner than a week's time, at the very earliest. He asked Farrimond to think it over. That evening Farrimond returned to see Lees. He told him that he wanted in: if Captain Michael Lees was deploying, so would Corporal Albert Edward Farrimond. It now only remained for the SOE's Maryland office to clarify the nature of their coming operation.

SOE'S Italian mission had been codenamed Maryland by its chief, Commander Gerald 'Gerry' Holdsworth, for a very specific reason. A still-waters-run-deep type, Holdsworth – a seasoned mariner and a former rubber planter from Malaya (now Malaysia) – nursed a deep passion for the things he cared about, plus an occasionally explosive temper. He'd been described variously as being 'as brave as they come', 'half hero, half pirate', and an 'expert in clandestine warfare in all its aspects'.

A former film-maker, Holdsworth had been recruited into SOE by the traditional 'tap on the shoulder' method. He'd played a key role organising and commanding the 'Helford Flotilla', a collection of small boats that ferried the earliest SOE recruits to and from occupied France. Its base was a farmhouse called Ridifarne, on the secluded Helford River, in Cornwall, from where the flotilla set sail. The Ridifarne HQ had been run by Holdsworth's wife, Mary, herself a top expert in the use of explosives for demolition and sabotage work.

Fittingly, Holdsworth had named SOE'S Italian mission after her, and he cared about it as passionately as he did its namesake. He was backed to the hilt by Major General Gubbins, SOE's chief.

'It is desperately important to encourage resistance in northern Italy by every means possible,' Gubbins had urged. Likewise, General Alexander had exhorted SOE to unleash maximum efforts against the enemy, and he had gone as far as speaking to the Italian resistance leaders directly, urging 'violent and sustained' attacks.

That their work had borne fruit was perhaps best gauged by the reaction of the enemy. By the summer of 1944, German intelligence had reported some 20,000 dead, wounded or missing at the hands of the partisans. None other than Field Marshal Kesselring – Hitler's chosen commander in Italy – had started to refer to the Italian resistance in the following haunting terms: 'Our Wehrmacht [unified armed forces] is being stopped by a shadow.'

By October Kesselring had become so concerned that he decreed 'a week of anti-partisan war'. He'd ordered his best forces, equipped with tanks, flame-throwers and artillery, to take the fight to the hills. When such measures failed to secure a definitive victory, Kesselring – with Hitler's encouragement – ordered his men to resort to widespread brutality.

'It is the duty of all troops and police in my command to adopt the severest measures,' he announced. 'Every act of violence committed by the partisans must be punished immediately.' He ordered 'a proportion of the male population' to be shot, while pledging to 'protect any commander who exceeds the usual restraints'. Hitler added fuel to the fire, ordering ten partisans killed for every German casualty.

Winston Churchill – a key proponent of irregular warfare across occupied Europe – was privy to Kesselring's orders. Codebreakers working at Bletchley Park had decrypted the German commander's messages, sending them directly to the British prime minister. They made for grim reading. In August 1944, in the village of Sant'Anna di Stazzema, SS troops had machine-gunned 560 men, women and children, as reprisals for partisan operations. Then, in late September, at Marzabotto, they had per-petrated one of the single greatest massacres of the war, wiping out over 700 villagers, including the priest.

These were far from isolated examples, and the level of bes-tial horror visited on remote Italian populations was terrifying. It reflected the growing desperation of Kesselring. For many this was seen as being out of character for a commander of his long experience. A decorated First World War veteran who had masterminded the rebuilding of the Luftwaffe, Kesselring had commanded the Condor Legion in the Spanish Civil War, the forces of Nazi Germany that had fought alongside the Fascist armies of General Franco.

At the outbreak of hostilities in 1939 he had orchestrated the invasion of Poland, Holland and France. From there he'd gone on to oversee the invasion of the Soviet Union, earning Hitler's very highest regard. Kesselring had vowed to the Führer to fight for every inch of Italian soil. He was a diehard believer in the Nazi cause and had recently adopted a policy of hanging any would-be German deserters. Allied commanders respected, if not feared, his military acumen.

Come the winter of 1944, Kesselring worried about the partisan threat more than ever. It was a phenomenon that he absolutely hated and reviled – irregular, unpredictable guerrilla operations by forces that could melt into the mountains. He branded Italian resistance activities 'a degenerate form of war', deserving 'the utmost severity'. In short, Kesselring was rattled.

A high-level Allied report, written from the enemy's perspective, spelled out the 'Reasons Why the Germans Stay in Italy'. It read: 'If we wish to defend the Reich it is better to defend the frontier as far south as possible and do the fighting on someone else's soil . . . The important industrial output of North Italy contributes to our war effort . . . Italy is one of the Axis partners and nearly our only Ally left. It would be a serious blow to the political morale of our own people to abandon Fascist Italy.'

Aware of all this, SOE Maryland's chief, Holdsworth, fought tooth and nail to counter any directives that might pour cold water on the work of the Italian resistance. He had few doubts what the 150,000-odd partisans positioned north of the Gothic Line could achieve, if properly armed and trained. Crucially, they could 'harass German lines of communication by sabotage and guerrilla warfare and . . . impede the withdrawal of German forces from Italy, in order that the Allied armies might be able to get at them and destroy them.'

Heaven forbid that they should be stopped, and by what amounted to outright abandonment by the Allies. This was doubly so, for in the winter of 1944 Allied forces were under-strength, compared to those of the enemy. In December, the Allies had nineteen divisions facing Kesselring's twenty-seven, and while the Allies enjoyed air and sea superiority, the terrain, the weather and the Gothic Line itself favoured the enemy.

Allied commanders reckoned that Kesselring's attempts to crush the partisans were tying down eleven divisions. Militarily, their role was utterly critical, and so far Holdsworth and his ilk had succeeded in beating off the naysayers. Mike Lees had been promised his new mission courtesy of such efforts, but for how much longer the believers could persevere was anyone's guess.

In early December Lees was briefed on his coming deployment by Major Charles Macintosh, head of the SOE's Florence headquarters. Lees mission was critical: he was to parachute to join the partisans positioned to the rear of the Gothic Line, at the exact point at which the Allies planned to achieve their vital breakthrough.

The cold, snow-bound months of winter 1944 had become known as the 'winter of disappointment in Italy'. Churchill had been promised that the war there would be over by Christmas. Instead, the Gothic Line had held. The fighting had been relentless and the few territorial gains had been won at enormous cost. Troops were exhausted, morale was low and the weather bitter. If Lees could foment havoc in the enemy's rear, Allied forces might achieve the elusive breakthrough.

Lees' mission – codenamed Envelope – came with one or two unfortunate caveats. As Macintosh was at pains to point out, Lees was being sent in to join another SOE agent, a Major Wilcockson. Wilcockson was of an age and rank that fully justified his posting, whereas Lees, a twenty-three-year-old captain, apparently was not.

Once in the field, Lees would be under the orders either of Wilcockson, or another SOE agent, Major Jim Davies, who ran a neighbouring mission. Davies had served in the Burma jungle, before deploying to Greece with the SOE and working closely with the resistance. On the upside, he was a die-hard believer in the potential of partisan warfare. On the downside, Lees didn't particularly relish the idea of being under anyone's direct control.

Still, a mission was a mission – and this one was not to be sniffed at.

Lees and Farrimond were to be dropped during daytime to a point just a few miles behind the enemy front. They would do so during broad daylight, and Lees could only imagine that the partisans were in real strength and must hold considerable territory. Inserting that close to the Gothic Line, they were bound to see serious action and would need to liaise closely with Allied forces on the opposite side of the lines.

As Lees studied his maps, his enthusiasm grew: the terrain was high, broken and mountainous, so ideal for guerrilla operations. To Lees' mind, the potential to wage war here appeared unlimited. But while he thrilled to the prospect, he didn't feel that he'd exactly hit it off with Macintosh. The man had a somewhat effeminate manner, Lees decided, and a 'limp and clammy hand'.

Macintosh had seen action, before becoming chained to his desk at SOE's Florence headquarters. In August 1944 he'd driven into enemy-held Florence in an armoured car borrowed from the Americans, with a large white Angolan rabbit called Poggibonsi perched on top of the Vickers machine gun. It was vintage SOE. The 27-year-old Macintosh was of New Zealand extraction, and was tall, broad-shouldered and charming. Women, apparently, went wild about him. On paper, he and Lees should have hit it off, but it hadn't exactly felt that way.

A few days after his mission briefing Lees was woken at five o'clock in the morning. He dressed quickly, pulling on underclothes and battledress, plus the plethora of kit vital to such a mission: binoculars, compass, fighting knife, revolver, water bottle and medical gear. Over it all went a thick woollen flying jacket, which in turn was zipped inside a set of overalls, fashioned without any buttons or tags that might snag in a parachute harness. Lees knew that he would be thankful for all the layers: outside it was bitterly cold and it would be especially so at altitude.

For today's deployment – as with his previous SOE missions –

Lees was laden down with an extra burden: money. In addition to the several million Lire he was carrying, he'd been given a bag of gold sovereigns. That he'd tied in a handkerchief and stuffed into an ammo pouch on his belt, while thick wads of Lire were jammed into his every pocket.

It struck Lees how ludicrous the situation was: his pay, all thirty pounds a month, would be dribbling into his bank account, yet he here he was entrusted with a king's ransom in cash and gold. If he cared to steal it, no one could possibly prove that he had done so. But how else was SOE supposed to fund such operations?

The previous night he and Farrimond had transferred to Rosignano Airfield, located a few dozen kilometres south of the SOE's Florence HQ, which was situated in a villa on the outskirts of the city. At Rosignano, the US 64th Troop Carrier Group had established a flight of Douglas C-47 Skytrains – the DC-3 in civilian parlance; dubbed the 'Dakota' in British military service – the classic twin-engine transport aircraft of the Second World War. From Rosignano the 64th's mission was to service the needs of special operations across all northern Italy.

Alongside the ranks of Dakotas there were one or two other, more curious airframes. One was a distinctive Nardi FN.305, a sleek Italian two-seater trainer and liaison aircraft, which in 1939 had achieved a world speed record. The other was even more instantly recognisable: it was a spindly, long-legged Fieseler Fi 156 *Storch* – Stork – a single-engine German spotter plane with an unrivalled short take-off and landing capability.

Both aircraft had seen service with the Italian air force against the Allies. Now, they'd been repainted in friendly colours to meet the SOE's needs. They were perfect for executing ultra-clandestine flights behind the Gothic Line, and especially as they boasted a pilot of untold renown. Lieutenant Furio Lauri was an Italian fighter ace credited with twelve Allied kills, including one Lancaster bomber. He'd been shot down twice, once by a Hurricane and once by anti-aircraft fire. Both times he'd survived.

By the time of the Italian surrender he'd been awarded the War Cross for Military Valour and the Italian Crown, plus the Order of the German Eagle, among other decorations. Regardless, he'd signed up with the Italian resistance and it wasn't long before the clandestine operators had come calling. Lauri had been approached by both the SOE and the US equivalent, the Office of Strategic Services (OSS). He'd decided to work with the British, hence his installation at the Rosignano airbase on SOE business.

As he strode out to the waiting Dakotas, Lees paid those former-enemy aircraft small heed, little realising what a crucial role they would play on his coming mission. He clutched the flying suit closer to his six-foot-two frame. The sky was grey, the weather bitingly cold. Three aircraft were being readied: one was already packed with Lees and Farrimond's weaponry and kit, while the others were stuffed full of arms, ammo and supplies to drop to the partisans.

As Lees clambered aboard the American transport aircraft he was struck by how different this deployment was from those that had gone before. When heading into Yugoslavia, and later to join Major Temple, there had been rich theatre and drama in the moment. He remembered his 1943 departure, flying out to join the Yugoslavian Chetniks. The dark, gaping bomb-bay of the Halifax – the route via which agents had had to exit the aircraft – had been somehow so symbolic: a gateway into another world, one wherein all the normal rules of warfare were to be torn up and burned to a cinder. They'd dropped into a world where anything goes.

By contrast, there was something curiously flat and unemotional about climbing aboard a purpose-built aircraft like the Dakota and settling into a relatively comfortable seat. As the aircraft roared into the skies, Lees had to remind himself just what he was flying into here: he was going in to wage total war. Their destination lay less than 200 kilometres north, and he had to focus and get into the zone.

With a flight of powerful P-51 Mustang fighters as escort, the Dakotas crossed the coast before turning north. Faint flashes from a coastal hill battery revealed that they had crossed into enemy territory. The shells burst harmlessly far below their 20,000 feet cruise altitude. In perfect arrow-shaped formation the three-aircraft rumbled on towards the high mountains, as a pair of Mustangs broke off and dived to strafe the enemy gunners.

Lees studied the terrain below. He could see tiny puffs of white smoke: the opposing sides, hurling artillery barrages at each other's lines. He had crossed this war-blasted landscape barely three months earlier, executing his daring mission on foot, yet Allied and enemy positions hardly seemed to have changed at all in the interim. The stranglehold had to be broken, and Lees hungered to play his part.

The aircraft began to bank this way and that, threading a path between the highest, snowbound peaks. Beyond, the vast plain of the mighty River Po – the longest river in all of Italy – opened out before them. If Allied forces could break through to that, they could steamroller across it with their armour.

Lees thoughts were pulled back to the present by a cry that echoed through the Dakota's hold. 'There it is! There it is!'

He glanced through the aircraft's open doorway. A distinctive pattern of red dots was visible on a high snowfield. The Dakotas began to circle in line astern, spiralling down towards that point. The distinctive red dots resolved themselves to be salvaged parachutes. Figures dashed among them, now and then stopping to wave at the approaching aircraft.

The Dakota's aircrew clipped their safety straps to the hold, to prevent themselves from being thrown out accidentally. They began to stack Lees and Farrimond's kit beside the gaping doorway. Lees clambered to his feet, making one last check of his parachute harness and the kitbag strapped to his leg. It contained all his personal equipment, and was fitted with a quick-release mechanism, which would enable him to lower it on a twenty-foot rope, so it would hit the ground first, taking the impact of its own weight.

Three runs were executed over the DZ, during which the despatchers hurled out the supply containers. On the approach to the fourth, Lees struggled to the open doorway, hampered by the heavy kitbag. He took up position, glancing behind. The redoubtable Farrimond was right on his shoulder. He looked up, to check his parachute line was firmly attached to the cable running along the roof of the hold. It would trigger his chute automatically just seconds after he jumped.

He turned back to the howling void, as the floor tilted, then gently righted itself. Moments later he sensed a distinctive flutter, as the pilot throttled back the engines and the red light flashed on: prepare to jump.

The red switched to green.

With both hands gripping the side of the doorway Lees cata-pulted himself forwards, the fuselage of the aircraft flashing past in a blur.

An instant later he was tumbling into the thin and icy blue.

Chapter 6

A few weeks after his return to Britain, Major Farran was given a completely new operational area and command. He was to take charge of a recently formed SAS unit, No. 3 Squadron, and to deploy with them to Italy. There, they were to be placed under a highly unorthodox chain of command.

In Italy Farran was to report directly to the Special Operations Executive, but for its battle orders, Farran's squadron was to fall under the direct command of US General Mark Clark, the comparatively youthful and hard-charging commander of the Allies' 15th Army Group, whose forces were tasked with the liberation of northern Italy.

It was a most unusual proposition – that a full SAS squadron, some sixty-strong, would be placed under the orders of the American high command. But with Allied forces outnumbered and very possibly outgunned along the Gothic Line, nothing that might help break that bloody impasse was being ruled out, no matter how unorthodox or irregular.

Farran viewed his new mission with great enthusiasm. While he would miss his old squadron – Big Jim Mackie, among many other unique and irreplaceable characters – his new command had great promise. Raised from fresh – mostly airborne – volunteers, the men of No. 3 Squadron had been trained by one of the best, Major Oswald 'Mike' Rooney. Major Rooney was one of the longest-served veterans of British Commando and special forces operations, having raided targets from as far apart as Norway, the Channel Islands, France and Italy.

Rooney had been forced to surrender his command of No. 3 Squadron, due to injury. He'd parachuted into France on post D-Day operations, but had broken his back in the process. His loss was very much Farran's gain. Rooney's men were young, fit, well-disciplined and raring to go. Mostly in their early twenties, many had yet to see action and were keen to prove themselves. In Farran, they sensed they had a commander who would enable them to do so.

Anyone with a view to getting down and dirty on – or behind – the *Gotenstellung* had to be in Florence, the jumping-off point for combat missions. In its sumptuous villa, set within the Fiesole suburb of Florence, the SOE had established their forward operating base, and the US 15th Army Group had likewise established a headquarters in the city.

Farran would report to two equally distinctive individuals. One, Colonel John Held Riepe, was the square-jawed US Army officer in charge of all special and irregular warfare along the Gothic Line. Colonel Riepe – US Military Academy West Point graduate of the class of 1924, and a cavalry officer – was forty-three years of age, so only five years junior to his commanding general, Mark Clark. He was cut from similar cloth: rigorously professional, driven and unrelenting, Riepe was prepared to pull out all the stops to out-think and outfight the enemy.

Of course, the reputation of the British Special Air Service went before it and Colonel Riepe was a self-confessed aficionado. In Major Farran and his No. 3 Squadron SAS, he sensed he'd been sent a commander and a body of men that could truly deliver, if only the right kind of deployment could be found for them. Colonel Riepe was determined to furnish just such a mission, Florence being the springboard for all Allied special operations and partisan missions north of the Gothic Line.

The other figure who would decide Farran's fate was Major Charles Macintosh. Macintosh had been with SOE since the first Allied landings in Italy, and he'd forged a reputation as being the daring agent who had penetrated war-torn Florence in the US armoured car that he'd borrowed, proving that a telephone cable could provide communications links to the partisans in the northern half of the besieged and starving city.

Superficially, Macintosh and Farran shared many traits. It was odd, then, how the two seemed to rub each other up the wrong way. At first, Macintosh declared himself delighted to have the tough and daring special forces unit at his disposal, and with the potential to link up with SOE agents and partisans. But he soon got wise to Farran's distinctive temperament: the SAS commander was impulsive, dismissive of orders of which he didn't particularly approve and hungry for action, and Macintosh began to worry that Farran's arrival might prove something of a poisoned chalice.

'I was somewhat concerned,' Macintosh concluded of the SAS major. His worries were chiefly for the SOE's behind-the-lines intelligence-gathering networks, something that he viewed as almost of more importance than offensive operations. 'Our Intelligence networks ... were in a very delicate security situation, and security was not one of the SAS['s] strongpoints,' Macintosh remarked.

According to him, the very nature of the SAS and Farran's own character meant that 'codes, safe houses, agents and such things would weigh lightly in their plans, which, in any case, were very short term.' Macintosh saw himself and his SOE agents as playing the long game, while Farran was intent on causing maximum havoc and mayhem as quickly as possible.

One night in Florence, Farran dragged a reluctant Macintosh away from his desk on a trawl of the city bars. After a good few drinks the SAS major got into 'a couple of scraps' and Macintosh began to take an even dimmer view of the man. As Farran would be the first to recognise, the years of back-to-back missions had left him somewhat on the edge. He drank too much. He had developed a dark side. His recklessness was coupled with a growing merciless-ness for his enemies that some found disturbing. But as his actions across France had proved – and especially at Châtillon – this was a commander who very much got the job done.

Here in Italy Farran hungered for a mission that might enable his No. 3 Squadron SAS to strike a decisive blow. Farran was convinced that his men could play a seminal role, enabling Allied troops to punch through the *Gotenstellung*'s defences and precip-itating the enemy's rout. He knew that no such behind-the-lines operation would be possible without the help, guidance and firepower of the local partisans. He also knew that the Italian resistance was riven with rivalries, but where was that not the case? From Norway to Greece and from France to Yugoslavia, it pretty much came with the territory.

As far as he understood it, about two-thirds of the partisans were nominally communist, while the remainder were right-wing 'democrats'. Tensions often ran high between the two, especially over Allied weapons drops. But Farran didn't particularly give a damn. He'd have done a deal with the Devil himself, if it enabled him to fight the reviled enemy.

He didn't doubt that the Italian resistance – armed, trained and led by SAS soldiers – would prove just as capable as the French Maquis had done. All he needed was to secure a mission that would enable him and his men to link up with a suitable band of fighters. Farran longed for that mission; he burned for it, and for a very specific reason.

Several times throughout the war – most recently in France – Farran believed he'd been gifted a second life, so miraculous were his escapes and his survival. He was determined to make maximum use of it. Throughout late November and early December 1944, he lobbied tirelessly; repeatedly made his case; trod the corridors of the SOE and US Army offices in Florence without let-up. Sooner or later he felt certain he would land the kind of deployment he sought.

A previous mission, codenamed Operation Galia, had more than demonstrated how a crack SAS unit, when married up with the SOE agent on the ground, could wreak havoc in the enemy's rear. That mission had come about almost by chance, and largely due to the extraordinary exploits of one individual.

British Major Gordon Lett had escaped from an Italian prisoner of war camp in 1943, headed into the mountains and raised his own force of partisans, completely independent of any Allied support. Before the war Lett had been an accomplished mountaineer, and he was a natural at this kind of work. Incredibly, he was recruited into the SOE in July 1944 while still commanding his band of partisans and having never returned to Britain.

In November 1944, Kesselring ordered a daring counter-attack to strike the Allies where he perceived them to be at their weakest, on the far western end of their offensive line. The Allied high command learned of the threat, and turned to the SOE for a solution. It just so happened that Major Lett had established his partisan operation – codenamed Mission Blundell Violet – in exactly the area of interest to the enemy.

A troop of SAS under the command of Captain Robert 'Bob' Walker-Brown prepared to parachute into Lett's area of operations. This was no small undertaking: it would be the largest single drop of men and supplies undertaken by the SOE to date. Walker-Brown was charged to hit the enemy's lines of communication and supply, stirring up a hornet's nest in their rear. That in turn should scupper Kesselring's planned counter-attack, by tying up swathes of his troops.

No better commander could have been allocated to such a mission: Walker-Brown was himself an escaped POW, and he'd been recruited into the SAS on the strength of his own spirited getaway. Serving with the Highland Light Infantry he'd been wounded in the June 1942 Battle of the Cauldron, in the North African desert, and taken captive. He'd ended up in the Campo Prigionieri di Guerra 21, situated at Chieti, in the foothills of the Apennine mountains.

An ingenious and masterful set of tunnels were excavated, through which Walker-Brown and fellow POWs planned to slip beneath the perimeter of the camp. Amid the confusion of the signing of the Italian armistice, he and six others managed to hide there and break out. On 5 October 1943 Walker-Brown finally reached Allied lines. Subsequently recruited into the SAS, he had parachuted in to join Major Farran in France, just before his audacious assault on the German garrison at Châtillon.

There, Walker-Brown had accounted for himself admirably: so well, in fact, that just a month later he was tasked to command a mission of Operation Galia's import. Galia had proved a spectacular success. Walker-Brown and Lett led a combined SAS-partisan force through deep snows, rugged terrain and freezing, ice-bound conditions. Fording treacherous mountain streams and scaling peaks up to seven thousand feet in height, they'd marched for days on end to strike the enemy at a time and from a direction he believed impossible.

Repeatedly they'd ambushed German transport convoys, mortared enemy positions, mined roads and machine-gunned infantry columns. They executed a perfect series of butcher-and-bolt raids, of which Churchill would have been inordinately proud. The Germans reacted by launching a massive *rastrellamento* – raking through – committing 10,000 troops to surrounding the joint SAS-partisan force and annihilating it.

Walker-Brown and his SAS managed to slip the noose. They went on to capture a German officer, forcing him at gunpoint to act as their guide. They made it back to Allied lines having lost very few men, and having scuppered Kesselring's much-vaunted counter-offensive. Walker-Brown won a DSO for his achievements, the citation for which stressed his 'unparalleled guerrilla skills and personal courage'.

In short, he was driven, unconventional, impatient of political correctness, occasionally prone to cussedness and blessed with a devilish wit. Following Galia, he had a very high view of the Italian partisans, whom he found to be possessed of 'quite remarkable courage, bravery and endurance . . . after all it takes a very brave man to decide that a very small force of British parachutists is a wise thing to back, when his home and his family are surrounded . . .'

In many ways Walker-Brown and Farran were cut from similar cloth. In Italy, they would form the dream team, joining forces on a mission of untold audacity and daring. But all of that lay sometime in the future. For now, Farran was struggling to convince someone – anyone – that his No. 3 Squadron had a vital role to play. They were here, fresh into theatre, armed to the teeth and raring to go.

All they needed was someone to champion them.

Chapter 7

It was 2 January 1945 when Michael Lees, drifting beneath his parachute and blown somewhat off course, landed in an icy mountain stream. His radio operator, Bert Farrimond, ended up snagged in a nearby tree, its branches frosted with snow. With help from Lees and the partisans, Farrimond was brought down from the treetops uninjured.

They'd landed on the flank of a wide, open valley. Beyond the high peaks to the south, the crash of artillery fire echoed noisily. It struck Lees as being unbelievable that they could have parachuted so brazenly, this close to the front line. As far as he could tell, this was a heavily populated region; paths led off to left and right, and they were thick with locals leading mule trains, ready to load up the newly arrived supplies. Half a mile further down the valley the SOE agent – or British Liaison Officer (BLO) as they were known in the field – had his headquarters.

That all this could be taking place in broad daylight and in plain sight of the enemy unsettled Lees, but he reassured himself the BLO had to know what he was doing. With an escort of heavily armed partisans, he and Farrimond set off, making for his base. They'd not been walking long when they rounded a bend and came face-to-face with a tall man wearing thick glasses. The iconic tommy gun slung over his shoulder marked him out as being British, as did his bearing.

The figure gestured apologetically. 'How do you do?' he called. 'I'm Wilcockson. So sorry I wasn't there to meet you chaps in person, but no one told me you were coming.'

It was true. No one had thought to warn Wilcockson to expect Lees and Farrimond. He'd been awaiting a resupply drop only, and he'd entertained few hopes that even that would materialise. Since his deployment in September 1944, Wilcockson had succeeded in calling in just one air-drop of twelve containers, so little more than a single plane-load. He and his local fighters had survived months of terrible winter privations, after which, he reported angrily, 'the Partisans' morale was nil'.

They had been left bereft of boots, ammunition, winter clothing and rations. By Wilcockson's own admission, they saw themselves as being 'handicapped by a British Mission and alleged supply officer whose record to date was . . . a pitiful show.' It was hardly Wilcockson's fault. A former artillery officer, Major Ernest Hulton Wilcockson had carried out small-arms and explosives instruction at one of SOE's training schools, before going on to smuggle agents into enemy-occupied Crete. He was committed, experienced and capable.

But here in northern Italy he had fallen foul of the same malaise which had struck down Canadian war reporter Paul Morton – the growing rift over whether to back the Italian resistance to wage war against the enemy. During the winter months air-drops had dried up. So few and far between were they that Colin Gubbins had railed against the failures, and Gerry Holdsworth had resorted to almighty shouting matches with those in power, declaring it 'a bloody poor show'.

The statistics spoke for themselves. In June 1944, 221 tonnes of supplies had been dropped to the partisans, with even more in July. But come the autumn, resupply missions had fallen off a cliff-edge. By October they were down to a third of the summer numbers, and worse followed. It was a situation in which it was 'impossible to supply even ... minimal needs', the SOE complained, 'and this has meant disaster to many an excellent group'.

Finally, Roundell Cecil Palmer, the 3rd Earl of Selborne and Britain's Minister for Economic Warfare – so the political chief of the SOE – raised the issue directly with Churchill. 'When you have called out a Maquis into open warfare,' he wrote of the Italian resistance, 'it is not fair to let it drop like a hot potato. These men have burned their boats and have no retreat. If we fail them with ammunition, death by torture awaits.'

This was no hyperbole. Across the eighteen SOE missions presently in place north of the Gothic Line, there was a feeling close to open rebellion. One BLO wrote: 'If Command has no intention of being interested, it should not have promised arms and materials or have sent Allied Missions to give false hopes ...' Others spoke angrily of being 'abandoned, and that therefore the only thing to do was to hide'.

Wilcockson's autumn and winter reports echoed this sense of hopeless neglect. Lack of air-drops had made the 'prestige of the British Mission reach rock bottom and all-out efforts come to [a] virtual standstill . . . The position of the Partisans' supplies . . . [is] now extremely critical and any offensive operations against the enemy [are] impossible.'

This was the dire situation into which Lees – and Farrimond – had unwittingly parachuted. Regardless, they made their way to Wilcockson's headquarters, situated in the small mountain village of Gova. Before the war Gova had been a popular winter sports resort, boasting two fine hotels. Wilcockson had chosen to base himself in one, and Farrimond was delighted to learn that it still had electricity with which he could power up his radio.

As Farrimond went about establishing communications with Macintosh, at SOE's Florence headquarters, Wilcockson proceeded to brief Lees. The partisans that he was scheduled to join were called the Reggiani, after the town of Reggio Emilia, some thirty kilometres away. They'd not seen action for months, their morale was at rock bottom and their supplies and kit were in a pitiful state. It wasn't the rosiest of pictures.

'So where are the nearest enemy?' Lees asked.

'The plains are thick with them and they have garrisons strung along the main roads,' Wilcockson explained. 'The nearest is about two hours' march away.'

'But surely they must know you're here,' Lees objected. 'I'm surprised they allow you to exist so close to them.'

'Don't worry,' Wilcockson reassured him, 'they've not got the troops to spare for a full-scale attack. We've had no trouble for months now.'

Lees remained sceptical. The weather was still relatively fine for winter in these parts, but sooner or later it would break and then the real test would come. With only a few inches of snow on the ground, the partisans were still able to move relatively freely. Thick drifts and freezing conditions would change all of that. He didn't doubt that the enemy lacked the troops to man the Gothic Line and to clear out the pockets of resistance permanently, but they could launch swift, stabbing attacks to disrupt operations.

'Well, make sure your patrols are watchful tonight,' Lees warned Wilcockson. 'I'm allergic to Germans. Wherever I land they always seem to cause trouble in a day or so.'

While it had been said with a smile, Lees wasn't joking. Within forty-eight hours of deploying on his first mission, in Yugoslavia, the enemy had swooped. Lees had escaped by the skin of his teeth, but three of his party of fellow Brits were left dead or mortally wounded. Likewise, upon parachuting in to join Major Temple's mission north of the Gothic Line, Lees, Morton and Long had been under fire and fighting a series of desperate battles within hours of their arrival.

Of course, such fierce actions would have made for great newspaper copy, if only Morton had been allowed to publish his stories. As it was he had been silenced and Lees had a new and pressing mission to execute.

Wilcockson outlined the strength of the partisan forces. There were four separate brigades, of which three were communist and one hailed from the right-wing Christian Democrats – known as the *Fiamme Verdi*, or the Green Flames. When serving with Major Temple, Lees had grown accustomed to how Italians of apparently opposing political views seemed to operate happily together, so he wasn't unduly concerned. The overall commander of the partisans was a former Italian Army officer, Colonel Augusto Monti, who Wilcockson described as being pleasant enough, but hardly a live wire.

That evening Lees, Farrimond and Wilcockson dined in the hotel, waited on by a servant in formal dress and with a table laid for several courses. The food was first class: spaghetti steeped in wine with grated cheese, omelettes made with real butter, and each course accompanied by a fine vintage. The aperitif was a Marsala – similar to sherry – followed by a sparkling red, and to finish an excellent bottle of Sassolino, a strong aniseed liqueur made locally.

They had eaten far better than in so-called 'liberated' territory. Lees was amazed, especially as they were surrounded by the enemy. It was somehow so unreal, and he was determined to get down to some real war-fighting as soon as possible. The very next morning he planned to set out for Colonel Monti's HQ, to get a better sense of the lie of the land, not to mention the fighting calibre of the partisans.

But Lees awoke to find that the weather had turned. A thick blizzard was howling outside. Dressed in every item of warm clothing that he could muster, Lees headed for the hotel's front door. It was jammed solid with snow. He found an alternative exit on the lee side and stepped into the icy blast. His exposed skin was assaulted by freezing, stinging gusts, his boots sinking into the thicker drifts.

Wilcockson suggested they postpone the trip, at least until the storm blew itself out. Lees remained adamant that a start should be made. With a guide leading the way, they set forth into the tempest. The snow was falling so fast it was impossible to see from one side of the street to the other. They'd been struggling through thigh-deep drifts for half an hour or so, when the guide confessed that he couldn't find the way.

Lees wasn't entirely surprised. If they didn't retrace their steps they would be obliterated by the storm, and they mightn't even find the hotel again. By the time they reached it, their clothes were stiff with ice and all were frozen to the bone. They gathered by a crackling fire to thaw out, after which Farrimond went about raising Florence headquarters. He was in excellent spirits, despite the abortive trek, and declared that this was just the kind of mission that he'd been hoping for.

Unfortunately, his good spirits were to be short-lived.

A signal came back from Macintosh at Florence headquarters, which Farrimond duly decoded. It was addressed to Wilcockson, and it suggested that Lees had overstepped his orders. He had not been sent in to take over control of the Reggiani partisans. Any suggestion he'd made to that effect was wrong. While the message fell short of ordering Lees to withdraw – just – he'd had the rug pulled out from under his feet in spectacular fashion, and barely twenty-four hours after his arrival.

Lees sent back a typically robust missive. 'I should like to point out that this message was received by Major Wilcockson and my wireless operator, and has been the cause of considerable embarrassment . . . If it is considered that I have come into the field to pursue a position not recorded, I should be delighted to return and account for my actions . . .'

Of course, Lees had only just got his boots on the ground and he sensed an opportunity for real action here; to achieve great things. The last thing he wanted was to somehow attempt a return to Florence, to face some kind of dressing down for whatever obscure reasons. Indeed, both he and Wilcockson were left dumbfounded. The source of the growing tension – and confusion – from headquarters eluded them.

In an effort to head off the enemy at the pass, Lees telegraphed: 'Have placed myself under orders of Major Wilcockson.' He added, with emphasis, that this message 'has been read by Major Wilcockson' – so in other words, the two SOE officers were in full agreement. Lees made clear that the entire exchange should also be copied to London, as he sought some top cover from senior SOE figures.

Unbeknown to Lees, there were hidden reasons behind SOE Florence's apparent antagonism. Their hands were becoming increasingly tied. In recent weeks, none other than General Alexander himself had issued a series of orders, which on the face of it telegraphed that the military, too, was turning its back on the Italian resistance.

Alexander's directive – broadcast direct to the senior partisan leadership – had told them to 'stand-down' for the winter months. Not only that, they were to go home and conserve their ammunition and abandon all offensive action. Even more shocking, the broadcast had been made without consulting the SOE. The fear that drove Alexander's proclamation – of the Italian partisans being 'Reds' and being poised to seize power – emanated from the Foreign Office, but the orders, coming from General Alexander himself, caused utter consternation.

'Despair and confusion filled the minds of Partisans and Liaison Missions . . .' SOE Maryland bemoaned. Key partisan leaders expressed disgust at such an order. 'The battle continues and must continue,' declared one. 'There must not be a weakening of the Partisan effort, but an intensification . . .'

Faced with a growing backlash, Alexander made a telling admission. His 'go-slow' order was not of his – not of the military's – making. 'You have to realise,' he told one foremost resistance leader, who raised bitter objections, 'I am a soldier, not a politician.' It was all entirely political, and the naysayers – those who were arguing for the Italian resistance to be abandoned – were gaining the upper hand.

On 8 January 1945 a two-page memo marked 'SECRET' was circulated to the British military's Chiefs of Staff. Signed simply 'A Cadogan', its author was the Foreign Office luminary Sir Alexander Montagu George Cadogan, one of the central figures driving British policy. Scion of a titled and wealthy aristocratic family, Cadogan cited in his memo Anthony Eden, the Foreign Secretary, and one of Churchill's key deputies.

Cadogan's memo pulled no punches. He wrote: '[F]rom the political perspective the situation was potentially dangerous . . . we could not overlook the danger that the Communists who, by all accounts, are by far the best-organised of the anti-Fascist parties . . . would make a view to capturing so useful and powerful a machine, with a view to building it up as a rival of the Italian government in Rome.' That 'useful and powerful machine' was the Italian resistance, armed and organised by the SOE.

The memo went on to warn of the dangers of 'creating the essential elements for a civil war . . . While not wishing to dispute the value which . . . may be attached to the services which the Italian guerrillas in the North have rendered . . . the Secretary of State feels bound to take into consideration the possible political repercussions which may result if these guerrillas are built up beyond a certain point. He feels, therefore, that the Chiefs of Staff ought to watch the situation . . . with the utmost care.'

Increasingly, the British military's hands were tied by their political taskmasters in London. The Chiefs of Staff responded to Cadogan's directive by issuing their own orders, marked 'TOP SECRET', directing the BLOs to take the partisans in hand. 15 Army Group declared that 'future policy regarding the resistance movement in northern Italy will be to . . . concentrate on the supply of food, clothing, boots and money, rather than arms and ammunition . . .'

By January 1945, the Chiefs of Staff were referring to the 'serious problem' of the 'resistance question' in Italy, which needed to be 'thrashed out'. The focus was rapidly shifting towards a perceived need for 'the rapid disarmament and absorption into civil life . . . of all Italian Patriots,' and the 'prevention of fighting between

Patriots and Fascist forces . . . when the Germans withdraw from those parts of Italy they at present occupy.'

Michael Lees had parachuted in to join a band of partisans who, along with their BLO, had been subjected to the miseries of such directives. A wild man of action, it stood to reason that Lees wouldn't accept the status quo. As he had on previous occasions, he would find a way to fight. After all, this was a man who, when ordered to abandon offensive operations with the guerrillas in Yugoslavia, had resorted to solo sabotage missions.

Those at headquarters were getting cold feet at Lees being dropped into theatre. Charles Macintosh, chief of SOE's Florence mission, felt bound by such orders, much that he might abhor them. 'No new orders were forthcoming and the proclamation was to serve as our official guide to the Partisans throughout the winter,' he remarked. In other words, go-slow it was, at least until someone decreed otherwise.

Of course, Lees – and Wilcockson – were privy to little if any of this bigger picture stuff. Marooned in a largely deserted and snowbound hotel, and with the enemy to all sides, little of what was happening made any sense to them. In which case, they decided, they would simply bash on regardless. There was, after all, a war to be fought.

The morning after the snowstorm Lees awoke to a wonderfully still and sunlit dawn. It was just what he needed to lift his spirits. After wolfing down a breakfast of fresh eggs and bacon, he set out following the tracks villagers had beaten through the snow. The scenery was bewitchingly beautiful, but the going proved tough, and it was evening before they reached Colonel Monti's head-quarters. The journey had taken fully eight hours, demonstrating the extent to which winter conditions would hamper operations.

Colonel Monti had established his HQ in the priest's house in Febbio, a village set high in a cleft in the mountains. Only one track led into Febbio, while a narrow twisting path crawled towards a high mountain pass on the far side, now rendered impassable by the snows. It was a veritable fortress, and the colonel's headquarters was seemingly a hive of activity.

A large stone building set on the village outskirts, the priest's house turned out to be a warren of rooms. As Lees entered, he could hear the clack-clack of typewriters to all sides and the chatter of women's voices, as orderlies darted to and fro with stacks of papers. To Lees, it was doubly incongruous. He might have expected this in safe, liberated territory, but a mobile guerrilla headquarters this most definitely was not.

Colonel Monti was a man in his early fifties, tall and distinguished-looking, with a clipped cavalry officer's moustache and swept-back greying hair. Charming and well-mannered, he didn't strike Lees as being the forceful and dynamic character that a leader of irregular forces needed to be. Over dinner, the colonel briefed Lees on the forces under his command, which supposedly amounted to some 2,000 men-at-arms.

'What about defences?' Lees queried. Again, he'd been struck by how dismissive all seemed to be of the enemy threat.

'Oh, that's all taken care of,' the colonel replied. Where their positions were not shielded by the mountains, they had partisan units holding key paths and roads. But of course, if the British could drop in better weapons – mortars and heavy machine guns, for example – they could be rendered doubly secure, the colonel argued.

'What about sabotage operations?' Lees probed. 'What kind of things have your men been up to?'

It was now that the colonel became evasive. He kept trying to change the subject, waxing lyrical about the intelligence they had gathered and propaganda leaflets distributed around the towns. Lees kept pressing him, and finally the colonel admitted that over recent months offensive action had been woefully thin on the ground.

He offered excuses, some of which – such as their lack of ammunition – were entirely valid, but still Lees suspected that much was not as it should be with the Reggiani partisans. They were living in the mountains but not *fighting* in them. He worried about how he might catalyse them into action. Getting proper supply drops was key, but so too would be reigniting the partisans' belief in themselves and their ability to wage war against the enemy.

Lees sensed that the partisans needed a jolt into action. A kick up the proverbial backside. As luck would have it, they were about to receive it, but not from him. It would come from the enemy, and much sooner than even he had imagined.

Early the following morning Lees set out to return to Wilcockson's hotel base, in Gova. It was another glorious day and he had an unusual escort – a village priest turned guerrilla fighter. The warrior-priest's real name was Domenico Orlandini, but everyone knew him by his nom de guerre, Don Carlo. Don Carlo had founded the local right-wing partisans, the *Fiamme Verdi*, and he'd earned something of a reputation for fearlessness.

The priests tended to constitute the backbone of the Italian resistance. Like many, Don Carlo was a stickler for the weekly mass. One Sunday he'd been officiating with a pistol tucked under his cassock, when a messenger arrived to say that the enemy was approaching. With a remarkable coolness Don Carlo had detailed a patrol to break off from the service and take on the enemy, while he finished mass, after which he'd joined them in battle.

From the path's vantage point Don Carlo proceeded to point out the key features. To their backs lay Monte Cusna, the second highest in the Apennines at 7,000 feet, its humped expanse thick with snow. To their left reared Mount Prampa, a little over 5,500 feet, with one of the few roads that cut through the region snaking around its lower slopes. To their front lay the village of Villa Minozzo, which had been twice burned by German troops in reprisals for partisan actions. Beyond that lay the Secchia river, one of the Po's main tributaries, and beyond that again lay the nearest German garrison.

'What's the strength of the garrison?' Lees asked, as he eyed their position through binoculars.

'About three hundred, normally,' the priest answered. 'But I hear a battalion of *Brigate Nere* arrived last night.'

The *Brigate Nere* – Black Brigades – were more formally known as the Auxiliary Corps of the Black Shirts' Action Squads, a Fascist militia loyal to Mussolini. Equipped with standard Italian Army uniforms, they tended to favour items of German military dress. They wore a distinctive badge: a death's head skull with a dagger gripped between its teeth, very similar in design to the SS's own *Totenkopf*. Raised to fight the Allies and the partisans, they'd proved ill-disciplined and ineffective, earning a reputation for brutality, especially against civilians.

But Lees' chief concern was what the arrival of this battalion, some three hundred-strong, might signify. 'Any idea why they've been brought in now?'

Don Carlo shrugged. 'Who knows? Maybe to reinforce the

front line, though *Brigate Nere* don't normally serve a front-line role.'

They set off again. The route before them had been well trodden, and it carved a path between deep banks of snow that glittered in the fine January light. It was mid-morning when, without any kind of warning, they rounded a bend and came face-to-face with Wilcockson. Behind him stretched a long mule train, and Lees could see that his wireless set, weaponry and other kit was loaded aboard one of the heavily laden pack animals.

'Hello, moving house or something?' he called.

Wilcockson stopped and stared. 'Good God, haven't you heard? The Jerries put in an attack last night . . . They captured Gova this morning and we only just managed to get out in time. You're a bloody Jonah, you are! Your arrival's broken our luck.'

Wilcockson's 'Jonah' reference was to the biblical figure pop-ularised in the story of Jonah and the whale – more commonly referring to a person who brings bad luck. It struck Lees as being a little unfair. After all, he'd warned Wilcockson to be doubly vig-ilant. It also struck him that despite Colonel Monti's expansive set up, they'd received zero warning of the enemy attack.

Clearly, whatever kind of bush telegraph the partisans relied upon to spirit warnings around these hills, it wasn't working very well. As Lees garnered a hurried briefing from Wilcockson, what news there was appeared worrying. Resistance by the partisans was piecemeal and chaotic, Colonel Monti's so-called leadership seeming non-existent. There was an air of panic, as enemy forces closed what looked to be a carefully set trap.

They'd sent in a full division of German troops – some 10,000-plus soldiers – on a massive sweep of the territory. Organising such a push must have taken weeks, so it was sheer coincidence that it had happened a day or so after Lees' arrival. Enemy commanders had clearly been awaiting the first heavy snowfalls, in the hope of trapping the partisans and wiping them out.

Advancing from the east, they had overrun the key defences on that flank of the valley. Simultaneously, the *Brigate Nere* – the same force that Don Carlo had identified – had advanced from the north, crossing the Secchia river and thrusting deep into the valley. Even the high mountains to the south had proved no block to the enemy: a battalion of Austrian alpine troops equipped with skis were even now assaulting Febbio, site of Colonel Monti's HQ.

In short, Lees and the warrior-priest had escaped by a combination of sheer luck and good timing. But only so far. Panic seemed to be the order of the day, and partisans were donning civilian clothes in an effort to escape. Worst of all, little reliable information was available about the exact whereabouts of the enemy. In short, the legions of the resistance had buckled, broken and run.

Blind to enemy gains, the only option open to Lees and Wilcockson was to avoid every track and path, no matter how little used. Only by so doing might they evade the enemy. So began a nightmare march, as long bursts of gunfire echoed across the terrain. Struggling through the deep snow they dropped towards the valley floor, beyond which lay the uncertain refuge of the high ground. To reach it they would need to push north across the Secchia and the main road, which hugged the river's course.

It was dusk by the time their exhausted party reached the nearside river bank. The scene was utterly bleak: a deep carpet of white fringed the roaring waters, which snaked through flat, open, windswept terrain, with flanking mountains to either side.

The small village of Costabona lay just ahead of them, a satellite of the larger Villa Minozzo. If the enemy were watching, now was the time when Lees and his party would be hit, out in the open and devoid of cover as they were.

To make matters worse, one of the mules refused to enter the water. Nothing would persuade the pig-headed animal to move. As daylight faded and the moon rose eerily from behind the hills, that lone mule remained stubbornly immobile. In desperation, Lees, who'd spent much of his youth riding on his family's Dorset estate, climbed into its rough wooden saddle, but even he couldn't budge it. There was no option but to unload the obdurate beast and pile the extra kit onto aching shoulders.

Thus doubly encumbered, Lees waded into the raging, waist-deep waters. Inching ever further and with feet struggling for purchase on the boulder-strewn river bed, he staggered through the icy torrent. He reached the far side, throwing an evil glance in the mule's direction. It stood resolute, seemingly laughing at their predicament.

They began to climb towards the road, which ran along the spine of a low ridge. The approach was steep, the snow sculpted into wind-driven drifts, the moonlight glistening off their surface. Dressed in their dark clothing, the long column of men – and the mules – stood out for many miles around. If the enemy were smart, they'd have placed sentries along the road to guard the back door to their trap. Lees couldn't imagine that they hadn't done.

Struggling through the thick drifts and bowed under their loads, the column of figures moved at a snail's pace. Lees felt utterly exposed. It struck him that a pair of German machine-gunners sited on the road could mow them down with ease. Unbelievably, they reached the ribbon of tarmac only to discover that it was unguarded. For some inexplicable reason the enemy commanders had failed to lock and bolt the exit.

It was twelve hours' solid marching before they reached Ranzano village, higher up the mountainside and a place of relative safety. They'd slipped through the noose, but few felt any sense of triumph. As they collapsed exhaustedly, they noticed a ragged line of fighters emerging from the moonlight. It turned out to be Colonel Monti with his headquarters staff, who had likewise fled before the enemy onslaught.

They stumbled past in disarray. Figures trudged forward, their weapons strapped to the mules, their feet painful from frostbite. But as Lees watched them shuffle past, he felt a curious upsurge of hope. Perversely, a part of him felt glad that this rout had come so quickly. No longer could Colonel Monti and his deputies pretend to be leading a potent and effective guerrilla force. The Reggiani partisans needed rebuilding from scratch, and Lees felt confident that he had the ability and the experience to do just that. By demolishing any semblance of battle-worthiness, the enemy had done him a favour. Sometimes, you had to destroy to start anew.

Over the next forty-eight hours Lees went about putting flesh on his plans. He called a meeting with Colonel Monti, explaining just what he intended: they would rebuild the guerrilla movement, armed, trained and fully equipped to take the fight to the enemy. As delicately as he could, he explained how dissatisfied he was with the colonel's leadership, and how he would need to take over command.

To his credit, the colonel was in enthusiastic agreement. If he could remain the nominal figurehead, he would happily give Lees the lead. If nothing else, this would prevent the communists from seizing control, which they had been agitating to do for some time. That was the last thing that anyone wanted. The Reggiani partisans had to remain resolutely apolitical and to concentrate totally on taking the fight to the enemy.

In this regard, the British captain and the Italian colonel could make common cause. Of course, by seizing command Lees didn't doubt that he would be seen as going against orders, but he really didn't give a damn. He was here to wage war, and right now the partisans weren't capable of doing so. Only by taking control could he turn that around.

It would be days before the Germans departed the Reggiani valley. While Lees couldn't know it, they were here on Kesselring's personal orders, charged with exterminating the Reggiani partisans. Exhibiting what Lees observed was a typical Teutonic lack of lateral thinking, they combed the partisans' known hideouts, burning villages and looting, but never thinking to widen the net or to leave ambush parties in wait.

Lees was likewise busy, but utilising a somewhat more outside-the-box mentality. He got Farrimond to radio through a shopping list of kit and supplies, chief among which was explosives, while he set about raising an elite sabotage squad. He chose as its head one Glauco Monducci – war name 'Gordon' – formerly an Italian alpine trooper, so a man well versed in mountain warfare. Monducci was tall, strong and confident, not to mention striking-looking with his long dark hair. Armed with a letter of authority from Lees, he was despatched on a tour of the surviving partisan bands to recruit forty of the best fighters.

Lees told Gordon not to return until he had those men. In exchange, he would ensure that they would be fully equipped with arms and ammunition from the first air resupply, presuming that he could persuade Florence to send flights. They would be trained in all forms of sabotage, something in which Lees himself was an expert. That done, they would be sent out to train the various partisan bands, after which they would be unleashed upon the enemy.

That done, Lees sought to organise an intelligence-gathering apparatus. There were to be no more surprise attacks by the enemy. He wanted to be forewarned and forearmed of everything the Germans might be up to. Lees appointed Giulio Davidi as the head of his intelligence service. Davidi had adopted the nom de guerre 'Kiss', which was inordinately peculiar, even among a band of fighters who seemed to affect the oddest war names.

Kiss was no Romeo. In an otherwise unremarkable face, his one arresting feature was a pair of huge, icy, penetrating grey eyes. He had a slow and very deliberate way of speaking, and a strangely secretive manner, which made him an obvious choice as spy-master. Lees explained that he didn't just want information brought in. He wanted a body of agents who could be sent out with urgent messages, or on bespoke spying missions. Kiss was adamant that it was the female partisan members who would be best suited to such tasks.

Lees agreed. From what he'd seen, the women had courage and front in abundance, and they were clearly not averse to using their not-inconsiderable feminine charms to hoodwink the enemy. Equally important, a pretty woman 'innocently' pedalling a bicycle through a German position could pass without suspicion, where any number of men might fail. Lees and Kiss decided to christen the female recruits their *Stafettas* – 'couriers' in English.

Twelve days after having been despatched, Gordon returned.

He'd managed to garner twenty recruits for his elite sabotage force, and somehow he'd managed to arm them, including acquiring two Bren light machine guns. Though half the number that Lees had asked for, they were a first-class band of toughs, and he certainly favoured quality over quantity. Arming them had been a touch of genius, especially as Lees had been warned that he would receive no air-drops until he had returned to his base of operations.

Two of the recruits struck Lees as being particularly promising. One, called Reubens, was a wiry little hard-case who'd worked for years as a doorman at a shady Paris nightclub. The other, a Sicilian, had a particularly stirring story. Captured by the enemy, he'd been taken to their base to be beaten and tortured. He'd managed to break free and leap through a second-floor window. Miraculously, he'd escaped unharmed, but the brutality he'd suffered had left its mark and he hungered to exact revenge.

Lees and Gordon christened their elite force the *Gufo Nero* Brigade – the Black Owls. In Lees' mind he wanted them to operate along SAS lines, executing highly mobile hit-and-run attacks, melting into the hills before the enemy had a chance to retaliate. That was the kind of tactics that he figured the target-rich Reggiani valley was crying out for.

Two weeks had passed by the time Lees' Stafettas reported that the enemy were in the process of withdrawing. He formed up his column to march back into the Secchia valley, putting Gordon and his Black Owls in the vanguard. They proceeded as a fighting patrol, with the mules carrying their all-important radio in the midst of the column. Upon nearing the main road, Gordon sent his Bren-gunners ahead to secure the crossing.

As Lees flitted across, he felt a thrill of excitement. He was returning 'home', to a region from which he fully intended to unleash merry hell. But first, he was to make an unexpected acquaintance . . . The column was nosing its way into the heart of the valley, when they came across a bunch of partisans wearing the red star of the communists. Lees had just begun to question them in his pidgin Italian, when a quite extraordinary figure stepped forwards.

Round-shouldered, portly, and leaning on a heavy alpenstock – a primitive, long-handled ice-axe – he was instantly recognisable as being non-Italian. Something of a cross between a hobbit and a mountain troll, a pair of bulging blue eyes peered through jam-jar glasses, above a bearded red face, which came complete with a permanently open mouth and drip on the end of a hooked nose. Lees couldn't help but be intrigued.

'How do you do, sir,' the mystery figure announced, in some-what archaic but crisp English. 'I am Fritz Snapper, Reserve Lieutenant of the Royal Dutch Army.'

Lees could barely contain his laughter. While he'd stumbled upon any number of nationalities in the Italian mountains, he couldn't for the life of him conceive of how a Dutch soldier had ended up with this ragged band of communist partisans.

'How the devil did you get here?' he asked.

Snapper endeavoured to draw himself to his full height. 'I have the honour, sir, to have been attached to the Reggiani partisans for some months now, in an honorary capacity.'

That, plus the Shakespearian English, was just too much for Lees. He sat down in the snow and practically wept with laughter. As Snapper remained remarkably unperturbed, Lees felt he'd better recruit him.

He waved an arm at his column of fighters. 'You're such a tonic, you'd better stick around. Will you do me the honour of joining us . . . in an honorary capacity, of course?'

Snapper looked almost tearful. 'That, sir, is a compliment which it gives me the greatest pleasure to accept.'

With that, Fritz Snapper – alpenstock in hand – formed up next to Lees, and they marched onwards. Lees was keen to hear the man's story. It didn't disappoint, and from just about anyone else Lees would have found it utterly unbelievable. In May 1940, as the German blitzkrieg had steamrollered across Holland, Snapper, a Dutch Army lieutenant, joined the Dutch resistance, before deciding to make his way to Britain and the real war.

For some reason, he'd reckoned the best way to get there was via neutral Switzerland, where he'd sought in vain for a flight. The odd aircraft did of course leave for England, but seats were reserved for far more important personages than Lt. Snapper. After a year's wait he decided he'd cross the Alps, find his way into Italy and from there to Tunisia, to join up with British forces in North Africa. The plan fell through on a small oversight: Fritz Snapper spoke barely a word of Italian. He was picked up by the Italian Fascist police and charged with being an Allied spy. Taken to court, the case fell apart when the Italian judge ruled that even the British wouldn't be stupid enough to send a man to spy on a country whose language he didn't speak. Saved from execution, Snapper was sent to a POW camp. There he managed to convince the camp commander, a German, of his love for all things German. He was duly released, and promptly made his way into the mountains to join the partisans, fully intending to show the Germans what he really thought of them.

Lees sensed that Snapper was 'quite mad', but who wasn't among this ragtag band? More importantly, he'd carved out for himself a unique niche with the partisans. Snapper had taken charge of running a courier network via which messages were spirited across the lines. Incredibly, this service – often employing young boys who could slip through undetected – proved highly effective. In time it would enable Lees to write a missive to Florence headquarters, with the confidence that it would be delivered in three to four days.

For his part, Snapper saw in Lees the salvation of the Reggiani partisans. After months of non-existent supply drops, near-starvation and in-fighting, they were desperate for a figure behind whom to unite. Lees was it. He was the unifying force that the partisans were crying out for. Snapper would write of his arrival that the 'new BLO for Reggio Emilia saved the situation . . . Capt Lees completely understood Partisan mentality.'

Love him or loathe him, Lees was the man for the job.

Chapter 8

Inspired by Operation Galia's achievements, Farran tried to go one better by striking at a prime target – the Brenner Pass, which cuts through the Alps, providing the vital rail links from Austria into northern Italy. Appropriately codenamed Cold Comfort, the mission's objective was to blow up the high mountainside, causing a massive landslide that would block the railway lines, significantly disrupting supplies to the Gothic Line.

But sadly, Cold Comfort was to prove as cheerless as its name suggested. Led by the fearless Major Ross Robertson Littlejohn MC, operation Cold Comfort employed a similar troop-sized – twelve-man – force as had Galia. But there the similarities ended. Widely scattered in the drop, the men found themselves among unfriendly locals of essentially German extraction. For days Littlejohn and his team fought against inhuman conditions, hunger and exposure, as the atrocious weather prevented any resupply drops.

Littlejohn was no stranger to such hardships. He'd won his MC in June 1944, having stormed Sword Beach in the D-Day landings with No. 4 Commando, a unit that suffered fifty per cent casualties. Not content with surviving that, Littlejohn – then a captain – went on to launch a solo assault on a German bunker, attacking it with grenades, becoming injured and isolated in the process. Playing dead, he'd avoided capture by German troops, who prodded him with bayonets, eventually crawling 2,000 yards to reach friendly lines.

By September 1944 he'd made a full recovery and had volunteered for the SAS, which led him to Cold Comfort. Eventually, Littlejohn – just twenty-three years of age – and one other patrol member, Corporal Joseph Crowley, were captured by an elite German ski unit. The two men, last seen engaged in fierce combat with the enemy, would be executed under Hitler's notorious 'Commando Order', which stipulated that 'all enemy troops encountered . . . during so-called commando operations . . . armed or unarmed, are to be exterminated to the last man . . .'

The order – issued in October 1942 and personally signed by Hitler – reflected how enraged the Führer had become at the successes of Churchill's butcher-and-bolt raiders. It ended with a chilling warning to any who might dare oppose it. 'I will summon before the tribunal of war, all leaders and officers who fail to carry out these instructions . . .' Each copy was stamped: 'This order is intended for commanders only, and must not under any circumstances fall into enemy hands.' It was classified 'MOST SECRET' and was to be committed to memory, after which all printed copies were to be destroyed.

With Littlejohn's capture Cold Comfort imploded – the Brenner Pass remaining resolutely open. One of those who did miraculously survive the mission was SAS Private Robert 'Bob' Sharpe. Upon parachuting into Cold Comfort, Sharpe had had his kitbag torn away, leaving him bereft of much of his equipment. He'd been forced to bivouac wrapped in his chute, in a snow-hole excavated at the base of a tree. Sharpe and others had been dogged by kit failures: issued with no specialist alpine equipment, their boots had proved next to useless. They'd ended the mission dressed largely in scavenged German Army gear.

Sharpe and others returned to Allied lines angry and disillusioned at such failures. Farran hadn't escaped their ire. He felt plagued by guilt at the loss of such brave men as Major Littlejohn, plus the horrendous trials and tribulations suffered by the others. He hungered to make good; to score a signal success in Italy, fearing that he'd ordered Littlejohn to undertake a mission of which he himself would have fought shy. It was the old terror coming back to haunt him – that after the long years at war he'd become 'windy'.

Major Littlejohn's mission had failed for one crucial reason, as far as Farran was concerned, apart from the appalling weather: lack of local support on the ground. He vowed the same mistake would not be made again. He approached SOE's Charles Macintosh, in Florence, asking who among his SOE agents could best accommodate an entire SAS squadron, one that would be embraced wholeheartedly by the partisans.

Oddly, Macintosh seemed somewhat less than enthusiastic at the proposition. Privately, he doubted whether his men in the field – his British Liaison Officers – would welcome Farran's squadron, whose arrival would doubtless disturb the status quo. The news of several dozen SAS parachutists dropping in would be inflated by enemy spies until reports cited hundreds, risking savage German reprisals, which was the last thing anyone needed right now. Or at least, so Macintosh reasoned.

Some BLOs, certainly, had no need of such potent support as Farran and his SAS offered. Many, like the SOE's Major William McKenna, had been given predominantly non-offensive roles. Embedded with partisans to the far western end of the Gothic

Line, at Val d'Aosta, McKenna's Clarinda Mission was charged with 'anti-scorch' work, which was intended to prevent the enemy from sabotaging key targets as they withdrew, a tactic known as 'scorched earth'.

The Allies had drawn-up a list of vital installations that were to be safeguarded at all costs, chief among them being hydro-electric plants, and BLOs like McKenna had been tasked with their protection. As the weather was atrocious and parachuting wasn't an option, McKenna had been forced to trek in over the Alps, using skis wherever possible. That alone was an incredible feat, and all to stop the Germans from blowing up key dams – something that would have a catastrophic impact on the Italian people.

McKenna – formerly of the Royal Berkshire Regiment and SAS – had been mentioned in despatches for service with the SOE in Sicily, back in 1944. Long-serving and battle-hardened, he mastered his defensive anti-scorch role with aplomb, recruiting thousands of partisans. He trained them in anti-aircraft drills, using Bren guns to shoot down aircraft, just in case the enemy came at them from the skies. When a group of German soldiers did attempt to sabotage a power station they were summarily caught and shot.

Charles Macintosh reached out to the agents he had serving in the area where Farran was keenest to deploy – to the rear of the central section of the Gothic Line. Two, Major Jim Davies and Major Charles Holland, demurred. Long-experienced at SOE work, they expressed reservations that Macintosh could well appreciate. For his part, Farran reacted with incredulity. To his mind, their lack of hunger to take the fight to the enemy was unconscionable.

But the third individual seemed to be of an entirely different mind set and came back with an altogether more enthusiastic response. Lower in rank, younger and arguably less worldly-wise, Captain Michael Lees had only recently inserted into his area of operations. Via Bert Farrimond, his radio operator, Lees sent back a crystal-clear response to Farran's offer of SAS troops: 'Send as many as you can!'

Macintosh had already formed his own opinion of Lees. He believed him to be the 'most impatient and headstrong of the BLOs'. Considering there were over a dozen such agents spread across northern Italy, those were harsh words indeed. There was little love lost between Macintosh and Farran, either. Once Lees had sent his message of unqualified welcome, Macintosh feared that this – *Farran plus Lees* – would turn out to be a marriage made in hell.

Once in the field, Farran would outrank Lees. He was also several years his senior and a legendary figure in his own right. 'Together, they would be a bloody menace,' Macintosh concluded, somewhat churlishly. 'I consoled myself with the thought that it was the Hun who should be worried.' There was one other complicating factor, as far as Macintosh was concerned. Major Farran was banned from deploying with his troops, yet he felt convinced that the SAS commander would find some way to join them, regardless.

'It was clear that contrary to orders, he was thinking of jumping with the squadron,' Macintosh would write of Farran. 'It was also clear that once in enemy territory he would act as he pleased . . .'

In one respect Macintosh was right: Farran had been forbidden from deploying, and by none other than London headquarters. In part, the ban resulted from his previous injuries, which rendered him unfit for front-line duties, at least in the eyes of some. In part, it reflected the acute lack of availability of experienced SAS officers, and the pressing need to keep some at headquarters, to oversee wider strategy and command.

Armed with Lees' unqualified message of welcome, Farran went about clearing the forthcoming mission, codenamed Operation Tombola, with Colonel Riepe, the American commander in charge of special operations. In the process he quietly slipped in a request that he be allowed to lead his men in the field. While the colonel gave his blessing to Tombola, he categorically refused Farran's entreaty.

Painfully short of experienced officers, he needed Farran in Florence, Riepe explained. Farran acted as if he had accepted the colonel's strictures with good grace. But in truth, he knew in his heart that very shortly only a slender thread would be hanging between himself and a court martial.

Of course, Farran had heard the rumours about Michael Lees. He knew of his 'wild man' reputation. But that simply reflected that he was a man of 'sterner calibre', as far as Farran was concerned, and his positive attitude spoke volumes. Lees had been awaiting just such an opportunity, and he was convinced that the arrival of an SAS squadron would boost partisan morale hugely. He promised to recce potential targets immediately.

If Lees' actions were as good as his words, Farran felt certain that he'd found his kindred spirit. In time, he would go on to judge Michael Lees as being 'the best partisan Liaison Officer in the whole of Italy'. High praise indeed from a man of Farran's standing.

His deployment set, Farran went about selecting the force to join him on the ground. No. 3 Squadron SAS had deployed from England under-strength, and especially with regard to the senior ranks. Farran would need to beg, borrow and steal officers from wherever he could find them.

With no Big Jim Mackie to serve as his bulletproof right-hand man, Farran sought out another of the old and bold – Captain James 'Jock' Easton, a grizzled, battle-worn Scot with a heart of gold and guts of steel. By rights, Easton should not even have been available. Just returned from two years as a POW, he was supposed to be enjoying a safe desk job in Florence. But typically, when Farran suggested a bit of fun and games behind enemy lines, Easton jumped at the chance.

Farran's main challenge was one of comprehension: a rough diamond hailing from the tough streets of Falkirk, Easton was blessed with a thick accent. When issuing orders in pidgin Italian garbled by his broad Scots, it was a wonder any of the locals got the barest gist, especially as his every utterance tended to be laced with a good dose of ribald cussing. But Easton had the pedigree that a mission such as this – challenging, ambitious, unprecedented – called for.

One of SAS founder David Stirling's 1941 originals, Easton had soldiered across the scorching deserts of North Africa, raiding scores of enemy bases and airfields. Wounded and taken prisoner, he'd escaped in Italy and made his way to neutral Switzerland, and from there to the French resistance. He'd subsequently fought his way through France, making it back to England. In short, Easton constituted Farran's safe pair of hands to backstop the coming mission.

With Easton thus purloined from his desk job, it made perfect sense to recruit another SAS officer who by rights also shouldn't have been available. One look at Lieutenant James Arthur 'Ricky' Riccomini's résumé accounted for why Farran held him in such

Where it all began. In 1940 Winston Churchill called for Special Duty Volunteers to 'set the lands of the enemy ablaze'. Cue David Stirling and his Special Air Service (SAS), the butcher and bolt raiders *par excellence*.

More secretive than the SAS, the Special Operations Executive was Churchill's shadowy 'Ministry for Ungentlemanly Warfare'. The SOE taught assassination, sabotage and all the dark arts of war.

SOE agent Captain Michael Lees, pictured with his wife Gwendoline (also SOE), was charged to make this dirty war a reality. Parachuted into Yugoslavia, he linked up with resistance fighters, blowing up and derailing enemy trains. Often working alone, he would earn the nickname Mike 'Wild Man' Lees.

Severely wounded and taken captive in 1941, Major Roy Farran (seated, in jeep) executed a daring and epic escape. Already an SAS legend, in the autumn of 1944 he took his SAS squadron deep behind enemy lines in northern France on a daring mission codenamed Operation Wallace.

Farran led the spectacularly successful attack on the German garrison at Châtillon, housed in a grand chateau. Hunted remorselessly by the enemy, Farran and his men had to go to ground in woodland, jeeps becoming bogged in autumn mud. They survived by the skin of their teeth.

In preparation for D–Day, Churchill charged Allied forces to launch a thrust into the 'soft underbelly of Europe' – Italy – to force the enemy to fight on many fronts. But by autumn 1944 the advance had stalled on the fearsome defences of the Gothic Line, a stretch of high terrain across Northern Italy's Apennine Mountains honeycombed with trenches, tunnels and bunkers. Below, Churchill (in pith helmet) surveys Italian lines.

In September '44 SOE's Mike Lees was parachuted behind the Gothic Line to link up with the Italian resistance and foment havoc in the enemy's rear.

Lees led a highly unusual force, including war artist Geoffrey Long (who drew these images and is pictured in the sketch above), plus war reporter Paul Morton (right). Long and Morton were charged to file stories about how the partisans were raising merry hell. Armed by air-drops from SOE, they ambushed German forces, before driving hell-for-leather for the safety of the mountains, providing Long and Morton with gripping stories.

After weeks in the field Lees was tasked to cross the Gothic Line, spiriting vital intelligence to the Allies. Moving on foot, he would have to pass through many kilometres of gun-emplacements, machinegun nests, bunkers and minefields, plus towns blasted apart by fighting.

In autumn '44 SAS Major Roy Farran (front right of photo, with captured German weapon) deployed to Italy. With Allied forces bogged down on the Gothic Line, the dash and daring of the SAS was in high demand. Farran was placed under joint command of SOE plus those American forces charged to break the Gothic Line.

Supreme German commander in Italy, Field Marshal Albert Kesselring (with staff), vowed to give no quarter. One of his greatest problems was the Italian resistance, who'd accounted for some 20,000 German casualties. Backed by Hitler, he ordered savage reprisals against villages he accused of harbouring the partisans.

Farran launched his first mission, Operation Cold Comfort, a daring sortie to block the Brenner Pass, the key resupply route for the Gothic Line. It proved disastrous. Despite linking up with partisans, his SAS force – pictured above – was harried across snow-swept mountains.

After Cold Comfort, Farran was plagued by guilt. Banned by high command from deploying, he vowed to do so anyway, leading a force of volunteers including 'Churchill's Spaniards' – war-bitten Spanish fighters. Raphael Ramos, kneeling second right, Juan Abadia, on his immediate left, and Francisco Jeronimo (not pictured) were Spanish Civil War and French Foreign Legion veterans.

high esteem, and why he hungered to have him join the Tombola team. Tall, sandy-haired and always with a ready smile, Lieutenant Riccomini had had some kind of war.

One of five brothers hailing from Kent, Riccomini had volunteered for 'The Snowballers', a Scots Guards battalion formed to help the Finns fight the Russians, in what had become known as the Winter War. It was early 1940 and Russia was allied to Nazi Germany, under a 1939 Non-Aggression Pact. The Snowballers were formed to soldier in Finland's cause, to deter Russian aggression. With Finland being largely snowbound, Riccomini was trained in alpine warfare, but the battle proved short-lived, and in March 1940 Finland signed a peace treaty.

Posted to Egypt, Riccomini was captured while on a reconnaissance mission and sent to an Italian prison camp. After repeated escape attempts he was sent to Italy's equivalent of Colditz, for the real 'bad boys' – Campo PG 5, at Gavi, in mountainous north-west Italy. Then in September 1943 he was one of a group of POWs being moved north by train to Austria. He and others sawed a hole in the side wall of the cattle truck in which they were travelling and jumped for it. Having made his getaway, Riccomini – half Italian, and fluent in the language – headed for the hills, along with fellow escapee Lieutenant 'Pete' Peterson.

Using forged papers the two soldiered with the partisans for many months. In his most memorable operation, Riccomini led a guerrilla unit disguised as Fascist troops to sabotage a railway bridge. Setting explosives stolen off the enemy, they waited for a troop train before detonating the charges. In his diary Riccomini wrote: 'There was an almighty explosion, a whooping crescendo of sound, followed by a screaming of metal and indescribable splintering crashes. The world was flooded with scarlet followed by a pall of thick blackness.'

Riccomini was finally betrayed by a Red Cross representative, who'd promised to get a Christmas letter to his wife, Joyce, in England. They'd married in October 1939, spending precious little time together over the war years. That Red Cross agent doubled as a Nazi spy, and a truck load of German troops arrived. Riccomini and Peterson escaped by jumping from a second-floor window, after which they scaled an Alpine pass and made it to Switzerland. There, Riccomini was duly recruited by the SOE as an 'agent in the field'.

In August 1944 he crossed into France, linked up with the French resistance and attacked the German's 90th *Panzergrenadier* Division. Finally making it back across the lines, the SOE recommended that Riccomini should be 'SOS wef' – struck off strength, with effect from . . . 26 September 1944. They suggested that he take permanent sick leave for the remainder of the war, such was the toll the behind-the-lines missions had taken upon him.

Instead, Riccomini penned a report very much to the contrary. 'I would welcome an opportunity for further work of this nature . . . I speak and write both German and Italian . . . May I request an interview with Lt.Col. William Stirling, SAS. I was with his brother, Lt. Col. David Stirling, in PG 5 Gavi, Italy, and was recommended by him for appointment to the SAS Regiment.'

Taken into the SAS, he quickly won renown for his unbreakable good spirits: 'Nothing ever got him down and his great sense of humour was a real tonic in hard times.' Not long after joining the SAS he was flown to Italy. Being a former POW and very probably known to the Germans, he'd taken on the somewhat facetious cover name of Lieutenant Richard Hood.

Riccomini deployed with Captain Walker-Brown on Operation Galia, for which he earned a Military Cross. The citation read: 'He was a personal source of inspiration and encouragement to his men. His conduct could not have been excelled in any way, being far above the normal call of duty.' Having only recently returned from Galia, Riccomini was supposed to be on leave and he had every reason to reject Farran's approach. Instead, he agreed at once to the SAS major's invitation to join the Tombola party.

Still short of officers, Farran went hunting. In a nearby infantry depot he delivered a recruitment speech of Churchillian proportions, calling for volunteers for special duties and offering little but 'sweat, blisters and frostbite and the probability of being shot as spies'. One of the first to step forward was the smallish, quietly spoken, pipe-smoking Lieutenant Arthur David Eyton-Jones. A member of the Royal Sussex Regiment, Eyton-Jones had deployed to Italy fresh out of training, and he'd yet to get his boots dirty.

When war broke out, Eyton-Jones – hailing from Brighton, on the south coast of England – had been at Jesus College, Cambridge. He was a keen rower and had indulged his dreams of forging a career in agriculture. Coming from a long line of clergymen, he was breaking the mould by looking to a future working the land. Now, some five years later, he found himself in Italy stepping forward to volunteer for the famed SAS, along with a dozen other would-be recruits.

Apart from his infantry training, Eyton-Jones' war experience was restricted to a stint in the Home Guard. He'd been stationed around Bath, on a hillock watching out for German invaders. For several nights a bird had stubbornly sung from its place of hiding, keeping Eyton-Jones awake. Finally, he'd cracked, unleashing a shot from his .303 Lee Enfield rifle. The bird flew off unharmed, but the rifle shot triggered an invasion alert, for which Eyton-Jones was severely reprimanded.

In the summer of 1944 he'd embarked for Italy on the troopship *The Empress of Scotland*. He was commanding thirty infantrymen, and they were supposed to link up with their parent regiment, the Royal Sussex. Instead, the ship had been forced to zig zag to avoid U-boat attacks, and the soldiers were plagued by sea-sickness and delayed by the heavy seas. They reached Italy too late to join their regiment, which had already deployed to Greece.

Eyton-Jones was understandably frustrated. His family had titled roots, there being a baronetcy and a Buckinghamshire mansion in the lineage. It was there, waited on by twenty staff, that the teenage Eyton-Jones had listened to Neville Chamberlain announcing the declaration of war on Germany. The housekeeper had been summoned and ordered to introduce rationing based upon First World War lines. His great aunt, the Honourable Gertrude Aird, had donated £5,000 to fund a Spitfire, which had been named 'Gerty' in her honour.

Lieutenant David Eyton-Jones, still just twenty-one years of age, longed to play his part. Farran weeded down the volunteers to just two: fortunately, Eyton-Jones was one of them. The other, Lieutenant Kenneth 'Ken' Harvey, hailed from Rhodesia (now Zimbabwe), in southern Africa. If anything, Harvey had even less war experience than Eyton-Jones. He was just nineteen years of age, so barely out of his school uniform.

As Farran's No. 3 Squadron was just days away from deploying, there would be precious little time for any specialist training.

Indeed, Eyton-Jones and Harvey would have to parachute behind the lines with no practice, on their first ever jump from an aircraft. Farran told them not to worry. In the SAS they found the best way to learn was live, on the job as it were.

But in truth, No. 3 Squadron was a relatively newly raised unit, and Farran craved experienced operators. The ranks were also plagued by malaria, contracted during previous operations. Farran figured as many as seventy-five per cent of the men had been hit by the debilitating disease, and he'd ordered those affected to take mepacrine, an anti-malarial drug. He needed experienced recruits, and much of the kind of irregular warfare skills he sought were vested in the regiment's 'international brigade'. Fittingly, perhaps, as Field Marshal Kesselring had once commanded the Condor Legion fighting on the side of Franco's Fascists in the Spanish Civil War, Farran sought out veterans who'd fought on the other side – men who'd been soldiering in one form or another for approaching ten years.

About a dozen Spaniards were serving with the SAS, and two were immediately available. They had the most incredible stories. Lance Corporal Robert Bruce – real name, Justo Balerdi – and Parachutist Frank Williams – real name Francisco Jeronimo – had fought for the Republicans, the democratic left-leaning forces in Spain's 1936–39 civil war. Upon the Fascist victory they'd escaped to France, where they were interned by the French authorities. They were given a stark choice: join the French Foreign Legion, or rot – and starve – in the internment camps.

Hailing from Sestao, a town lying on the outskirts of Spain's northern port city of Bilbao, Justo 'José' Balerdi had worked as a telephonist prior to the outbreak of the conflict. Francisco Jeronimo came from the opposite end of the country, Málaga, on

Spain's southern coast, where he'd been an apprentice electrician. They bonded in surviving the harsh privations of the French internment camps, in contrast to which the rigours of the French Foreign Legion looked immensely preferable. Posted to Syria – then a part of French North Africa – they hungered to join the fight against the powers of Nazism then sweeping Europe.

Following Germany's lightning victory over France, fate turned against them. All Spanish members of the French Foreign Legion were ordered to be sent to German-held soil. Knowing they faced execution or the concentration camps, the officers turned a blind eye as many deserted. Francisco Jeronimo and Justo Balerdi joined a sixty-strong force of Spaniards determined to make it to British territory. They 'deserted' en masse, taking their weapons with them and headed for British-held Palestine in a convoy of army trucks.

Having reached the first British checkpoint, a sentry tried to bar their way: with no papers they couldn't be allowed through, he argued. A figure jumped down from the rear of one of the vehicles and knocked the man unconscious, after which the trucks thundered past. Two maverick British officers, Colonel George Young and Lt.Col. Stephen Rose, happened to be in Palestine at the time, recruiting for the newly raised Middle East Commando. Making a virtue out of necessity, the Spaniards were taken en masse into No. 50 ME Commando. War-bitten guerrilla fighters and experienced Legionnaires, they made for ideal recruits.

They first saw action in Operation Abstention in February 1941, a raid on Castelorizzo, an island in the eastern Mediterranean. A suspected Italian sea-plane base, the commandos struck by total surprise, Italian resistance crumbling. They'd seized the key objective, Paleocastro Fort, perched atop an 800-foot cliff that dominated the harbour, its garrison surrendering. But failure to land reinforcements left the two hundred men of 50 Commando under siege from air and the sea, hounded by warplanes and motor-torpedo boats.

With ammunition, water and food running low and casualties mounting, the survivors were lifted off the beaches under cover of darkness, in a daring evacuation by Royal Navy warships. Three months later 50 Commando were back in action, in the battle for the Mediterranean island of Crete. Under ferocious assault by German paratroopers, Crete fell, with Francisco Jeronimo and others being taken prisoner.

With his shock of unruly black hair and dark, good-humoured eyes, Justo Balerdi – Robert Bruce – could easily have passed for a local Cretan, but as luck would have it he'd just been pulled off the island, so he missed the fate that befell so many of his comrades. Realising their Spanish backgrounds would spell a death sentence, the Spanish commandos decided to claim that they were Gibraltarians, a plausible tale given their accents.

Francisco Jeronimo, similarly dark-haired and intense of gaze, had no intention of being held captive for long. He broke out of the Cretan POW camp and spent long months hiding out in the mountains, along with other escapees. One was a British colonel whom Jeronimo befriended, helping him fend for himself in the hills. When they were finally rescued by a British warship, the colonel invited Jeronimo to join his regiment as his personal batman. The Spaniard's response was typically emphatic: 'I polish the shoes of no man.'

Hospitalised with malaria after their stint in Crete, it wasn't until late 1943 that Jeronimo (and Balerdi) were able to volunteer for the SAS. There they linked up with a third Spaniard, a former policeman and comparatively grizzled veteran called Juan Torrents Abadia. Realising he was too old for parachute training, Abadia had lied about his age, reducing it by four years to blag his way into the SAS. None other than the commanding officer of 2nd SAS, Lt.Col. Brian Franks, would write of him: 'An excellent soldier. Reliable, willing and respectful. Was an Officer in the Spanish Republican Army. First class individual.'

Abadia 'fathered' the younger Spanish recruits through their earliest months in the regiment, during which they were asked to change their identities. Over drinks in a bar, they were advised that taking British war-names might be advisable. There was a cloak-and-dagger justification: former Spanish freedom fighters could expect no mercy from the enemy, if caught. But it was also as much for the sake of convenience: the British found it hard to pronounce – let alone remember – their real names.

Juan Torrents Abadia – the elder of 'Churchill's Spaniards' as they were known – chose the surname Colman, for he was the spitting image of Ronald Colman, the iconic 1930s actor who'd starred in such classic movies as *Beau Geste* and *A Double Life*. Jeronimo and Balerdi favoured the names of famous British warriors – Francis Drake, Walter Raleigh or Robert the Bruce. Robert Bruce was allowed: it fell to Balerdi. But Drake and Raleigh were seen as being just a little too obvious. Francisco Jeronimo had to settle for the typically English – and somewhat un-warrior-like – Frank Williams.

On Francisco Jeronimo's remarkably brief signing-up papers, where it asked for the parish, town and county of his birth, two brief words were inscribed: 'NO – SPANISH'. With his change of name, 'GERONIMO, FRANCISCO' was struck out by hand, the words 'WILLIAMS, FRANK' replacing them (Jeronimo's last name had been misspelled by the military). His army number was duly altered to 1304867, and that was it – ID change complete. A similarly brief exercise switched 'Justo Balerdi' to 'Robert Bruce'.

After SAS training in Scotland, Balerdi – Robert Bruce – was first into action, being dropped on 5 August 1944, as Major Mick Rooney's signaller for Operation Rupert. Rooney's forces shot up a troop train and linked up with the French resistance to launch a series of harassing attacks, before finally withdrawing on 10 September.

Jeronimo (now Frank Williams) also saw action that August with the SAS. He was deployed on Operation Trueform, with orders to 'harass the enemy with a priority on the destruction of petrol tankers, petrol dumps etc'. Linking up with the French resistance, the thirty-seven-strong SAS patrol was guided to a German ammunition dump. There, Jeronimo – Frank Williams – shot dead the sentries with a Bren gun. 'The explosion was terrific,' the official report concluded of blowing up the dump.

Trueform was a great success: in addition to the enemy killed, seventy-eight Germans were taken prisoner, five ammo and fuel dumps destroyed, scores of trucks, half-tracks and field guns put out of action, and only three men lost. In operations in France Colman had also distinguished himself, saving the lives of three fellow SAS operators – Arthur Huntbach, Taffy Rogers and Jock Sinclair. In short, Churchill's Spaniards had earned for themselves a sterling reputation.

Those long-serving Spanish veterans had just the kind of experience that Roy Farran craved, for Operation Tombola. Abadia – Colman – was off serving in pastures far from Italy, so he was ruled out. But Robert Bruce and Frank Williams – fluent Italian speakers to boot – were available to deploy as part of Farran's team. Whether they were fit and ready for such a behind-the-lines mission was another matter entirely, though.

On a previous operation Frank Williams had been faced with the worst of all dilemmas. Even as they'd been ordered into action, an eighteen-year-old partisan had turned and bolted. They had a phrase for losing one's nerve in the SAS: it was called 'crapping out'. Though Williams had tried to forgive the boy, it had been a moment of intense fear and risk, as the lad's flight could have alerted the enemy, and 'we would all have been dead', he reflected.

Williams had been asked by one of the partisan commanders what they should do with the errant fighter. 'He's only eighteen,' the partisan leader had pointed out.

Williams face had hardened. 'Shoot him.'

The partisans refused, a decision for which Williams would be eternally grateful. Reflecting on this dark moment, he realised that he had been waging war behind the lines, dodging bullets, captivity and worse for too long. The blood, the brutality and savagery had seeped into him. Normally a bright, light-hearted fellow, Williams feared it had become a dark stain on his soul. But surely, he figured, the war must come to an end soon. Williams reckoned he could weather one more mission, and he and Bruce signed up for Tombola.

To round off his international brigade, Farran chose to take Lieutenant 'T. G. Stephens' – his anglicised nom de guerre – an Austrian Jew and long-serving SAS member, who was fluent in German, which should prove useful where they were heading. Plus he approached another Operation Galia veteran, a grizzled Italian sailor called Luigi 'Pippo' Siboldi. In spite of his sixty years of age, Siboldi had guided Walker-Brown through the mountains as they'd harassed the enemy on Operation Galia. Having done so, he'd been quietly recruited into the SOE.

Farran felt sure that Siboldi's skills and experience, not to mention his ready smile, would prove useful for Tombola. Team sorted, he didn't believe that a man among those recruited was a 'passenger'. Each promised his own worth. 'It was a collection of old toughs,' Farran would write of his team, the newbies Eyton-Jones and Harvey included. 'I loved every one of their cracked, leathery faces.'

Prior to departure for the mission, he led his entire No. 3 Squadron on a fifty-mile trek across the Apennine mountains. Not all would deploy. Some would be weeded out during this final trial. Sixty-odd men returned aching, footsore and weary. They knew now what those lucky enough to be chosen should expect. The heady scent of methylated spirits – alcohol, with a foul-tasting colouring added, to render it undrinkable – filled the barracks, as desperate attempts were made to harden the soles of battered, blistered feet. Rucksacks were packed and repacked, in an effort to refine loads. Non-essential items of kit were binned, to cut weight. Above all, an atmosphere of fevered excitement filled the air.

The DZ that Farran's advance party would drop into for Operation Tombola had been codenamed Swell Crimson. Fittingly, Tombola had originated in southern Italy, being similar to the British game of bingo or a raffle. It was a form of gambling, and Farran didn't doubt that the coming operation was a gamble of the highest order.

But not a man among his 'collection of old toughs' could wait to get started.

Chapter 9

Michael Lees chose as his headquarters the small hamlet of Secchio, set equidistant between Colonel Monti's HQ – which he re-established at Febbio – and the warrior-priest Don Carlo's base, from where he commanded the Green Flames. Secchio consisted of a clutch of houses perched in a valley formed by a tributary of the main Secchia river. At the head of the valley lay a flat, open area where Lees would establish his DZ.

Don Carlo introduced Lees to Don Pietro Rivi, the Secchio village priest known to all as 'Don Pedro'. Don Pedro volunteered his home as a base for Lees' mission, despite the dangers this brought him and his family. The priest was thin and seemingly retiring, but appearances can be deceptive: he was in truth a heartfelt Italian patriot. The previous summer he'd raised a group of partisans, and with weapons they'd managed to beg, borrow and steal they'd ambushed an enemy patrol (not entirely successfully, but at least they'd tried).

Don Pedro's elderly mother, who lived with him, would treat Lees and his team as if they were her own flesh and blood. This sense of kindred spirits was accentuated by the faith Lees shared with the priest, his family and the wider village. Brought up a strict Catholic by his eccentric and devout mother, Lees had been made to wear red for the first eight years of his life, signifying 'the blood of Christ' as his mother had told him. His sister, Dodo, had worn bright blue, to signify 'Mary the Queen of Heaven'. Any issues Lees had were to be dealt with by prayer, his mother advised. It was not the easiest of boyhoods.

But here in the Secchia valley, Lees found his Catholic faith helped build bridges with those that he had come to lead to war. There was no better way to break the ice than sharing Sunday mass. Secchio had a fine defensive layout, and Lees intended it to be a permanent base of operations. Gordon chose to billet his Black Owls in Secchio's former school, while Kiss placed his Stafettas in a farmhouse on the outskirts of the village, where he could better guard their moral fortitude.

It was early February 1945 by the time Lees had got his plan-of-action agreed with all parties. The Reggiani partisans would fortify the Secchia valley, from where they would sally forth on hit-and-run operations. Each of the four partisan brigades was allocated a section of the valley perimeter that it was to hold at all costs, and a segment of enemy territory where its job was to wreak havoc and mayhem.

In the face of bitter opposition from Colonel Monti, Lees slashed his HQ staff by half. Responsibility for provisioning the partisans was devolved to brigade level. The plains were rich in food and wine and when they fought – and vanquished – the enemy, the partisans were to seize provisions. Conversely, if they didn't fight they would go hungry. In return, Lees promised to provide weaponry, including heavy machine guns, to hold the valley, and to clothe and supply the partisans for war.

In the past, 'theft' from the drop zones had been a serious cause of bitterness and resentment. Rival bands had been in the habit of seizing everything. To put a stop to this, Lees recruited a wonderful old ruffian called Ettore Scalabrini – known as 'Scalabrino' to all. Scalabrino boasted a thick, tangled white beard and carried an ancient-looking shotgun. He was the type who would have been a mountain bandit in another age, and indeed he'd spent years in America working the remote and lawless frontier minefields.

Lees could barely understand a word of Scalabrino's English, which was peppered with colourful American curses, but somehow they made each other understood. Prior to the much-heralded receipt of their first resupply drop, Lees warned Scalabrino that if one container went missing then he would have him shot. Scalabrino countered that if one pair of socks went missing, a lot of other people were going to get shot before him.

As it turned out, Scalabrino was far from joking.

It was the second week of February 1945 by the time Lees had persuaded Florence headquarters of their urgent need for a resupply. On 7 February he penned a long and notably conciliatory letter to Major Macintosh, to be taken by courier across the lines.

'Just a line to wish you all the best, and say that everything is going well,' Lees began. 'At the moment things are getting almost beyond us . . . As you know we're handling a lot of W/T traffic, about ten messages most days . . . Then there's intelligence . . . dropping grounds, and God knows what . . . Personally, I'm far more interested [in] and better at the more active side of the job . . . but we're very satisfied really.'

By sounding a mollifying note, Lees hoped to secure delivery of the first major resupply drop for many months. As good fortune would have it, the sheer scale and muscularity of the American cargo fleet now assembled at Rosignano Airfield meant that requests for arms and supplies could hardly be stymied much longer. The Dakotas would be lying idle, their American aircrews frustrated, their commanders perplexed beyond reason.

Early on the morning that the drop was scheduled, Lees was heading to the DZ when he heard a wild outbreak of fire. The rattle of rifles, sub-machine guns and heavier weapons echoed alarmingly across the valley, as the first of the Dakotas swooped low over the valley. Fearing that a perfectly timed enemy attack had been launched, Lees broke into a run.

He reached a vantage point, only to hear the sharp blast of a whistle, at which point the firing abruptly ceased. The unmistakable figure of Scalabrino strode into the middle of the DZ, where containers and parachutes lay thick on the ground. It turned out that he'd posted men to all sides, with orders to open fire without warning to dissuade any would-be thieves. Under the cover of their guns Scalabrino checked that each and every package was present and correct. Though a little draconian, his methods ensured that Lees was never to lose a single container.

Resupplied with ammo and explosives, Gordon's Black Owls sallied forth with sabotage in mind. Shortly, they were pouncing on enemy convoys, striking under cover of darkness and always at a different location. This was butcher-and-bolt at its best. At the same time Kiss's Stafettas were out and about, hoovering up the intelligence. Lees found himself inundated with details of enemy positions and movements, and he was often awake into the early hours, collating all.

Condensed into summaries, most could be telegraphed by Farrimond to their Florence headquarters. In no time the W/T specialist was working fourteen-hour days, encoding and transmitting those urgent missives. With any that were too long to be sent by radio, Lees summoned the Tolkien figure of Fritz

Snapper, alpenstock in hand, to organise a courier to sneak across the lines.

In short, by the third week of February 1945, Lees had taken control absolutely – despite Florence warning him not to – and his forces were well and truly going on the offensive. But still he wasn't satisfied. Still he hungered to do more. As luck would have it he was about to receive a highly unusual visitor, one who would give him a sense of how he might expand the scope of his operations in unforeseen ways.

Captain Neil Oughtred parachuted in on a top-secret mission, codenamed Cisco Red II. Like Lees, Oughtred – formerly of the Lincolnshire Regiment – had served in Yugoslavia, and he dropped in with his own radio operator, Sergeant Ted Fry. Upon arrival Oughtred explained they were an advance party charged to set up a discreet SOE intelligence cell. They were doing so with one aim in mind: to receive Major Bernard James Barton, an SOE agent with a long history of assassination missions.

Targeted assassinations were a rare, but necessary, weapon in the SOE's arsenal of ungentlemanly warfare. In 1942, SOE had masterminded Operation Anthropoid, the assassination of SS Obergruppenführer Reinhard Heydrich, a favourite of Hitler and a main architect of the Holocaust. Then, in early 1944, they'd orchestrated 'Rat Week', a coordinated series of assassinations against senior Nazi figures across Europe. In recent months, much planning had gone into an assassination attempt on Hitler himself.

Barton – just twenty-four years old and formerly of the Buffs (Royal East Kent Regiment) – was known either as 'Lucky' or 'Killer' to his comrades. He'd first demonstrated his penchant for assassinations during a raid in February 1944 on the German-held island of Brač, in the Adriatic Sea. As the citation for the DSO he'd earned made clear, he'd deployed with the intention of 'finding the German commander of the troops there and killing him'. He'd linked up with local partisans, who'd smuggled his Sten gun into the target's location hidden in a bundle of sticks and strapped to a donkey.

Barton followed, sneaking his way past the German checkpoints disguised as a local shepherd. He'd entered the commander's house at dusk, searched it and located the dining room, 'where he saw a German officer. He at once opened fire and killed him with two bursts from his silenced Sten gun.' The man he'd killed was indeed the Brač garrison commander. Barton slipped away and hid in caves for several days, before he could be taken off the island.

For that mission he was granted an immediate DSO, though the write-up is marked: 'NO PUBLICITY TO BE GIVEN TO THIS CITATION'. Even in war, assassinations were a risky and highly controversial business. In November 1944 Barton had been parachuted north of the Gothic Line, on a mission to assassinate General Heinrich von Vietinghoff, a Hitler lookalike who had taken over command from Kesselring in Italy, while the latter recovered from injuries received in a car crash.

Barton's citation for his bar to his DSO (second DSO) takes up the story. Though deserted by his guide and interpreter, Barton 'continued alone to search for his objective . . . his journey took him into the towns of Reggio and Modena, where German patrols, Fascist checks and house-to-house searches were made at every stage . . . Major Barton spent over a month in the area moving short distances at night and living by day in barns, stables and holes in the ground.' During one period he spent ten days hiding in such a hole, and gave up only when he had absolute proof that General von Vietinghoff had moved his HQ out of the area.

Now, in mid-February 1945 Barton was scheduled to return for a second assassination attempt, only this time hosted by Michael Lees. Lees thrilled to the proposition. More to the point, it opened his mind to other tantalising possibilities. He called a meeting with Kiss, and ordered him to use his Stafettas to locate, identify and document the enemy's key headquarters, those housing senior German commanders. As far as Lees was concerned, they would offer the juiciest targets.

The more he considered such a possibility – the concept of targeted assassinations – the more one area intrigued him. On the fringes of the plain around the town of Reggio Emilia, Lees had heard reports of a foremost enemy headquarters, but every piece of fresh intelligence seemed to contradict that which had come before it. It was frustrating and alluring in equal measure.

As chance would have it, Gordon had just recruited two unusual new figures to the Black Owls. Both were German soldiers who had deserted, due to their disillusionment at the Nazi cause. Not only were they well trained and disciplined, but they proved extremely useful when called upon to confuse the enemy. A few shouted orders in German at exactly the right moment seemed to work wonders on sentries.

During the third week of February one of the Germans brought in a fellow deserter, who turned out to be Austrian. Due to the priceless intelligence he brought with him, this young Wehrmacht sergeant was henceforth known only as 'Hans'. Hans had served with the elite German 4th Parachute Division, but he came to Lees' attention when it transpired that he had intelligence concerning the elusive target that he sought.

Hans knew of a headquarters located near Reggio Emilia, which commanded an artillery regiment. But of far greater significance, he argued, was another HQ, which orchestrated command and control for a huge stretch of the Gothic Line. Hans knew only of its rough whereabouts, for the enemy guarded such secrets fiercely. It was staffed by senior generals, and Field Marshal Kesselring himself was said to put in regular appearances.

Feeling his pulse quicken, Lees briefed Kiss. Even if it meant dropping all other work, he wanted that elusive headquarters found. The SOE and SAS favoured two types of behind-the-lines missions: sabotage operations, and those designed to target senior officers, so cutting the head off the snake. As missions to decapitate the Nazi serpent went there would be none better, though the mystery HQ was bound to be extremely heavily guarded.

If Lees could find and hit that headquarters and kill the senior commanders based there, he would have out-Bartoned 'Killer' Barton, the SOE's chief assassin. But to do so he would need more than just his partisans, he reasoned. This called for a unit of British commandos or similar, to stiffen their punch and their resolve.

Lees set about finding out all he could about Hans the deserter – a typically blond and athletic Aryan type. Why had he deserted? What was his motive? Was there any chance he was feeding disinformation to Lees, as some kind of a trap? It turned out that Hans had a very compelling set of reasons to turn his back on the German military and unleash his ire on his former comrades. In short, he had been wounded deep in his heart.

It took all of Lees' powers of persuasion to get the deserter – often morose and brooding – to talk. He hailed from Vienna, Hans explained, where he still had a wife, but he never wanted to see her again. He had been away fighting in Stalingrad on the Eastern Front, when he'd received a letter from his mother, telling him that his wife was due to give birth to a child. Only trouble was, Hans had not been home to Vienna for two long years.

Hans asked his commanding officer for leave on compassionate grounds. That man, an ardent Nazi, had laughed in his face. He'd chided Hans for being selfish and possessive over his wife. She had done her duty to the Fatherland and to Hitler by making another soldier happy, he argued, and in conceiving a child for the Reich. In fact, if Hans were a good Nazi he should celebrate the fact.

'That is why I fight my countrymen,' Hans had concluded, a line of argument that Lees – only recently wed – could relate to.

A few days later, Lees found himself at their Secchio base watching Farrimond decode a message from Florence. 'Please report on possibilities of dropping a force . . .' his W/T operator scribbled on a cypher pad, as a fine spring sunshine streamed through the windows.

There was a knock at the door. Kiss walked in, glancing from Farrimond to Lees with those big, bulbous grey eyes of his. 'Excuse me, sir,' he began, in his slow, ponderous way, 'but I've got the information you requested.'

Lees was amazed. 'Well done, but how the devil did you manage it and so quickly?'

Kiss allowed himself the rare hint of a smile. 'Well, one of the Stafettas is a very . . . beautiful young lady. She is not . . . averse to love. Last night she returned from Castelnovo, where she paid a visit to the officer commanding the garrison.' Kiss reached out with a slip of paper for Lees. 'She . . . obtained this information in the course of her duties.'

Lees grabbed the paper and ran his eyes across it. 'There is an important German headquarters at Villa Rossi, in Botteghe,' he read. 'It is the HQ of 5 Corps and serves as headquarters of the 14th Army. General Feuerstein is living in the villa. Last week Marshal Graziani visited him there.'

Lees stared, dumbfounded. He could hardly believe it. By chance, his area of operations happened to include territory that housed what had to be one of the enemy's most important headquarters for the whole of the Gothic Line. It was incredible, but seemingly true, unless of course the Stafetta had erred in her amorous endeavours.

A 'Corps' would amount to some 25,000–50,000 men; an 'Army' 100,000–150,000. In short, this was the HQ for fully four of the enemy divisions manning the Gothic Line. More importantly, those four divisions held the key section where Allied commanders planned to launch their spring offensive. If Lees could hit it, and comprehensively, he could decimate enemy command and control at exactly the point Allied commanders intended to punch through.

The enemy commanders mentioned in the message were well-known. Marshal Rodolfo Graziani, the First Marquis of Neghelli, was a die-hard Fascist fiercely loyal to Mussolini. His position – that of Marshal – outranked a general, so he was about as senior as one could get in the Italian military. For his part, General Valentin Feuerstein was an Austrian commander in charge of the 2nd Mountain Division, a unit of elite alpine troops. One of Kesselring's trusted deputies, Feuerstein had played a key role in the Battle of Monte Cassino in the spring of 1944, wherein fearsome German defence had cost the Allies dear. He was a holder of the Knight's Cross of the Iron Cross, one of the highest military awards in Nazi Germany.

In all his operations to date, Lees had never once taken on any target anything as remotely ambitious as this. He would need to scrutinise the information. He'd need to gather further intel on the HQ's defences. He'd need absolute certainty. But if the Stafetta's note turned out to be anything like accurate, this was a chance too good to be missed. It was an incredibly tempting target. Irresistible, in his mind. At one fell stroke Lees and his partisans might strike a blow to change the course of the war.

By the time Farrimond had finished decoding the incoming message from Florence, it seemed serendipitous in the extreme. 'Please report on possibilities of dropping a force of British SAS parachutists in your area to carry out attacks against enemy lines of communication.'

Never mind *lines of communication*, Lees told himself, he had a far better target in mind. He grabbed a message pad and scribbled out a short reply. 'Excellent idea. Send as many as you can!'

He turned to Farrimond. 'Get that one off soon as, Bert, will you?'

In a sense Lees was chancing his arm here. He had only the Stafetta's word for it about the target. But hell, faint heart never won fair lady.

Once the message was sent, Lees had one priority foremost in his mind: to prove that target once and for all. To do so he reckoned he needed to get sight of it himself. Not averse to sneaking about the Yugoslav mountains dressed as a peasant, Lees didn't doubt he could infiltrate the plains around Reggio similarly disguised. But before he could do so, the enemy would prove to have very different ideas in mind.

By now Kesselring himself was alert to the ferocity of partisan attacks emanating from the Secchia valley region, which had 'spread like lightning in the past ten days'. That February, the toll of bridges blown, convoys ambushed and trains derailed exceeded the total efforts of the Reggiani partisans for the preceding six months. In railing against this, Kesselring pointed to the 'more commanding leadership' at the helm of the resistance. Something would have to be done, he declared.

The day after Lees had received those two momentous messages – one from his amorous Stafetta, the other from Florence headquarters – the enemy arrived in force. Soon after dawn Lees heard fierce gunfire echoing up the valley. Reports came in that Don Carlo's Green Flames were in action, and Lees set out to help. He'd not gone far when a messenger arrived, carrying a missive from the warrior-priest himself. Two companies of Fascist *Brigate Nere* – Black Brigades – were attempting to push into the valley, but the Green Flames had it all under control.

Lees was doubtful. In any case, he sensed an opportunity to inflict a crushing defeat on the enemy, massively boosting partisan morale. Instead of heading back to his headquarters, he turned down a little side valley, making for one of the communist brigades. Upon arrival, he told Giovanni 'Gianni' Farri, its commander, to take his men and outflank the Fascist forces, so as to cut off any route of escape. Then they were to be annihilated.

Gianni was a short, squat, battle-hardened commander with a rough grip and ready smile. Lees had every faith in his abilities. Once he'd set out, Lees hurried off to stiffen Don Carlo's resolve. He arrived to discover the battle had reached stalemate. The enemy were hunkered down on the far bank of the Secchia, from where they were unleashing mortar and machine-gun barrages. Don Carlo's Green Flames were holding the nearside bank, and each time the enemy tried to advance they were cut down in the water.

Bearing in mind the Green Flames' spirited resistance, Lees' main worry was that Gianni's partisans might not get into position before the enemy decided to retreat. He told Don Carlo to stage a mock withdrawal. From each of his positions half a dozen fighters ran backwards, making sure they were seen doing so. Heartened, the *Brigate Nere* increased their fire. Just as they broke cover to advance, Lees heard the sound that he'd been longing for – the eruption of fire from the direction of the enemy's rear.

The trap had been sprung, the *Brigate Nere* surrounded. Knowing that the partisans would take no prisoners, they fought for their lives. It was two hours before a final grenade charge by Gianni's communists silenced them. Of the two-hundred-strong *Brigate Nere* force, less than fifty had escaped with their lives. It was a crushing defeat for the enemy and it sent exactly the kind of message Lees had intended: enter the Secchia valley at your peril.

With the enemy so chastened, Lees could return to his main focus: executing a reconnaissance of the newly discovered German headquarters. Several days had passed since Florence had mooted – and Lees had accepted – the offer of SAS paratroopers. There had been no further word of them, and Lees' Plan B was to hit the German headquarters, or at least the key commanders, with the forces he could muster here in the valley.

If they could log General Feuerstein's movements, there was no reason why Lees' Black Owls shouldn't ambush him. They were hitting road convoys nightly now, and Lees could see no argument why General Feuerstein's staff car shouldn't likewise end up riddled with bullets. They could always mount a full-scale attack on the HQ at a later date.

Lees had a new companion to accompany him on his

reconnaissance journey. Lance Corporal Phil Butler had only recently parachuted in to join his mission. Butler had been working locally as a schoolmaster before the war, learning to speak Italian while wandering about these mountains. Quiet, charming and with considerable intelligence-savvy, his other key attribute was his ability to march across the hills at a stiff pace. That was just to Lees' liking, for he hated being slowed down by anyone.

Leaving the ever-capable Farrimond in charge at Secchio, Lees and Butler prepared for the off. As they would be slipping into the heart of enemy territory, the key thing they needed was a convincing disguise. Due to his imposing physical presence, Lees had always found getting local civilian dress something of a challenge. In Yugoslavia, they'd been forced to search the mountains high and low for the tallest man around. Eventually one had presented himself approximating to Lees' height and girth.

He was persuaded to exchange his rough and much-patched trousers for Lees' combat pants, plus his gaily knitted stockings, fur coat and black woollen cap. Lees' feet were wrapped in the skin of a freshly slain calf, so forming the traditional footwear of the region, akin to a lightweight pair of moccasins. Thus adorned, he'd taken on the guise of a local. He'd faced one major problem: within minutes of his transformation he'd started itching horribly. He'd been forced to conclude that when he swapped his clothes back again, his uniform would be similarly riddled with lice.

Here in the Secchia valley, Lees settled for a less onerous form of a compromise. A pair of moth-eaten trousers were conjured from somewhere, plus a voluminous cloak. With that thrown over his battledress tunic and with his Sten gun – fitted with silencer – hidden beneath, he figured he could pass muster. Butler was similarly disguised.

They set out early, sticking to faint paths and tracks. It was a thirty-mile trek to their first port of call, Viano village, perched on the very edge of the hills. They reached it about midnight, creeping along the main street cautiously, for German patrols were known to billet themselves there. Their guide took them to a house standing a little apart, where one of Kiss's contacts lived. No lights were showing and all was silent within. The guide used the pre-arranged signal – a sequence of rings on the back-door bell – to alert those inside.

A voice answered from an upstairs window. 'Who's there?'

'Partisans,' the guide answered.

'Go away at once,' the voice hissed. 'I have nothing to do with partisans . . . The Germans were in the village today. They may come back at any moment.'

Lees stepped out of the shadows. 'I'm an English captain. Open up, please.'

As far as he was concerned, it was his Lire that were paying the man for the intelligence he supplied, so he had every right to demand a bed for the night. The window slammed shut. Moments later the back door opened and Lees and party were ushered inside.

After being served a meal, Lees and Butler were shown to a room they could share for the night. Lees decided to open the window, to let in some air. He detected movement in the bushes below. He hissed to Butler to call out a challenge, while he readied his Sten, releasing the bolt of his weapon with a sharp steel-on-steel rasp.

'Answer at once!' Butler cried.

'It is I, your host,' came back the fearful reply from the bushes.

Lees ordered the man into the open, and demanded to know what the devil he was up to.

'I am afraid to sleep in the house in case the enemy return at dawn.'

'So where are you going?' Lees demanded. 'If you inform on us, don't you know you will be shot!'

The man seemed genuinely distraught at the suggestion he might betray them. 'No, no, no. Never! I was just going to a farm close by.'

Lees was convinced the man was telling the truth, and he eased his finger off the trigger.

Early the following morning they made contact with Gordon, who was holed up in a patch of nearby woodland. The previous night he and his Black Owls had ambushed an enemy convoy, after an armoured car had driven over one of their mines. They'd destroyed two trucks, left the armoured car a smoking wreck, and had one man lightly wounded in the exchange of fire. All in all, it had been a good night's work.

From the shelter of the woods, Gordon sent out word for the leaders of the local underground movement to come. They arrived around midday, whereupon Lees proceeded to ask about the enemy HQ. It was situated in a hamlet called Botteghe, they explained, lying on the outskirts of the village of Albinea, some ten kilometres south-west of Reggio Emilia. They were able to furnish several more fascinating details, plus they offered a guide who could take Lees and Butler to within sight of the place.

Lees chose Gordon and 'Giorgio', one of the German deserters, to accompany them. After three hours' march through the darkness following a difficult and convoluted route, they reached an isolated farmhouse lying on a small hillock overlooking the plain. While Lees and Butler held back, Gordon went ahead to deal with the farmer. Issuing fearful threats, he informed the man that he needed use of the farmstead for twenty-four hours. No one was allowed to leave or enter on pain of death during that time.

As Gordon and Giorgio took turns standing sentry, Lees and Butler crawled into a hayloft and dropped to sleep. The following morning dawned bright and clear. The sun burned off the mist that clung to the low-ground, as Lees gazed out over a vast plain that stretched unbroken to the banks of the River Po. Directly to the north some ten miles away, Reggio Emilia shimmered in the early morning heat. A convoy of trucks crawled along a road.

Using his binoculars and map Lees began to identify the smaller, closer landmarks. A village here marked as 'Sundiano'. A large building there with a bright red-tiled roof – a farmstead marked as the 'Villa Spandoni'. Closer and to Lees' left, a clutch of homesteads, seemingly nothing more than a few cottages clustered around a crossroads. But just beyond those lay two large and imposing buildings, one constructed in rich red brick, the other in fine white stone. That had to be it – Villa Rossi; Red Villa – as identified in the Stafetta's note, plus a sister HQ building, Villa Calvi.

He pointed to the place. 'Is that Botteghe?' he asked the guide, feigning a passing interest.

'Si, Signor.' He pointed at the large red-brick building. 'And that is Villa Rossi. They say a general lives there.'

Lees drew a detailed sketch of the place, including the two grand villas, one of which came complete with its own chapel. Via his binoculars he studied Villa Rossi: it was a multi-storeyed fortress, graced by square-walled towers and arched windows, and surrounded by fancy, wrought-iron gates and railings with imposing pillared entryways. It had clearly been a wealthy country residence, before the enemy seized it. The neighbouring building,

Villa Calvi, appeared like a towering, white-walled mansion, and was equally impressive.

Before the two villas lay a small patch of woodland. If they were to attempt an approach unseen and undetected, that might offer good cover. At eight o'clock sharp, the roads, which had been thronged with traffic, suddenly became empty. The reason why shortly became clear: a flight of Thunderbolts roared into the airspace, searching for targets. The Germans clearly knew the hour the Allies sent over their first air patrols, and they timed their convoys accordingly.

All that day Lees and Butler hid in the hayloft, gazing through their binoculars. From all that Lees had learned, ambushing General Feuerstein's car was looking like a non-starter: the German commander varied his movements. He came and left at different times of day and night. His driver took different routes, and sometimes the general never left Villa Rossi for days.

Without a regular schedule, shooting up his staff car was going to be nigh-on impossible. Bar the SAS getting parachuted in, and launching a full-frontal assault on the two buildings, Lees didn't know how exactly they would execute the hit. Still, the recce had gone well and he felt buoyed. Something would shake out of it, of that he felt certain.

Come nightfall he and Butler left, paying the farmer handsomely for his pains. But they arrived back at their Secchio base to disappointing news. The insertion of the SAS parachutists was looking doubtful. Florence worried that sending such a high-profile force might prove counter-productive, by drawing the enemy's ire. Lees was enraged. He was the best judge of the situation on the ground.

He sent a very strongly worded message back to headquarters

to that effect. His anger was fuelled by what else he was to learn, following his return to his Secchio base. By chance, a German prisoner had been brought in by one of the communist brigades. A nondescript private, Lees left him to Fritz Snapper's questioning, alpenstock in hand. That evening, over dinner, Lees asked if the prisoner had had anything to say.

Snapper waved a hand, dismissively. 'Nothing much. He was in the Signals Corps, stationed at some place called Botteghe.'

Apart from Kiss, none of Lees' men knew anything about his intentions regarding the 14th Army's headquarters.

'Where is he now?' Lees demanded.

'I sent him to Febbio, to the POW pens.'

Lees eyed the Dutch Army lieutenant. 'I'm afraid you'll have to fetch him back at once. Go yourself, and for God's sake don't let him escape.'

Snapper, ever willing, set out right away, bringing the prisoner back directly. Lees proceeded to question him into the early hours. He could be a hard man when he had need, and he was ready to do whatever it took to make the man talk. Fortunately, the captive spoke relatively freely and knew the Botteghe headquarters intimately. A German private, he'd served as General Feuerstein's personal telephonist at Villa Rossi, so in his private residence. It was sheer good fortune that he'd fallen into Lees' clutches. He'd been out for a stroll when he'd stumbled into a unit of partisans who were returning from an ambush mission. Not being particularly warlike, he'd surrendered pretty much right away.

He knew everything. He knew the exact strength of the guard forces and where they were stationed. There were some five hundred at the two villas, with hundreds more in reserve, billeted at a barracks just a short drive away and with armoured cars and tanks in support. He knew the layout and role of the two buildings. He confirmed that the HQ oversaw command of German forces manning the Gothic Line from Reggio Emilia to the western coast, so for over a hundred kilometres, or around half of its total length.

From Villa Calvi there was said to be a hotline running direct to Berlin. Field Marshal Kesselring was known to visit the place twice a week, and he was very likely speaking to the Führer himself. While Villa Rossi – two centuries old, and formerly the properly of an Italian lawyer – provided accommodation for senior staff, Villa Calvi housed the 14th Army's communications, command and control set-up. In other words, it was the absolute nerve centre for four German divisions.

The prisoner had one other key piece of intelligence to depart. General Feuerstein had just been replaced, one General Friedrich-Wilhelm Hauk taking over. The blond, blue-eyed Hauk was a highly decorated veteran who had led the invasions of Poland and France in the early stages of the war. He'd won the Knight's Cross of the Iron Cross, in June 1944, for extreme battlefield bravery and leadership, before being posted to Italy that autumn. As assassination targets went, General Hauk was preferable in many ways to his predecessor, but the news of his arrival placed Lees in something of a quandary.

A few days earlier Kiss had presented him with an alternative plan to do away with General Feuerstein, as the SAS seemed to be so long in the coming. One of his Stafettas had just discovered that the general was a devout Catholic and a regular at Sunday morning mass. As Kiss knew the priest local to the area, he'd proposed that he hide himself in the priest's house on a Saturday night, overlooking the steps of the church. From there he'd proceed to shoot the general when he arrived for Sunday worship, with a silenced pistol.

The key to Kiss's plan had been slipping into the priest's house unremarked. They'd decided to disguise him as a holy man, which would provide the perfect cover. Lees had approached Don Pedro, his host, who had provided Kiss with a set of his own cleric's robes.

Kiss had already departed on his devilish assassination mission, not knowing that General Feuerstein had flown the nest. Unless General Hauk was likewise a devout Catholic, Kiss was going to return empty-handed, at which stage Lees would need those SAS parachutists as never before. He signalled as much to Charles Macintosh, at Florence headquarters.

'LEES to MACINTOSH. Have here German who is private telephonist to Lt-Gen HAUK of . . . Staff Corps HQ of 14 Army. Subject is intelligent and willing to talk and am sure he is genuine . . . Am absolutely set for attacking this HQ; can I go ahead either with SAS or partisans, using subject as guide? We have tremendous chance of success and this HQ is vitally important.'

The reply Lees received was surprisingly enthusiastic: '15 Army Group sanction attack . . . Submit plan of attack for possible coordination air support . . . Will SAS be involved?'

Lees replied confirming all points, and strongly requesting that the SAS parachutists be sent in. He received confirmation that an advance force would be despatched the very next day, under the command of an SAS captain. Lees had no idea what lay behind this apparent change of heart at headquarters. In truth, he'd had assistance from several key figures behind the scenes in Florence.

One was Captain Walker-Brown, the brilliant commander of

Operation Galia. Walker-Brown had been lobbying in the background and working his magic on the Americans. Appointed as No. 3 Squadron SAS's liaison officer in Florence, he'd been arguing forcefully for the squadron to be sent in. Upon hearing of Lees' discovery of the Botteghe HQ, he'd recognised that here was a mission ready-made for the special forces raiders.

'It was planned,' he wrote of the Botteghe raid, '. . . in the hope that destruction caused in a major headquarters would result in some loss of control, however momentary . . .' In that moment, Allied forces massing to the south of the Gothic Line could seize the advantage.

Major Jim Davies, one of Macintosh's favourite BLOs, who commanded a neighbouring band of partisans, had also reported back most positively on Lees, saying that he had totally resurrected the fortunes of the Reggiani partisans. Davies wrote: 'I am sure they would be most effective, even decisive, in attacks on the trans-Apennine communications.' Of Lees' HQ assault plan, he noted: 'LEES . . . doing very well. I have discussed SAS question . . . He wants them for the Corps HQ and will get everything teed up first.'

In Secchio, Lees remained oblivious to such behind-the-scenes manoeuvres. Hardly a politician or diplomat, he didn't particularly give a damn about such things.

All he cared about was getting the mission of a lifetime done.

Chapter 10

It was dawn on 4 March 1945 when Major Farran clambered aboard the lead flight of six Dakotas bound for the Secchia valley. Some forty minutes later, he found himself at the open doorway of the aircraft, buffeted by icy blasts. As they swooped low over a mountain pass, Farran could see tiny black figures outlined against the sparkling, sunlit expanse of the snowfields.

Behind him, five fellow parachutists were bunched up close, each weighed down with heavy kit. As one, they staggered when the aircraft hit a patch of fierce turbulence. Farran noticed their nervous glances, as they stared down at the barren terrain flashing past, and at the pair of P47 Thunderbolts flying escort, close on their wingtips. He could well appreciate their nerves.

It had been three days since their last contact with Mike Lees, the SOE's man on the ground. As the area was crawling with enemy, a lot could have happened in the interim. And even if the pilots did find the DZ and it was in friendly hands, the partisans might have failed to leave the proper designation of markers. If that happened, should they leap regardless? The weather was bound to break soon, so there was no knowing when they might get another chance.

Farran held the US aircrews who flew the Dakotas in very high regard. During Operation Galia, Colonel Hardt, their squadron leader, had personally flown a mission of untold import. Harried through the ice-bound mountains, Walker-Brown's men were sick to death with dysentery and scabies – a horrible infection caused by mites that burrow beneath the skin. Hardt had piloted a lone, unarmed Dakota through deep, fog-bound valleys, dropping Captain John 'Jock' Milne, an SAS doctor, into their isolated location, saving many lives.

Likewise, Farran had every confidence in today's aircrew. He'd been jammed in the Dakota's doorway buffeted by the freezing slipstream for a good ten minutes, when he felt the aircraft lose altitude and start to circle. Sure enough, the point below was marked by a distinctive arrangement of coloured parachutes showing red and yellow in the snow. Tiny figures darted about, busy with last minute preparations. The DZ lay at the head of a long, narrow valley, above which towered the unmistakable form of Monte Cusna.

Smoke drifted lazily from one or two villages scattered across the terrain. Farran studied them closely, trying to ascertain if they had been burned out in a recent *rastrellamento* – raking through. The red light flashed on, marking the ten-minutes-to-jump point. Farran turned to the six men behind him: each forced an uncertain smile.

Jock Easton, Farran's second-in-command, seemed the calmest. Hardly surprising, as he was one of the genuine old and bold. Behind him, Kershaw, a British Olympic bobsleigh competitor before the war, gave a thumbs-up and shouted something, but his words were torn away on the wind. It was Kershaw's first parachute jump, but no doubt he would be very much at home once in the snowfields. After Kershaw came the two war-bitten Spaniards, Robert Bruce and Frank Williams, arguably the most experienced of the lot in irregular warfare. But even they looked nervous.

The men's disquiet underscored one of the main reasons that Farran had decided that he *would* be joining them today, regardless of orders to the contrary. He needed to lead from the front, to set an example. But even so his guts were knotted tight with nerves. For a moment he wondered if he could back out. God knows, he had every excuse – not least of which, he would be jumping against orders. But if he bottled it, his men would know the real reason and it might deter them from making the leap themselves.

More to the point, Farran would be judged by his peers. He'd not been too windy to send Captain Littlejohn and team into the freezing darkness above the snow-bound Brenner Pass, on operation Cold Comfort, but he would have been too windy to jump now. At the end of the day it was neither duty nor patriotism that stiffened Farran's resolve: it was his relationship with his men and that age-old desire to stand high in their regard, and to lead from the front.

He braced himself at the doorway, feeling the cold burn of the air against his fingers. He leaned further forwards, the slipstream tearing at his face. He tried to remember how to do this: *feet and knees together as you jumped*. He consoled himself with the thought that in many ways it was easier to go first. That way, you didn't see the man before you dive into the howling void, something that was so utterly unnatural that it went against your every instinct.

As he peered at the ground flashing past, Farran sensed they were too low. The gleaming white flank of Monte Cusna towered above them. He turned to speak to the despatcher, but the words froze in his throat. The man thumped Farran on the shoulder, and indicated that the light had switched to green. After a moment's hesitation, he threw himself forward.

There was a second's gut-wrenching panic, before the parachute snapped like a yacht's mainsail catching the wind and it
blossomed above his head. Farran found himself drifting towards
earth, the white folds of the valley rising to great heights on either
side. He reached for the pin that held his kitbag fastened to his
leg, and ripped it out, letting it fall on its retaining rope. As he
did so, a voice yelled beside him, exultantly.

'Whoa Mahomet! Whoa Mahomet!'

It was the curious war-cry of the British 1st Airborne Division,
something that the paratroopers had picked up from the locals –
and no doubt bastardised – during the 1942 Operation Torch
landings in North Africa. Farran laughed. It was Kershaw who
was yelling, and to Farran it signalled that his men were with him
in spirit, as well as in body.

As the ground drifted up to meet them, he spared a thought for
the predicament he was in, although there was no getting back
into that aircraft now. He'd told the American aircrew an utterly
fanciful story, one that he'd begged them to deliver to headquarters as straight-faced and sober as they possibly could. They were
to report the sad tale that Major Farran had unexpectedly fallen
from the aircraft, even as the others had jumped.

He wondered how long the ruse would hold. Once it was discovered that he'd 'fallen' with a parachute strapped to his back
and his kit and weaponry slung on his person, he figured the
game would be up. He would be in grave danger of ending a
distinguished wartime career with a court martial. The one thing
that might mitigate his disgrace was the success of the coming
mission, for which so much depended on the man on the ground
here, Michael Lees.

Farran had heard much about Lees and his reputation as a

force of nature. He was 'the best and yet the wildest, most difficult to tame and the most domineering mission commander in northern Italy', as Farran understood it. He couldn't wait to see Lees in action.

Farran's kitbag had barely reached the end of its rope, before he felt it thump down with a hollow plop. Moments later he hit the snowy ground, which proved to be deceptively hard. He rolled twice, coming to rest with the breath knocked out of him and lying on his back. He reached up and tried to get his parachute under control, which was billowing wildly and threatening to drag him away.

Fortunately, a figure appeared to help. Cloaked in baggy battledress, he looked barely out of his teens.

'Buongiorno,' he cried, as he helped Farran wrestle with the chute. 'I am Bruno.'

Moments later, Bruno had hoisted Farran's kitbag onto his shoulders and was climbing up the slope towards the DZ, which was set a little way above them.

Farran struggled to his feet. 'Come back, you little brute!' he yelled, before promptly falling over again in the snow.

Over the past few days the surface had repeatedly thawed and frozen, making it as slippery as an ice rink, hence Farran's problems.

Bruno returned, dropped the kitbag, and helped the struggling SAS major to his feet. All around them freshly released supply containers drifted to earth. Some broke free from their parachutes and came screaming down like bombs. Farran thanked his lucky stars he wasn't under one of those.

By a combination of crawling and sliding he reached the DZ, only to find that not one of his men was in sight. A tall fellow with a giant white beard seemed in charge. Upon spying Farran he saluted smartly, and introduced himself as 'Scalabrino', but that did little to dispel his Robin Hood air. Still, he struck Farran as being the most soldierly of any present. The remainder – presumably, Mike Lee's finest – were as long-haired and bearded a bunch of ruffians as ever he'd laid eyes on.

They were a distinctly motley crew, sporting items of uniform from just about every nation that had fought in this war: British, American, Italian and German. The one unifying feature appeared to be the lengths of colourful parachute silk each had wrapped around his neck, as a makeshift scarf. That, plus the fact that every single one of them was armed to the teeth – bristling with knifes, daggers, grenades, pistols and tommy guns.

As initial impressions went it left something to be desired. Only Scalabrino impressed. The efficiency with which he had mule trains and oxen sleds collecting up the supplies was striking. Farran asked if he'd seen any others from his stick. 'Yessir,' Scalabrino replied, indicating a nearby village. Farran spied Kershaw wandering up the track. He was hatless, his uniform was torn and he was a little dazed-looking, but he managed a broad smile.

Kershaw reported that they'd been dropped over the village itself, landing among the roofs and hard, icy streets. In the process, Jock Easton had injured his shoulder. Kershaw himself was only saved when he landed on a snowy roof, slid off and a comely Italian woman happened to break his fall. Bruce, the Spaniard and former Foreign Legionnaire, had smashed his carbine upon landing, but otherwise he was in relatively good shape, as was his fellow Spaniard, Williams.

Farran spotted Jock Easton stumbling up the track, looking white as a sheet. He was in the company of a second figure, a

Lieutenant Smith. Farran had met Smith in Florence several weeks earlier and he'd warmed to the man. A Scot, he seemed either to be talking non-stop or to lapse into long silences. Wholly at home in the mountains, Smith was acutely shy and prone to fits of depression. He had been dropped in recently to assist Lees, and Farran wondered how he was faring under the command of such a man, serving in his not-inconsiderable shadow.

Easton was in great pain, and he collapsed and vomited into the snow. Farran, Smith and Kershaw carried him to the nearby village, a tiny place called Casa Belocchi. There, Bruno the teenage partisan volunteered to fetch the nearest doctor, which might take some time. While they waited they put Easton to bed, and Smith led them to a nearby café for breakfast.

A wizened old crone blew twigs into crackling flames, and lit oil lanterns. Shortly, she'd rustled up a fine breakfast of chestnut bread, fried eggs and red wine. This was Farran's first introduction to chestnuts, a staple of the poverty-stricken villagers. Their coarse mountain bread was studded with chestnuts, to help bulk it out.

Houses lined the village square, linked by steep cobbled paths slippery with ice. From the outside, they looked like hovels. Inside they were spotless, each boasting an open charcoal fire and dancing oil lanterns. In a way, they reminded Farran of the neat little white-painted cottages you'd find all over County Tyrone and South Down – the part of Northern Ireland that his family hailed from.

As he sipped his wine, Farran marvelled that such a place and such a life could exist, so close to the German lines. Everywhere he looked figures were busy hauling supplies through the streets. The place was alive with partisans and their local helpers, while a force of newly arrived parachutists breakfasted in the village café, yet the enemy were but a short march away. It was all so utterly brazen, with the main front just the far side of the mountain.

They'd never have got away with this in France, Farran reasoned. Smith, in garrulous mood, explained how things worked around here. The partisans held the mountains, the enemy the plains. If the partisans caused too much trouble, the Germans tended to mount a *rastrellamento*, but they were only ever short-lived. The enemy just didn't have the forces to man the front line and to drive the partisans out of their mountain redoubt.

'Are they all Reds?' Farran queried, remembering his Florence briefings.

'Most of them call themselves communists, but . . . they don't really know what communism means.'

'Are they holding on to seize power when the war's over?' Farran asked. Again, it was something he'd heard talk about in Florence.

Smith shrugged. 'That may be partly it.'

A sudden burst of gunfire echoed through the streets, cutting their conversation short. As Farran and his men reached for their weapons, Smith told them not to worry. It was just a bout of high spirits. Overjoyed with the drop – fully five plane-loads – the partisans were celebrating as only they knew how.

Of course, the spirit of resistance would run deep in these mountains, Farran reflected. The locals were the descendants of Garibaldi's originals, those brave Italian souls who had fought centuries back to liberate and unify the Italian nation. In 1860 the famed Italian commander General Giuseppe Garibaldi had raised a volunteer army, to march on southern Italy, in the celebrated Expedition of the Thousand.

With a thousand volunteers he had defeated a much larger regular army, leading to the unification of a hitherto divided nation. General Garibaldi was a fierce advocate of democracy, tolerance and liberty, and he'd won international renown particularly in Britain and the USA. His volunteer fighters had worn red shirts, as their one distinguishing feature, and they had named themselves the Garibaldini. The general's present-day descendants, the communist partisans, referred to themselves by the same name.

At last the doctor arrived. A tall moustachioed individual, he appeared somewhat servile and frightened. Farran did his best to put the man at ease, before stiffening Jock Easton's spirits with a good draft of red wine. That done, the doctor seized his injured arm and twisted it behind his back. There was a sharp crack and the dislocated shoulder was forced back into place. Agonising though it doubtless was, Easton appeared instantly happier. With his arm bound up in a sling, he should be good to move.

Farran noticed the crowds thronging the streets seeming to part ways spontaneously. A tall figure mounted on a fine brown mare rode forwards, making a beeline for the café. Farran didn't doubt for one moment that this was the illustrious Mike Lees, the man upon whom everything now depended. Swinging with ease from his saddle – he used to hunt regularly with the South Dorset Hounds – Lees towered over the locals. They cheered his arrival, like a football star at a big match.

Lees was wearing a stylish, sand-coloured American windbreaker jacket, topped off by a dashing black beret. No doubt about it, he looked the part. He strode forward and grabbed Farran's hand, pumping it so enthusiastically that he wondered whether his soldiering days were over.

'Delighted to see you,' Lees began. 'I didn't think they'd ever get around to sending British troops. No one warned me you were coming, but it's just as well if the other chap is hurt.' By that he meant Easton.

'Didn't you get a message from Florence?' Farran asked.

'Got a message. Said there was going to be a drop, so I sent Smith. Didn't say you were coming. Don't believe half of what they say, anyway. Sometimes they say there's going to be a drop and nothing turns up. Didn't know you were coming yourself.'

Farran's blue eyes twinkled mischievously. 'No one knew. In fact, my chief refused permission, but I thought I'd come in the plane and see the chaps jump. Well, you know how it is . . . I thought I'd wear a parachute, just in case we had trouble. I was standing by the door and someone tripped over me, and bless my soul there I was in the air. And a man on a parachute can hardly go upwards, can he?'

Lees saw Farran's left eye droop momentarily, in the vaguest suggestion of a wink. 'Of course, there's no way I could get out again, is there?' Farran ventured. 'I'm supposed to be doing a desk job in Florence – chairborne!'

'Well, there's a courier service that regularly crosses the lines,' Lees replied. 'But it's very dangerous,' he added, with emphasis. '*Very dangerous indeed.*'

'And we'll be liberated soon?' Farran prompted.

Lees nodded vigorously. 'Oh yes, I expect so. Very soon, I expect.'

Both men burst out laughing.

'In that case I think I'll have to stay,' Farran declared. 'Now, tell me about this place you want to beat up. I'm itching to get at it.'

'Good show!' Lees enthused. 'Lots of targets for you, actually. The Army HQ's a sitting duck. At last we can get cracking. These farts are bloody useless. You lot will shake 'em up. Farts is what we call 'em – you know, bastardisation of "partisans". No strength and gone with the wind.' He laughed. 'I've arranged for Colonel Monti to come over tonight. He's supposed to be the CO around here. Let's get moving. My base is at Secchio, three hours from here.'

Farran explained that Jock Easton was walking wounded, and Lees immediately offered his horse. He turned to Scalabrino to outline what was required.

'See this old scoundrel,' Lees continued, once he was done explaining, 'he's the only fart I trust in the whole valley. He'll account for everything, down to the last pair of bootlaces.'

'So what are the plans now?' Farran asked.

'Andiamo.' – Let's go. 'We walk to Secchio. It'll take three hours. Do myself pretty well there. Lodge with the priest. You'll see.'

Secchio village was pointed out to Farran – he could see it perched on the far side of the valley. It looked about five miles away. How could it take three hours to get there? he asked.

Lees' shoulders shook with laughter. It took three hours or more to cross the valley, no matter where you tried, he explained. With that Lees was off, heading up the narrow, rocky path that led out of Casa Belocchi. As he strode ahead, he started to sing in a stentorian voice:

> *The cow kicked Nellie in the belly in the barn,*
> *And the old man said it wouldn't do her any harm . . .*

Caught up in his enthusiasm, Farran grabbed his heavy kit, wondering how on earth he was going to keep up with the almighty great strides of this giant of a mountain man.

That evening, Farran and his men were shown to their billets scattered across Secchio. In the priest's house, the SAS major was led to his room by Don Pedro's elderly mother. He threw open the window and gazed over the scene. It was captivating. Beyond the goats and chickens in the back yard rose the flanks of a mountain, its slopes tinged purple in the evening haze. Oil lanterns flickered in cottages to left and right.

As Farran marvelled at the apparent peace here, a chill crept in to the room. This was far from what he was used to as a soldier's billet: the flowery wallpaper and crucifix adorning the wall; the crisp white sheets on the bed. Next door, a hot bath was running. Dinner was to follow. He lay back and laughed at the ceiling. This was the oddest way to begin operations behind the lines that he had ever known.

He wondered if Lees had somehow grown soft; if the SOE's man-on-the-ground here had somehow got it all wrong. Gung-ho, larger-than-life and battle-hungry, Lees didn't strike Farran as being the type to mess up. Regardless, he resolved to carry a carbine with him at all times, just in case.

But for now, more pressing matters beckoned. Farran needed to count a massive pile of cash. His rucksack was stuffed full of Lire – operational funds. As he flicked through the thick wads, he reflected upon how unlikely he was ever to be this wealthy again. Trusted implicitly with such a vast sum, little if any book-keeping was going to be possible. But he was too bound up in the spirit of the moment to wonder how a small portion of those funds might benefit his life in the future.

Downstairs, Lees was waiting over a dinner of ravioli. He offered Farran a choice of grappa – a strong, grape-based brandy – or Sassolino, the locally-made aniseed liqueur. Farran chose grappa, having acquired a taste for it on previous behind-the-lines operations. Fittingly, the priest's dining room had a giant portrait of the original General Garibaldi gracing one wall. Don Pedro looked on, bemusedly, as the two men got down to business.

The partisan leadership would be wary of Farran, Lees warned, as they'd been of him upon his arrival. The key was to allow individuals like Colonel Monti to appear as if still fully in command, while leading quietly from the shadows. The enemy were likely to know soon enough that Farran and his advance party had dropped in, which led around to the main point of interest for Lees.

'How big a force do you plan to bring?' he asked.

'Around fifty, with everything up to heavy mortars. That's a lot for us. We may even get jeeps and a howitzer dropped in before we're done.'

Farran had discussed such possibilities with Walker-Brown. He believed the US Willys jeep the 'greatest invention of the war'. Getting jeeps parachuted in would lend them the vital mobility upon which fast, hit-and-run guerrilla operations thrived. Getting a big 75mm howitzer dropped in would open up a whole new world of possibilities in terms of targets.

Lees leaned forward eagerly. 'Look,' he whispered, 'let's have a go at the German headquarters ... Ever since arriving I've wanted to attack it. That's why I pleaded for British troops, never dreaming they'd send some. I know all about the place ... Are you game for a really big show like that?'

'If you think we can do it, we'll take it on,' Farran replied.

Even as he'd said it, Farran had felt a flutter of nerves. For years now he'd grown accustomed to brewing up enemy convoys, blowing bridges, wrecking trains and shooting up aircraft on the ground. But taking on a heavily guarded army headquarters was a different matter entirely. The nearest Farran had ever got to anything like this was his wildly successful autumn '44 assault on the German garrison at Châtillon – but even that was small fry compared to what Lees was proposing. The headquarters of the German 14th Army was in a whole different league, and as far as he was aware the SAS had never attempted anything as remotely ambitious as this.

As Lees outlined its fearsome defences – several hundred German troops, boasting armour and anti-aircraft guns – Farran felt ever more daunted. When Lees explained its exact location, situated out on the plain of the Po and surrounded by enemy garrisons, he was doubly unsettled. But faced by Lees' unbridled enthusiasm, and benefiting from several refills of grappa, all Farran could do was live up to his fearsome reputation as a highly decorated and fearless SAS commander, drinking toast after toast to the coming mission.

Lees summoned Gordon, the Black Owls' chief, to join them with his accordion. Farran was struck by the man's appearance. His battledress displayed a black owl badge stitched onto one pocket – the newly minted emblem of their elite unit – and in his belt was tucked a pair of daggers and a matching pair of pistols. With his fingers flashing over the accordion's keys, Gordon began to sing in a rich, ringing tenor, belting out revolutionary songs, some of which dated back to the days of the original Garibaldini.

Gordon sang romantically and passionately, Italian style, and Farran found himself caught up in the spirit of the moment. Shortly, he was doing his best to croon along. The carousing was brought to a halt with the arrival of Colonel Monti, who had ridden from Febbio to make the SAS major's acquaintance. At first the colonel seemed guarded, as Lees had warned he might be, when introduced to 'Major McGinty', Farran's nom de guerre.

Farran offered up a bottle of whisky to break the ice, Lees producing some fine German cigars. He proceeded to regale his audience with the tale of how he'd come by them. There was a German Army deserter called Hans, Lees explained, who hated his former comrades with a vengeance. He'd taken to standing on the main highway seeking a lift, dressed in full German uniform. A truck would stop and Hans would hold it up at gun-point. The cigars had been purloined from one of his hijacked rides.

With the Scotch whisky flowing and German cigars glowing, the three commanders got down to business. Colonel Monti's foremost concern, it became clear, was that his prestige as chief of the Reggiani partisans was under threat. Lees handled the situation with remarkable skill, briefing Farran on the nature of the various partisan brigades, and translating everything for the colonel. Now and again he threw in a witty aside, which served to put Colonel Monti increasingly at ease.

There were four partisan brigades, Lees explained, amounting to some five hundred men-at-arms. In his view, the communist Garibaldini were the finer units, for they were led by commanders of more level temperament than the Green Flames. Gianni, Rames and Zito, the Garibaldini commanders, were rock-solid and dependable. Their fighting spirit was stiffened by Eros, the political commissar or chief of the Garibaldini brigades. A driven, fiercely ideological and somewhat difficult individual, nevertheless Eros had fought the Nazi enemy with enormous grit and courage over the years.

Lees moved on to outline the debilitating effect of the 'go-slow' and 'stand-down' orders issued by Allied high command, not to mention the winter shutdown in resupply drops. It had caused a sense of abandonment and betrayal, resulting in a complete loss of offensive spirit. What Lees had tried to focus on was turning all of that around.

As Lees talked, translating for the colonel's benefit, Farran could see the Italian commander fingering the stem of his glass uncomfortably. The colonel was impressed by the depth of Lees' understanding, if not a little discomfited by how completely he had seen through their façade. But he appeared far more discomfited to learn that a full squadron of SAS was scheduled to follow Farran, dropping in to join them.

'Whose command will they be under?' Colonel Monti ventured, addressing his question to Lees.

Farran jumped in. As the Italian colonel outranked him, he explained, he, Major Farran, would be under Colonel Monti's command. But as he had to take his orders from Florence, Monti's orders to Farran would have to originate in Florence headquarters. Convoluted and unworkable though this might be – Farran would obviously be taking his orders direct from headquarters – it was as fine a piece of weasel wording as he could muster.

'Then this is my understanding,' Colonel Monti ventured. 'You are under my command, but receive your orders from Florence.'

'Your orders to us originate in Florence,' Farran corrected him. 'And no one in the valley need know the details of this arrangement, of course.'

The colonel nodded. The peculiar arrangement seemed to pass muster. 'Very good. So, what now will you need?'

Farran explained that the first priority was a base for his SAS field headquarters, suitable for accommodating fifty men-at-arms. Easton and the rest would move in right away, preparing for the others to follow. Plus they'd need rations and some runners, to carry messages to and from Colonel Monti's HQ and to Lees' mission here in Secchio.

The colonel began to speak more freely now. The delicate negotiations done, he seemed far more comfortable. There was a disused church at Tapignola, he explained, just across the valley from Secchio. It was ideal for housing that size of force. The priest, Don Pasquino Borghi, had been a foremost resistance figure, until the enemy had arrested him. That had been in January 1944, when the priest had been officiating at a religious ceremony, the Festival of Saint Agnes.

A show trial followed, designed to demonstrate that even the clergy were not immune to the harshest of punishments for consorting with the resistance. On 30 January Don Pasquino Borghi had been executed by a shot in the back. Deprived of its priest, the church at Tapignola had fallen into disuse. In a sense, there was no more suitable a place to house those who would drop in, seeking vengeance. Farran couldn't agree more. His No. 3 Squadron SAS would be based in a church, whose priest had been executed by the Nazis. It was somehow so devilishly fitting.

Colonel Monti promised that supplies of food staples – spaghetti and flour – would be delivered there. He also offered six mules, to carry the SAS's kit and armaments. It was generous, for nearly all such beasts of burden had been commandeered by the Germans. Farran suggested they could also use the church as a base to train the partisans in the use of heavier weapons.

'Does that mean we are to receive more and heavier arms?' Colonel Monti queried.

'Of course,' Farran replied.

Florence recognised that the Reggiani partisans were of

unusually high calibre, he explained, which was why the SAS were being sent in. This was mostly hot air, of course, and Farran was chancing his arm by promising more and heavier weaponry. For all he knew, he might make contact with Florence only to be ordered out again, under threat of court martial. But it was a case of nothing ventured, nothing gained.

It was now that Lees aired an entirely new proposition. With the SAS's arrival, why not form a bespoke partisan brigade, one benefiting from top training and weaponry? It could be christened the 'Allied Battalion' and be permanently attached to the SAS. If it combined right-wing elements and communists, it would be truly apolitical. Barba Nera, a commander whom Lees held in high regard, could be appointed its chief, so directly under Farran.

As Colonel Monti seemed to favour the idea, Lees followed through with a further suggestion. 'What about the Russians? Surely, Modena's Russians would be far better under Major McGinty? That way, three companies would form the battalion: one British, one Italian and one Russian.'

Who on earth were the Russians, Farran wondered? But Lees was on a roll, and the good spirits and good liquor seemed to be doing the trick with Colonel Monti. He wasn't about to object. The colonel seemed to like the idea of adding the mysterious Russians into the mix. Swelled with the hundred men they could muster, Major McGinty's Allied Battalion would amount to some three hundred men-at-arms, SAS included.

Farran's head swirled. Given the time to train and arm them properly, this would truly be a force to be reckoned with. It wasn't the usual way the SAS went about doing things: small-scale, shoot-and-scoot raids didn't require a unit of that size and strength. But there was the 14th Army's Botteghe headquarters to be reckoned with.

Colonel Monti raised a glass to toast the *Battaglione Alleato* – the Allied Battalion. Lees winked at Farran and clapped his hands, summoning Gordon for a round of revolutionary songs. Farran was impressed by the skilful and adept way in which he had handled the delicate negotiations. There were clearly hidden depths to Mike Lees, to which his wild-man reputation didn't fully do justice. With Walker-Brown at base, to orchestrate air-drops, and Lees here on the ground, it struck Farran that this was a marriage made in heaven.

But only if headquarters swallowed the story of his miraculous survival – his accidental fall from the skies.

Chapter 11

Having slept well Farran was called for breakfast, where the question of the mysterious Russians was answered most emphatically. He was met by Lees and a stranger – a tall, dashing figure dressed in calf-high German Army boots, with a blue sailor's cap atop his close-cropped fair hair, and a strip of matching blue parachute silk knotted around his neck. He had a guileless, open face, and a surprisingly boyish air.

Farran warmed to the man's firm handshake and easy smile. This, it turned out, was Victor Pirogov, the commander of the Russian brigade of partisans, whose chosen nom de guerre was 'Modena'. Farran was struck by something else: a tall, dark and intriguingly silent woman was seated in one corner of the dining room, seemingly oblivious to her arresting beauty. It turned out that this was Modena's Italian mistress whom he took everywhere, even into battle.

Their arrival at Secchio was purely by chance: they had been riding through, heading to Febbio to plead for more and better arms with Colonel Monti. En route, and serendipitously, they'd dropped in for a chat.

Modena had a remarkable story. A former lieutenant in the Red Army, he'd been taken captive during fighting on the Eastern Front and sent to a POW camp in Austria. He'd escaped, crossed the border into Italy and proceeded to raise his own band of partisans. Mostly, they were former Russian POWs, though some had slipped away from the Todt Organisation, the Nazi forced-labour ministry which had thousands working to stiffen the Gothic Lines defences.

The Garibaldini had huge regard for Modena, presuming him to be an ardent communist. In truth, he was far more interested in leading his men in battle, or being seen with his pretty girl on his arm. Indeed, he struck Farran as being the ultimate swash-buckling adventurer, and if the rest of his partisans were cut from the same cloth, he could understand why Lees was so keen to have the Russians join the Allied Battalion. If they were to hit the 14th Army headquarters, they were just the kind of fighters he'd need.

Lees wasted no time in laying out their proposition to Modena, whose blue eyes shone with excitement. He expressed delight that 'proper soldiers' – the SAS – were dropping into the Secchio valley. He was confident of raising a force of a hundred of the finest Russian warriors, he declared. Indeed, he could recruit far more, for Russians were deserting daily from the 162nd Turkoman Division, a German Army unit formed mostly from Russian and Caucasus POWs. Given the choice between the concentration camps or fighting for the Reich, many had chosen the latter, but only for as long as it took to find a way out. Right now, they were flocking to the hills.

Farran told Modena to cap his unit at one hundred, to keep the Russian company in similar strength to the Italian one. Modena offered to contribute twelve mules as well, for his partisans were better equipped with the pack animals, which were crucial for mountain-based guerrilla operations. That agreed, Lees and Farran watched Modena mount up his big mare, his weapon slung upon his back, his mistress jumping onto the saddle in front of him.

As they waved farewell, setting off towards Febbio, Lees began to regale Farran with stories about the Russian's exploits. In the early days Modena had served with the Garibaldi brigades, when their fighters numbered in the few dozen only, earning a fearsome reputation. Upon forming his Russian brigade, he'd appointed Nikolai, a former Red Army sergeant, as his second-in-command. Apparently, Nikolai ruled the brigade as a British sergeant major would tend to – with a loud voice and a rod of iron.

Modena received sporadic liaison visits from another young Russian officer, who was Mike Lees' opposite number in Moscow. But since that man had little means to contact Moscow, some 3,000 kilometres away, and had such a vast area of territory to cover, his influence was minimal. On the ground it was the Western Allies – chiefly Britain and the US – who were pumping in the hard cash and the weaponry.

While Modena's enthusiastic embracing of the Allied Battalion was unlikely to go unnoticed in Moscow, he and his men had every reason to seek a closer alliance with the British and Americans. The Russians were known to look askance at any of their countrymen who had fought alongside Western 'capitalist' forces. By signing up to the Allied Battalion, Modena doubtless hoped that he and his men would be better shielded by Britain and the US, come war's end.

With the Russians on-board, Farran was struck by the linguistic challenges commanding the Allied Battalion might entail. Modena's Italian seemed about as good as his own, so pretty much non-existent. Apart from Russian, he also spoke German, which was of little help. It was all the more reason for Farran to speed the delivery of Lieutenant Stephens, their Austrian Jew, into the Casa Balocchi DZ. Fluent in German, Stephens could serve as the linguistic bridge to Modena and his men.

But Farran sensed that a Russian-speaker would also prove invaluable, especially if that person understood the Russian mentality. As it happened, he had just such a figure in mind. Karl Nurk was as colourful a character as ever there was, and while not strictly Russian, he was fluent in the tongue. He hailed from the republic of Estonia, sandwiched between Finland and Russia. Born in 1904, he'd served in the Estonian military, before deciding to attempt to cross the Sahara along with a fellow Estonian adventurer.

In 1925 they'd done just that, ending up completing the epic journey on foot when their camels died. Finding himself in East Africa, Nurk became variously a farmer and a big game hunter. He'd travelled to Britain at the outbreak of hostilities and volunteered to fight against the Russians in the Winter War, joining the British Volunteers, also known as the Snowballers (along with James Riccomini, who was already a stalwart of Farran's Tombola force).

Commanded by Orde Wingate, a passionate advocate of irregular warfare, the British Volunteers were backed enthusiastically by Churchill. As Nurk was a fluent Finnish speaker, he became invaluable to Wingate and served as his aide throughout the campaign. The spirited defence of Finland proved ultimately abortive, but Wingate was undeterred. His irregulars set out for Ethiopia to fight the Italians, with Nurk foremost among them.

There, Nurk had trained local Ethiopians in guerrilla warfare, scoring a series of daring victories. He was promoted to captain and won a Military Cross, being praised for 'conspicuous gallantry and devotion to duty'. Despite the terrible terrain and lack of water, his irregulars had surrounded and routed the Italians, taking 150 prisoners. 'This officer's determination and will to succeed are beyond all praise,' his MC citation had concluded.

By then, Nurk was in his late thirties, so an 'old man' compared to the likes of Farran and Lees. But he was far from done. Recruited into the SAS, he was wounded on operations in Yugoslavia, before parachuting into France in June 1944 and winning a DSO. In short, Nurk was just the kind of figure who would work well with the Russians, as they prepared to hit the 14th Army headquarters, which was exactly the kind of operation that Nurk would thrill to.

Farran was determined to get him dropped into theatre. The only trouble was, that would entail making contact with Florence headquarters, and getting Walker-Brown to pull some strings, putting up a request to London. And that in turn meant Farran raising his head above the parapet. He was worried he was going to get it summarily shot off, once those in command realised he was alive and well and doing exactly as they'd forbidden.

But first, there was another surprise visitor in Secchio. Word of the raising of the Allied Battalion was spreading fast, and Annibale Alpi – nom de guerre Barba Nera (black beard) – turned up. Short, portly, and seemingly dwarfed by a massive spade-shaped beard, he wore smart Italian battledress and a peaked Italian Army forage cap. A former sergeant in the Italian military, he had a certain presence and bearing. He'd served as the Reggiani partisans' quartermaster for an age now, furnishing their supplies and stores.

With the ground thick with enemy, it was far from easy soliciting food and other provisions. By all accounts, Barba Nera had done a fine job. Farran sensed that here was a man who could prove difficult, if crossed, but he was just the kind of skilled and resourceful organiser that the Allied Battalion would need. After some discussion Barba Nera agreed to serve as Farran's second-in-command, with key responsibility for providing rations and kit.

Farran sensed that Barba Nera was swayed in part by the money. From his pile of cash Farran had offered 75,000 Lire, to be paid on a weekly basis, to cover all provisioning and other non-weaponry requirements. In truth, this wasn't overly generous. Much had to be purchased at extortionate prices on the black market, and Barba Nera would also have to find fodder for their mules. But on the plus side of the equation, each resupply drop furnished highly valuable parachute silk, which he could barter in exchange for supplies.

They rounded off their negotiations with Farran demanding that all elements of the Allied Battalion – Russians, Garibaldini, Green Flames and Barba Nera's quartermaster corps, plus the SAS, of course – be ready to muster by 9 March, so just a few days hence.

'Arrivederci' – until we meet again – Barba Nera replied. Then he came stiffly to attention, placed his cap on his head and saluted crisply. The SAS tended not to go in for such formality, but as Farran told himself, wryly, they were all in the Italian Army now . . .

With Modena and Barba Nera squared away, Farran decided a visit to his new base at Tapignola church was in order. It lay due west across the valley and he decided to cross it 'as the crow flies'. He set out heading directly downhill, forcing a path through thick bush, clambering over huge grey boulders and slipping down vast expanses of scree. In places the snow lay waist deep, especially in the deepest gullies where the sun's warmth rarely reached.

The lower Farran plunged, the less sunlight there was, until he reached a narrow defile shrouded in permanent shadow. It was a place of bare rock, confusing echoes and little birdsong. He began to feel lonely and almost afraid. After what seemed like an age, he felt the icy waters of the Secchiello, a tributary of the Secchia, lapping at his boots. He waded across and began to climb the far side; away from the frozen depths; towards life; to light.

Farran sweated on the hard climb under a fierce afternoon sun. He scrambled up steep meadows cropped close by goats and sheep, pausing to gaze back at Secchio village. Tiny figures crawled like ants through the streets. It seemed so close he could barely believe the two hours it had taken him thus far. He turned back to the climb and stumbled onto a road. Gravelled and wide, it was navigable by jeep, which got his mind thinking along fast, mobile-raiding lines.

Farran paused to light his pipe. He could only imagine the road had been built by the Germans, in an effort to control – vanquish – the partisans. It was too fine for any common mountain track, but it was perfect for Farran's purposes if only he could get some jeeps dropped in. No doubt about it, he needed to break his silence and make contact with headquarters.

A short while later he reached the church. It sat on the outskirts of the village overlooking a quaint little meadow cut into the hillside. Constructed of grey stone, it had clearly seen better days. There was a gaping hole in the roof, and one corner was in danger of collapse. More importantly, Farran could hear voices echoing from the far side and shouts and laughter – exactly the kind of life that he sought.

He stole through the gate, to spy Jock Easton sitting on the grass with two striking-looking locals. Raven-haired beauties, they seemed to have made themselves well at home, as if they were already an integral part of the Allied Battalion. For his part, Easton seemed to have forgotten his recent injuries and to be in remarkably high spirits.

'Hello, Roy,' he cried. 'Plenty to tell you about, how we're getting this bloody dump into shape!'

Farran glanced at the two women. One had the most arresting look in her deep grey-blue eyes, offset by her very business-like battledress tunic with a pistol tucked into her belt. Her feet were bare, but her head was adorned with one of the SAS berets.

'And who the devil are *they*?' he asked.

'They're on establishment,' said Jock with a grin. 'They belong to Mike Lees, and they're called Stafettas. Eytie for "messenger". Whenever they want to find out what's going on, they send the girls for a look-see. They cycle through, flirt with Jerry, then come back and report. Intelligence squad, that's what they are. Believe it or not, they're under command of a fellow called Kiss.'

'How many are there?' Farran asked incredulously. He'd used such young women on missions in France, but never so blatantly.

'Three here,' Easton replied. 'They double-up by helping fetch water, clean and cook.' The grey-eyed Stafetta was called Norice, he explained. 'Smith says she's got all the devils of the world in her eyes.' Farran had to agree.

He told Easton he was a little concerned that all the pretty company and home cooking might make the men slack and lazy, and the enemy might take them by surprise. Easton told him not to be so silly. They were keeping a proper lookout. He showed Farran their quarters, which were in a barn attached to the church, the men billeted in sleeping bags laid out on a thick bed of straw.

Easton led Farran into a side-room, what had once been the church vestry. A bare-armed girl was bent at a giant cauldron, stirring spaghetti over an open fire. Smoke rose through a hole in the roof and drifted through the room. She smiled at Farran and waved her spoon gaily.

Easton led Farran on into the church itself. It was in a sorry state. Apart from the jagged hole in the roof, plaster peeled and sagged from the lime-washed walls. Easton motioned to a black stallion, which was tethered to a stone in the centre of the church, calmly munching hay. It was around fourteen hands, so some sixty inches tall, making it more like a Welsh hill pony in size, but still lovely in Farran's eyes.

'That's yours,' he announced. 'You'll need it with that gammy leg of yours.' Farran had never fully recovered from the injuries he'd sustained on Crete. 'I commandeered it from a war widow in Coriano, the next village. She wasn't too happy, but it was the only mount free in the whole of the valley, the rest having been taken by the Germans.'

'Gosh, Jock,' Farran declared, gratefully, 'but I'd rather walk than ride bare back.'

Easton grinned. 'Oh, we've fixed that. You'll be trotting across the valley like the Scots Greys in no time.'

He gestured at a figure in the shadows. It was Kershaw, and he emerged laden down with what had once been parachutist gear, but from which they'd fashioned a makeshift saddle. As he watched them fit it to the pony, Farran felt humbled. These were not the men that he had led through France, and he'd never trained or fought with the most of them, yet he felt as if he'd served with them for a lifetime.

The make-do tack was rounded off with a red and white rosette, courtesy of one of the Stafettas. His men had christened the steed Whoa Mahomet. Farran was overwhelmed. He rode Whoa Mahomet up and down outside the church to cheers from all, especially when he kicked him into a canter.

Easton wasn't done yet. He blew a sharp blast on a whistle, and four boys appeared from nowhere, lining up smartly. They wore battledress on the pockets of which were embroidered in black silk the motif of an arrow, with 'McGinty' stitched beneath it. On their shoulders in red thread were spelled the words, *'Chi osera vincera'*, a rough translation of the SAS motto, 'Who dares wins'.

Farran eased back his beret and scratched his head in amazement.

'These are the Arrows,' Jock announced, proudly. 'They're our runners. They go anywhere, even across the lines. All you have to do is whistle!'

Jock Easton was one of the old and the bold all right, and this was exactly what Farran had brought him here for. As well he knew, any fool could be uncomfortable in the field of battle. It took a genuine old soldier to achieve what Jock Easton had here in a matter of days. To top it all, he'd got Farran's signaller set up in a separate house nearby, where he could decode and encode his messages in relative peace.

After a hearty supper of spaghetti and red wine, Farran mounted Whoa Mahomet and rode off to the signaller's place. It was time to grasp the proverbial nettle and make contact with Florence. Fired by what he'd seen, Farran had all sorts of ideas running through his head. The Italians loved show and colour. He wanted distinctive berets, belts and even hackles – traditional feathered plumes – dropped in for his Allied Battalion. He wanted jeeps, plus he wanted a piper complete with tartan kilt and bagpipes, to pipe the partisans into battle.

He needed Stephens and Nurk, so he could communicate with German deserters and Russian partisans alike. He wanted heavy mortars, at least one howitzer, and scores of heavy machine guns. Normally, such requests – pipers, colourful hackles, British uniforms for Italian guerrillas – would have been rejected out of hand. Most hidebound staff officers would have refused point-blank. But Farran had Walker-Brown fighting his corner, and he felt certain that the former Op Galia commander would understand.

Farran's radio man was an old hand: it was Corporal Cunningham, the cool-headed operator who'd carefully rolled up his wireless aerial, despite the hail of bullets that had cut through the French woodland, during their September 1944 operations. Farran drafted out a signal, listing all that he could imagine Walker-Brown might conjure, and handed it to Cunningham.

Radio contact was established. At first there was utter consternation at Florence headquarters. SAS Major Farran had been reported dead, having fallen from a Dakota during the initial insertion, so how on earth could he be making contact from the field now? Had a man who'd fallen from an aircraft somehow survived? If so, how? Nothing made any sense.

Charles Macintosh, the SOE chief there, wasn't fooled for long. The initial report on Farran's 'air-accident' had noted that the SAS major had been 'helping despatch the men from the door of one of the Dakotas, overbalanced and fell'. All had presumed Major

Farran dead. Serendipitously, it now appeared, he'd had a parachute strapped to his back when he tumbled out, which was 'most unusual for an assistant despatcher', Macintosh observed, tartly.

By playing up Jock Easton's injuries suffered during the parachute drop – he had been slated to command the SAS party – Farran was able to argue that following his miraculous survival, it made sense for him to remain on the ground. He was needed here, and Florence headquarters – Charles Macintosh and US Colonel Riepe – should make a virtue out of necessity, not to mention Farran's extraordinary powers of survival.

By the time Farran took to Whoa Mahomet again, for the dusk ride back to Secchio, he figured the dust was beginning to settle over his seemingly miraculous resurrection. A distinctive figure trotted at his side, guiding the way. It was one of the McGinty's Arrows. By the time they'd reached Secchio, Farran had failed to acknowledge the boy, who seemed rather hurt. Didn't he recognise Bruno, he demanded, the first Italian ever to receive him in these hills?

Farran placed an arm around his young shoulders. The SAS commander apologised for his lapse of memory: it had been a busy few days. Bruno's spirits brightened, and he pledged undying allegiance to 'Il commandante Inglesi'. Farran responded by appointing Bruno as his official personal messenger and the keeper of Whoa Mahomet, to which Bruno appeared overjoyed.

As he led the horse away, the young partisan paused, then turned back. Could he possibly have a gun, he asked. Of course, said Farran. After all, Bruno was a soldier now. Bruno Gimpel was just sixteen years old, but he'd been born in London and spoke decent English. Farran felt inordinately proud of his motley force of many nationalities. Between these tall, shadowed mountains, everything as far as he could see was McGinty's – and Mike Lees' – kingdom. They were the chieftains of the valley, just as General Garibaldi had been in days of yore.

During Farran's absence, Lees had been busy. Kiss had returned from Albinea and his putative assassination mission. He'd turned up at Don Pedro's place still dressed in the cassock that the Secchio priest had loaned him – his cunning disguise. But the cloak was covered in mud, his dog collar was awry, and he didn't look in a particularly good mood.

'The bastard never showed up!' Kiss announced, angrily. He'd been awaiting General Feuerstein's arrival at Sunday mass, pistol in hand, unaware that he'd been replaced by General Hauk.

Don Pedro dissolved into fits of laughter. Lees had to admit, Kiss's discomfiture was somewhat amusing. 'General Hauk must be a bad Catholic,' he observed. 'Thus he was saved.'

'Oh no,' Don Pedro countered, 'it is because General Feuerstein is a good Catholic that *he* was saved. It is true General Hauk did not go to church.' He turned and gestured at a couple of the SAS men cleaning their weapons outside. 'But perhaps his life will not be spared, after all.'

That evening, Farran and Lees talked through their plans. Lees was keen to have Hans, the German deserter, ease their way into the 14th Army HQ, speaking German if there were any challenges. Farran suggested that if Walker-Brown succeeded in rustling him up a piper, the skirl of the bagpipes would leave an indelible British mark on the operation. That in turn might lessen the severity of any German reprisals, for the piper would signify that it was a British-led operation.

The one potential bugbear remained the Germans, and how they would react once they heard about the British parachutists' arrival. Lees – always the lateral thinker – had a suggestion. In recent months the SAS had been forced to dispense with their traditional beige berets, which they'd worn throughout the war. Instead, high command – somewhat pernickety and resentful of the elite unit's freewheeling ways – had insisted they wear the standard red beret of airborne forces.

Right now Lees figured they could make a virtue out of that necessity. What if the red berets signified that the parachutists were a team of British leftists – 'reds' – sent in to stiffen the Garibaldini's political backbone. Farran thought it a wickedly clever deception. Lees summoned Fritz Snapper, whom he trusted on such things, asking him to spread the word that the new arrivals had been sent by the British Labour Party, to liaise with the communist partisans.

Snapper, too, thought it a wonderful wheeze. Lees decided they should seal the deal with a bottle of grappa, and by the time Snapper departed on his black propaganda mission he was fired up with high spirits. So effective was he in spreading the word, that two ardent communists approached Farran shortly after to ask if it were true that he was the famous British Labour politician Sir Stafford Cripps.

Whether the enemy would swallow the story that the SAS were actually leftist emissaries was a moot point. But first, it was to be their own command who would try to scupper Lees and Farran's best laid plans.

While it was key to have a strong presence of partisans on the raid, so they would feel ownership of it and raise their fighting spirits, Lees and Farran were in no doubt that it would be the SAS who would be in the vanguard. That made it vital that the remainder of the squadron be parachuted in, along with all necessary weaponry.

But worryingly, SOE's Florence headquarters had been niggling Lees of late, warning him against 'making trouble'. He feared opinion at headquarters was turning against the planned raid, which certainly would cause huge amounts of 'trouble', if successful. Convinced he needed to nip such sentiments in the bud, on 6 March Lees penned a strongly-worded letter to Charles Macintosh, to be rushed across the lines by one of Fritz Snapper's couriers.

'Don't please think this is directed AT you, Charles,' he wrote, 'it is directed TO you, imploring you to get the powers that be to give us a break. I am terribly embittered to this sort of treatment, the same thing happened in Yugoslavia . . .' There, Lees had been ordered to drop his support of the Chetnik resistance fighters, which was the trigger that had prompted him to launch his solo sabotage operations.

'I have lost everything by joining this firm,' Lees continued. (The SOE was often referred to simply as 'The Firm'.) 'But I don't mind provided somebody will help me to fight the Germans, but when one is told in a signal "not advisable to make the fur fly" well, that is tantamount to making a pact with the enemy . . .' Even with Farran and his advance SAS party on hand, Lees found himself having to beg to be allowed to take the fight to the enemy.

Fortunately, his entreaties were endorsed by Major Jim Davies, the BLO operating with the neighbouring partisans. Davies had dropped over to Secchio for a chat. 'RORY is enjoying himself,' Davies messaged Florence. (Rory was one of Farran's nicknames.) 'He is growing his long hair and Jesus Christ beard, but his saintly appearance does not deceive the village maidens . . . Says he's going to make this his last fling . . .' he wrote of the 14th Army

HQ raid. 'I am all for it, so long as it is not let loose prematurely and goes off at half-cock.'

But despite such support on the ground, trouble was brewing. Wilcockson had been pulled out of the Secchia valley on compassionate grounds, and to all intents and purposes Lees had taken over his SOE command lock, stock and barrel. This rankled, and behind the scenes Florence was agitating to get Lees removed from the field. On 10 March 1944 Macintosh penned a note to Lt.Col. Hewitt, the newly-appointed chief of the SOE in Italy, Gerry Holdsworth having moved on. Macintosh's memo bemoaned Lees' 'usurping' of Wilcockson's command.

'Capt. M. LEES told me he is not going to be under command of Major WILCOCKSON . . .' Macintosh wrote. 'I had understood from signals from Base that Major WILCOCKSON was to command Capt. M. LEES.' With Wilcockson gone, such niceties of the chain of command were surely an irrelevance. Love him or loathe him, Lees was the man on the ground. But even so, pressure kept growing to somehow have him removed.

Hewitt, the new chief of SOE Italy, had penned the glowing October 1944 report on Lees, concluding that he was 'energetic, courageous' and 'ideally suited' to paramilitary operations. It seemed to cut little ice now, as Lees found himself battling against his own headquarters as much as the enemy. Matters broke out into open hostility, with Lees being 'invited' to leave the Secchia valley. He refused, penning an angry letter to Macintosh bemoaning the 'armchair crushers', who were intent on wasting 'the glorious possibilities of this show'.

Not mincing his words, Lees implored Macintosh – Florence headquarters – to back him. 'Dear Charles, I am sorry we have declared war on each other, but over this recent affair the way we have been treated is bloody . . . I realise and admit that by not accepting your invitation to come out I gave you a moral victory, but I did not accept because I realise that the firm would have jumped at the opportunity of putting in some BLO type who would sit here doing fuckall and give them a peaceful job with FANYs on their knees . .'

By 'FANYs' Lees was referring to the First Aid Nursing Yeomanry – cover for women serving with the SOE. The spat might seem somewhat rancorous and small-minded, and it was doubly so from the position of the Secchia valley, where Lees and Farran were poised to unleash merry hell, if only they could get the kind of support they required. Frustration levels were reaching boiling point, as Lees sensed the fates turning against them.

Indeed, the Lees family were about to suffer the first of several terrible misfortunes to befall them during the war. James Lees, Michael Lees' cousin, had been serving with the Special Boat Service, executing raids off Italy's Adriatic coastline, so not so very far from Mike Lees' domain. James was just a year older and the two cousins had been brought up almost as brothers, after the death of Mike Lees' father.

In early March 1945 James Lees had set out leading a small, canoe-born raiding force, to strike at an enemy-held island. They'd attacked, but the battle had turned into 'complete murder, absolute hell', reported one of his patrol members. 'Bullets firing all over the place and grenades going off . . . bodies lying on the floor.' Someone had cried out 'Tansy's down!' – Tansy being Captain James Lees' nickname. Mortally injured and taken captive, he'd died of his wounds.

James Lees had been revered by those he commanded. 'A smashing chap he was,' remarked one. 'A real gentleman. I couldn't speak too highly of him.' Likewise, Mike Lees was loved by those he led in the Secchia valley.

It was only the high-ups that seemed to have a problem with his cussed, plain-speaking ways.

Chapter 12

By his own admission, Roy Farran had developed a 'profound contempt for the staff' – those desk officers who stood in the way of getting the job done. Fortunately, he had connections in high places. Apart from the rock-solid backstop of Bob Walker-Brown, 'chairborne' in Florence, Farran had powerful top-cover in the form of Lt.Col. John 'Jackie' Profumo. The 5th Baron Profumo was then the youngest serving MP, and he'd been a vocal opponent of appeasing Hitler, becoming closely aligned with Churchill.

Having fought in the D-Day landings, Profumo had been transferred to Italy to serve on Field Marshal Alexander's staff, winning an OBE 'in recognition of gallant and distinguished service'. Farran was acquainted with Profumo – whose career had yet to be sullied by the sexual and political scandal that became known as the Profumo Affair – and knew him to be wholly supportive of special forces operations. Fortuitously, Profumo's role was to liaise with the Americans overseeing air-missions, which would be all to Farran's benefit.

By the second week of March 1945 the logjam appeared to be breaking. Among the first to be parachuted into the Secchia valley were several officers whom Farran desperately needed to boost the training of his Allied Battalion. Just days into his service with the SAS, virgin parachutist Lieutenant David Eyton-

Jones plummeted towards the night-dark terrain, hopeful that he might survive the landing, and that his pre-war agricultural studies at Cambridge might help with the handling of stubborn mules in these hills.

Captain John 'Jock' Milne also jumped, a man who had last parachuted into these mountains to tend to the desperately sick on Walker-Brown's Operation Galia mission. Milne was a battle-hardened war surgeon who'd served with Montgomery's Eighth Army in North Africa, after which he'd experienced the bloody horrors of the Allied advance up the spine of Italy. The scion of a foremost farming clan from Angus, on Scotland's eastern coast, the larger-than-life Milne was a gifted physician. Serving with the Royal Army Medical Corps, he'd been seconded to the SAS, where his ebullient good humour helped him operate under terrible conditions.

Both men would prove huge assets to the Allied Battalion, and both landed well on the moon-washed snows. Less fortunate was a second Galia veteran – the grizzled Italian sailor, Luigi 'Pippo' Siboldi, who'd been Walker-Brown's guide. A gust of wind caught his chute and he was dragged along the frozen ground, ending up dislocating his shoulder. Fortunately, Jock Milne was on hand to tend to him.

A massive quantity of supplies was delivered that night, as a squadron of Dakotas thundered overhead, threading long strings of parachutes across the dark skies. The scale and grunt of the drop sent a powerful message to the partisans, telegraphing that SAS Major Farran at least was blessed with the full backing of the Allies.

It was approaching midnight by the time the new arrivals had furled their parachutes and gathered up their kit for the trek to Tapignola. As they marched into the early hours, the young Eyton-Jones confessed that today was his birthday. Upon arrival at Tapignola they proceeded to toast Eyton-Jones with shots of grappa, celebrating the fact that he was all of twenty-two years old. High spirits were boosted when the 'comfort containers' arrived. Stuffed full of whisky, cigarettes and the all-important mail from home, they'd been parachuted into the DZ along with the weaponry needed to train a force of three hundred to wage war.

As Farran had known he would, Walker-Brown had worked wonders. One resupply container was packed full of battledress for the Allied Battalion recruits, plus hackles that had been originally earmarked for the Transvaal Scottish, a South African infantry regiment, but somehow syphoned off for Operation Tombola. Green and yellow were prominent in the Transvaal Scottish insignia, and the feathered hackles were reminiscent of the white and green of the Italian flag. Showy, colourful and symbolic, Farran was hugely satisfied.

Blessed with an innate understanding of human nature, its tendency towards tribalism and the need to belong, Farran was convinced that such tokens would help weld together his multinational force. With the Italians especially, much was about appearances. The fine uniforms and hackles would give them pride in their identity, and Farran saw no reason why the Italian brigades shouldn't follow the example of McGinty's Arrows, and adopt the *'Chi osera vincera'* motto. They too would have it sewn onto their battledress tunics.

Following that resupply drop it was as if the floodgates opened. During the third and fourth weeks of March scores more flights thundered into the Secchia valley, as Farran exploited his direct line of communication via Walker-Brown and Profumo to US General Mark Clark himself. While the British might vacillate, the Americans were proving typically bullish. They showed few qualms about arming and training the partisans to rise up in the enemy's rear, and in Farran they sensed they had a commander who meant business.

Over a forty-eight-hour period twenty-six SAS were dropped in, including Lieutenant Ken Harvey, another of those recruited in Farran's speech offering nothing but 'sweat, blisters and frost-bite and the probability of being shot as spies'. At just nineteen, Harvey had been serving with the Seaforth Highlanders, and he was blessed with that 'baby-faced beauty that is so typically English', Farran observed. He had no combat record to speak of, but Farran had high hopes. He'd gambled upon the nineteen-year-old being fresh into battle and desperate to prove himself.

Harvey was inexperienced, but sometimes a good dose of youthful recklessness was exactly what was required. With almost biblical eloquence he would write of his arrival at the Tapignola church base: 'It was a long and tiring march . . . particularly after all the excitement of an early morning operational jump . . . It was late that night when the last sleigh drawn by mules was unloaded and the supplies broken down. I crept into my sleeping bag having gathered some straw in the stable and, with the others, was soon sound asleep.'

Stephens the Austrian Jew was parachuted in, which meant that Farran and Lees could communicate more easily with their German deserter-recruits. Lieutenant Mike Eld was dropped in, one of the most experienced and capable officers in No. 3 Squadron and a man Farran felt he could rely on to hold the front line. Once they hit the 14th Army HQ, he didn't doubt that the

Germans would come seeking vengeance, and it would be crucial to defend their valley against all-comers. Lieutenant Eld was the man for the job.

Lieutenant James Riccomini was dropped in, following the largest single drop of Operation Tombola, which delivered twenty-four SAS operators in one go. Half-Italian, half-English and with a wife waiting for him back in Kent, Riccomini had not been home since his capture in 1941, his subsequent escape and joining the Italian resistance. Another Galia veteran, Riccomini was the one operator that Farran had sought with a vengeance. Brave and fearless to a fault, he would be perfect for spearheading the 14th Army HQ assault.

Corporal Stanley 'Sammy' Bolden, a Glaswegian originally with the Cameron Highlanders, was part of that twenty-four-man drop. Bolden, a Military Medal winner, had a wartime record almost to rival that of Riccomini. In March 1941 he'd volunteered for the Commandos, winning his MM during the ironically-named Operation Cartoon, a daring raid on an iron pyrite mine on the Norwegian island of Stord. Bolden had been wounded on the operation – which wrecked the mine and sank enemy shipping – but he'd continued fighting regardless of his injuries, for which he was awarded the MM.

Following recovery from his injuries, Bolden had married Sergeant Andre Chapman, who served with the Auxiliary Territorial Service (ATS), the women's branch of the British Army. Shortly thereafter he'd volunteered for the SAS. In training, Bolden was assessed as being an 'outstanding performer, keen and confident. Very good NCO. Morale A1.' Post D-Day, he'd joined Major Rooney's squadron on Operation Rupert, the raid on the ammo dumps in north-eastern France. One of Bolden's fellows concluded of him: 'He certainly was a tough egg!' In short, Corporal Sammy Bolden was just the kind of operator that Tombola called for.

One of the last in was Serjeant Sidney Elliott Guscott, a fellow Galia veteran who had made the most extraordinary efforts to join Team Tombola. Known as 'Gus' to his men, Guscott hailed from Pennymoor in rural Devon, where his parents owned the village store. He'd met Doreen, his future wife, at a local knees-up, both being keen ballroom dancers. They'd married and soon had a son, Ken, and daughter, Pauline, to care for, but the war had cut short their hopes of becoming ballroom dancing professionals, Guscott signing up for the Devonshire Regiment instead.

Guscott volunteered for an airborne unit, being subsequently recruited into the SAS. A 'good performer, cheerful and hard-working', he too parachuted on Operation Rupert as part of Major Rooney's squadron. Promoted to sergeant, the open-faced and guileless Guscott had commanded a troop of parachutists, but they got isolated from the main force. They resorted to living with the French partisans, surviving off what little supplies they had and the land.

By January 1945 Guscott was back in action, this time in northern Italy on Operation Brake, commanding a party of three – including Spanish Civil War and French Foreign Legion veteran, Private Raphael Luis Mansens Ramos. Born in 1919, Ramos was adopted at an early age, never knowing his real parents. He'd found his way into the SAS via a similar route to Francisco Jeronimo (aka Frank Williams) and Justo Balerdi (Robert Bruce). But in contrast to them, he'd refused to change his name for anyone, not even the Gestapo. Come what may, he'd stick doggedly to Ramos.

A native of Barcelona, Ramos's adoptive father had run a successful publishing business. Educated at a Jesuit – strongly Catholic – boarding school, Ramos had been brought up in a martial tradition and with a sense of service to the cause of global justice. In the battle of the Ebro, Ramos had been captured by Franco's forces, but he'd managed to escape. Fleeing to France, he'd found his way into the French Foreign Legion and from there to the British Army.

It was early December 1943 when Ramos volunteered for the SAS. Young, battle-hardened, hot-headed and hungry for action, he was a perfect recruit. He earned the reputation that when all others might be diving for cover, Ramos would be unloading with his machine gun. In his military references, Ramos was described thus: 'Character – very good. A fine war record . . .'

In Ramos, Serjeant Guscott was blessed with an ideal behind-the-lines guerrilla fighter. Guscott had led his Operation Brake team into a region adjacent to where Bob Walker-Brown's Operation Galia force had been operating. Via their wireless set, Guscott and his men had radioed back vital intelligence about enemy troop movements and targets, before linking up with the Galia party.

Ordered to assist Galia in every way they could, Guscott and his team remained in the field when Walker-Brown and his force withdrew. After promised reinforcements failed to materialise, Guscott opted to trek east through the mountains in an effort to link up with Farran. The SAS major viewed Guscott as 'the best sergeant in my Squadron . . . We had formed a battalion of Russians, Italians and British,' he remarked, 'and I wanted a good NCO to act as RSM so I ordered Sergt. Guscott to join me.'

'RSM' stood for regimental sergeant major, the man Farran

wanted to enforce order and discipline on his motley crew of fighters. He got a radio message through to Guscott, never imagining that he would be able to make it. But on 17 March, almost two months after he had deployed across the lines, Guscott arrived at Farran's Secchio headquarters. 'He walked across the mountains and covered sixty miles in . . . in awful country,' Farran remarked. Not only that but he had brought with him Raphael Ramos, another major bonus.

By now, over forty SAS had dropped into the Secchia valley or marched across the mountains, which left only one man outstanding, as far as Farran was concerned – his much-vaunted bagpiper. But finding a 'piper' at such short notice to parachute behind the lines was proving something of a challenge.

Finally, an approach was made to a young man serving in the 2nd Highland Light Infantry. As his nickname suggested, David 'The Mad Piper' Kirkpatrick had earned something of a sterling wartime reputation, which was all the more extraordinary considering his youth. But as far as he was concerned his job was to pipe the troops into battle no matter where they might be – on the front line or even behind enemy lines, for that matter.

'You're at the front with all the company behind you,' the plain-speaking Kirkpatrick would remark. 'That's why you're made the company piper.'

Something of a wild, troubled character in his teens – he'd earned a reputation for drinking and insubordination – Kirkpatrick had recently piped ashore a unit of commandos, as they'd stormed the beaches in Albania on a daylight raid from landing craft. Resting after the mission and assigned to a job in the stores, Kirkpatrick had been approached by the commander of his regiment.

'I'm looking for a piper to do a wee job,' he'd announced, enigmatically. 'I know you're more or less qualified for these things.'

'Aye,' Kirkpatrick had agreed, simply, 'I'm way fed up in the stores.' That was how he'd volunteered to be Major Farran's piper on Operation Tombola.

When Kirkpatrick's father found out that his son had taken on a mysterious 'wee job', he wasn't overly happy, but the die was cast. As soon as he could be made ready, 'The Mad Piper' was to be parachuted into the Secchia valley.

The British high command's attitude to the Italian resistance remained painfully schizophrenic. At the SOE's Florence headquarters they had often discussed plans to capture or kill Field Marshal Kesselring, yet at the same time they fought shy of their BLOs causing too much trouble. By the time Lees and Farran were readying the Allied Battalion to strike the 14th Army HQ, there was little chance of catching the German Field Marshal there.

On the night of 10 March 1945 Kesselring had been quietly removed from the Italian theatre and transferred to the Western Front. Hitler was anxious that Kesselring's withdrawal should remain secret, but maps discovered on the body of a dead German officer and smuggled out by the SOE confirmed that he was gone. Whichever high-level German officers Lees and Farran might hit, Kesselring would not be among their number.

Undeterred, they set a date for the 14th Army HQ assault: it was to take place on the night of 26/27 March 1945, so less than ten days away. Training at the church intensified, especially in the use of mortars, which would be key for the coming battle. The partisans forming the Allied Battalion – especially Modena's

Russians – proved remarkably quick learners. The Ordnance ML '3-inch' mortar was actually 3.209 inches – or 81.5mm – in calibre, and in the right hands it was a reliable and hugely effective weapon.

Now, at their Tapignola church base, the SAS gunners set out to ensure that it *was* in the right hands, no matter if it were former Italian farmers or Russian POWs. The Russians were particularly adept: they could lay out the constituent parts of the mortar on a ground sheet in exactly the same order as the instructor, after only one demonstration. It was all the more impressive considering that most lessons were being rendered in a colourful mixture of sign language, pidgin English and execrable Italian.

Within no time partisans of all nationalities were able to dismantle and assemble the mortars almost as well as their instructors. The one drawback was the limit that had to be placed on live firing. There was a shortage of ammunition, dictated by the simple logistics of flying in heavy crates of shells, plus there was the ever-present risk of the enemy hearing the loud explosions echoing across from the far side of the mountains.

Still, it wasn't exactly uncommon to detect the rattle of a distant Bren gun or the thud of a 3-inch mortar ringing out from Tapignola. Farran never stopped being jumpy about it. The enemy were positioned within a few miles in practically every direction. He feared a surprise attack. Yet still there was no response, let alone any attempt to interfere with the training.

As morale soared, so too did the opportunities for entertainment and fun. Gordon was a dab hand at the accordion, which always got the ladies on their feet. There were nightly knees-ups, especially at Secchio, where most of the Stafettas were based. The Black Owls boasted several fine fiddlers among their number, and the British soldiers soon found they were having the time of their lives, dancing to fine Italian ballads. They in turn tried to teach the locals the joys of Scottish reels and jigs.

In a sense there was little point trying to hide what they were about here. The red-berets-equals-communists-deception wasn't going to last for ever. On one level it was better to shout it from the rooftops, for the partisans tended to fight best 'when in the mood and not when ordered', as any number of BLOs had observed. Of course, that had to be balanced against the need not to betray to 'enemy Intelligence the true strength of one's forces', but getting the message heard was key to boosting morale.

To that end, the *Italia Combatte* (Italy Fights) radio broadcasts orchestrated by the SOE played a vital role. Partisans liked nothing more than to hear reports of themselves in action, ambushing the enemy. As the BLOs were at pains to point out: 'Resistance Movement Bulletins giving accounts of actions were listened to avidly, and did much to raise morale and make one Brigade vie with its neighbour in performing feats of arms.'

Still, Farran and Lees weren't entirely surprised when the first reports of suspicious enemy action filtered through to them. Two German battalions were advancing towards the mouth of the Secchia valley. It was worrying news, especially since the training of the Allied Battalion was still not complete. What Lees and Farran needed was stability, so as to round off their preparations for the coming assault, and that meant holding the valley.

Although it went against all doctrines of guerrilla warfare, they decided to defend their positions at all costs. If they lost the valley, the attack on the HQ would be all but finished. If the pressure became too great, they would retreat through well-prepared lines deep into the mountains, where it would be hard for the enemy to follow. Whatever else, they would do everything to keep the Allied Battalion together and primed to strike.

Fighting from fixed lines of defence wasn't the chosen form of warfare of either the SAS or the SOE. Still, extraordinary times called for extraordinary measures. With Colonel Monti's assistance, they set the valley's defences. At key outposts they sited one SAS soldier with detachments of partisans. Their role was to delay any German advance for long enough to get a warning to the Allied Battalion's Tapignola base, so that reinforcements could be rushed in.

To the far south-eastern boundary, in the shadow of Monte Pena, they sent Parachutist (the SAS equivalent rank of private) Murphy, with ten Russians, equipped with a Browning .50-calibre heavy machine gun and a pair of Brens. Murphy established himself in Civago village, just this side of the Gothic Line and the jumping-off point for Fritz Snapper's couriers.

Corporal Larley, who had been among the first dozen SAS dropped in, was despatched to the far western fringes of the valley, with ten Garibaldini and a 37mm anti-aircraft cannon, which was equally devastating in a ground defence role. From his vantage point Larley had a direct line of sight – and fire – to the nearest German garrison, situated on the main road.

Parachutist Wooding, one of those inserted in the mass, twenty-four-man drop, was another soldier who had impressed Farran. He was despatched north, posted alongside Don Carlo's Green Flames, to boost the forces guarding the main crossing points of the Secchia river. Wooding took with him a Browning machine gun and ten of the finest Garibaldini.

To Lieutenant Mike Eld fell the most important position of all. He was sent north of the river to guard the main road leading into the valley – the route by which any mechanised forces would attempt to punch through. Eld took with him ten SAS Parachutists, and he would link up with Gianni's Garibaldini partisans, whom Farran viewed as the most capable.

Eld's position was vital to the entire defensive plan, and Farran ordered him and Gianni to dig in. They were to hold that line until ordered otherwise. To Eld's unit fell the heaviest responsibility and likewise the heaviest weaponry: they had a 3-inch mortar, a heavy .50 Vickers water-cooled machine gun and a Bren. If Eld's line broke, they were to fall back towards Monte Cusna and the 3,000-foot Cisa Pass. There on the high-ground Farran tasked his men to construct a final defensive position, which they nicknamed the 'Cisa Box'.

The Cisa Box would be heavily entrenched, with the Allied Battalion's prized weapon, their M116 75mm pack howitzer dug in as the centrepiece. Walker-Brown had worked miracles getting that weapon dismantled, packed into parachute-ready parcels and dropped into the Swell Crimson DZ. Designed to be semi-portable – hence the 'pack howitzer' designation – the M116 could be broken down into pieces to be moved by pack animals, but as far as Farran knew this was the first time one had ever been parachuted behind the lines.

Farran placed young Lieutenant Harvey in command of the Cisa Box. His position was reinforced with 37mm cannons, heavy machine guns, ten Brens and mortars. As far as the partisans were concerned, it was at the Cisa Box that the Allied Battalion would mount a glorious stand and drive the enemy out of the valley. But in secret, Farran and Lees decided to explore a final, last-ditch line of retreat. If all else failed, the SAS and SOE would attempt to break out over the supposedly impassable heights of Monte Cusna.

Harvey was charged to get enough food buried in the deep snows on Cusna's slopes, so as to provision their force for up to three weeks on the run. 'The time was spent in perfecting our positions and laying caches along the escape route,' Harvey recalled. '"K" rations, biscuits, bully beef, 24-hour packs and Oleomarge were buried and the positions recorded. We also hid sacks of maps that would be most useful if . . . the Germans put in an all-out effort to clear out our small British force.'

'K rations' were US military 24-hour combat rations, while 'Oleomarge' referred to tubs of margarine. Lieutenant Harvey described his local fighters as 'Red Star partisans, communists to a man . . . The force at Cisa was now forty-eight and was, I considered, a strong one which I was proud to command.' They were equally proud of their howitzer, which had been nicknamed *Molto Stanco* – 'very tired' – due to the Herculean effort involved in manhandling it into such an elevated position.

With the Cisa Box sorted, it left one massive unknown. Was there a route over Monte Cusna, as a last-ditch means of escape? No one seemed to know, which meant that someone was going to have to attempt to prove it, one way or the other.

Farran sought two men to make the attempt. The first choice was obvious: Kershaw, the former Olympic bobsleigh man, was a dab hand in the snow. The other, David Eyton-Jones, was a somewhat less enthusiastic recruit. His only apparent qualification was that he had enjoyed a little skiing in Switzerland during his youth. When Farran ordered the two men to seek out a route over Monte Cusna, Eyton-Jones feared it was a true mission impossible.

Kershaw and Eyton-Jones sought out a local guide. Apparently, all thought them stir-crazy. There was no way across Cusna's snowbound heights, they argued. Even the Germans' alpine troops never attempted it, properly equipped as they were. Finally, at Casa Belocchi, the village adjacent to the Swell Crimson DZ, they managed via a combination of cajoling and liberal doses of red wine to get a local man to agree to act as guide.

He came fully equipped with skis, ski poles and snow goggles. Kershaw and Eyton-Jones had none of those things, and they refused the man's offer to provide any, knowing that it would be impossible to equip a force of fifty with such kit. If there was a route over Cusna's peak, it would have to be proved by trudging through the drifts in British Army footwear.

They set out. The snow was a clogging three-foot-thick layer that dragged at their every footfall. After several hours they reached the avalanche line, where fifty-degree slopes reared to the heights. It was there that the guide made it clear that he believed Kershaw and Eyton-Jones were stir-crazy, if they opted to continue.

'I advise you to turn back,' he announced, darkly. 'You won't make it.'

He made a quick sign of the cross before heading back the way they'd come, convinced that the two British soldiers were going to their deaths. In truth, Kershaw and Eyton-Jones didn't feel entirely confident that they weren't. It hadn't escaped their notice that Monte Cusna was known locally as *Uomo Morto* – Dead Man.

It took the entire day to reach Dead Man's summit. At times they were struggling through waist-deep snow, when the entire slope would suddenly begin to peel away in a thunderous roar, leaving the two figures clinging to bare and treacherous scree. It was almost dark when they reached the very peak. There, at some 7,000 feet of altitude, they would surely die if they didn't find shelter.

They began searching for a *rifugio*, a tiny mountain hut that they'd been told was somewhere thereabouts, but everything was covered in a thick blanket of snow. Trees, bushes, boulders – all had been subsumed by the snowfall. A handful of such refuges had been built by the Italian Alpine Club, but it was like searching for the proverbial needle in a haystack. Finally, they stumbled upon what they first mistook for a giant snowdrift, but which turned out to be the *rifugio*, snow piled to the eaves.

With frozen hands they began to shovel, in an effort to clear the door. It opened inwards but proved near-impossible to budge. There were several feet of wind-driven snow *inside* the hut. It had blown in via a grating set in the eastern wall. With sinking hearts the two surveyed the interior. It was as cold as a deep freezer, the fireplace was blocked with snow and there were no logs or anything that could be burned. Both men were utterly exhausted, and there was no way they could summon the energy to forage for firewood.

They unrolled their sleeping bags and laid them on the snow, before wolfing down some tins of Heinz self-heating soup. It came in oxtail, pea, tomato and mock turtle flavours, and a hollow tube down the centre of the tin contained a self-heating element, which boiled the contents in thirty seconds flat. Soup eaten, they crawled into their sleeping bags without bothering to remove their boots, and promptly fell asleep.

Sometime later Eyton-Jones awoke to a bizarre spectacle. Though dawn light filtered in through the side-grating, it appeared ethereal and muted, and he seemed to have been thrown into a grave of shadows. For several seconds he wondered if he had died and gone to heaven. It turned out that overnight he had sunk in his sleeping bag through the several feet of snow, coming to rest on the hut floor.

Faced with a long descent of the mountain, Kershaw and Eyton-Jones were desperate: they broke out the Benzedrine pills they'd been issued with. Known colloquially as 'bennies', they were issued as part of the standard SAS escape kit. A powerful amphetamine popular in London's glitzier nightclubs, with its euphoric stimulant effect Benzedrine could keep a man alert for days. The benefits were obvious, but it was only possible to fuel a man with amphetamines for so long: eventually the body would simply burn out.

Having taken two each, Kershaw and Eyton-Jones stumbled outside. In every direction the fierce spring sunlight glittered off the snowfields. Within moments, Eyton-Jones found that he was suffering from 'snow blindness'. He was assailed by intense pain and a stabbing headache. His vision clouded, and he felt as if he'd had a handful of sand thrown into his eyes.

It was glaringly obvious by now that Monte Cusna offered no easy escape route. Indeed, this had become a desperate survival mission. Kershaw, the former Olympic bobsleigher, decided their only option was to descend as quickly as possible. They should attempt to toboggan down the slopes, sliding on their backsides. He led the way, guiding Eyton-Jones, his feet spread wide and using his heels to steer a route around the occasional boulder.

Hours later the two men reached more familiar terrain, heralding their return to the Secchia valley. They were bruised, battered and sore and Kershaw had injured his leg when he caught it on a protrusion. Their boots had frozen solid, but they stumbled onwards, every step being sheer agony. By the time they reached Secchio, they were convinced they had frostbite. When they leveraged off their footwear, sure enough their toes were horribly blackened, the toenails swollen and cracked.

That, if nothing else, convinced Farran that relying on any escape via Monte Cusna would be ill-advised. It might provide a last-ditch route to safety, but how many of his men might survive such a crossing? If his forces were driven back from their defence of the valley, the Cisa Box would have to hold.

By the end of the third week in March, Lees and Farran believed they had done everything possible to prepare their defensive lines. At the same time, the Stafettas had been feeding back daily intelligence reports on the 14th Army HQ, allowing Lees to build up an incredibly detailed picture of the target. The two villas lay to the north of the Botteghe crossroads, which formed the epicentre of the headquarters' defences. To wolf whistles and catcalls, the Stafettas were daily cycling through there, taking note of all. Norice in particular was not averse to stopping and apparently flirting outrageously with the sentries.

As a result, Lees knew the names of most of the officers who served there and much personal information. Locations of anti-aircraft guns, machine-gun posts and sentries had been minutely plotted. Florence headquarters, alert to the intended target, had flown in up-to-date maps and aerial photos, which were dropped to their Secchio base by fighter pilots leaning out of their cockpit windows.

As the picture of the target continued to build, Lees and Farran's greatest worry was that the Germans would relocate it before they could strike. 'A damaging attack on a main headquarters would certainly be a big contribution to the Allied cause,' Farran would write, 'especially if it coincided with the main offensive.' But no strike could succeed if the Germans decided to move the location of their headquarters.

In the final plan of attack the Allied Battalion – SAS included –

would be divided in two. While a force 100 strong would hit the HQ, the remainder – some 200 troops – would remain in their positions to hold the valley, for without a refuge to retreat to theirs was basically a suicide mission.

The one-hundred-strong assault force would be made up of thirty Russians, forty Italians and twenty-four SAS, with Lees' Black Owls making up the remainder. They would muster at the extreme border of partisan territory, and from there advance to a vantage point overlooking the plain of the Po. Come nightfall, the force would split into three for the approach to the target. The Russians, under Modena, would form a protective screen, isolating the two villas from any reinforcements that might try to reach them.

Each of the other two columns would be led by ten SAS, men who had been selected for their raw aggression and spirit. They would force an entry into the villas, to be followed by the Italians, guns blazing. Mike Lees was to lead the assault on Villa Rossi, where the senior officers were billeted, while young Lieutenant Harvey would spearhead the hit on Villa Calvi. Farran, meanwhile, would establish a base between the two villas from where he could orchestrate operations.

The orders Farran issued to his Allied Batallion were uncompromising and stark: cause maximum death and destruction. The priority was to kill high-ranking German officers – General Hauk and his Chief of Staff, one Colonel Lemelsen, being the prime targets. No prisoners were to be taken, for that would only serve to hamper their helter-skelter retreat.

Farran's chief worry remained the enemy's reaction, which he feared would be swift and determined. Accordingly, he allowed just twenty minutes for the parties to execute the raid, during all of which time Modena was to have his Russians spray the roads leading to the villas with machine-gun fire. Like that, he hoped to keep the German heads down and prevent them from bringing up reinforcements.

After wreaking havoc and ruin, the raiders would enter the 'run' phase of the attack – so fleeing for the mountains, wherein two-thirds of the Allied Battalion would shield them from pursuit. But once they had started to withdraw the real battle for survival would begin. They would be faced with a twenty-four-hour forced march over terrain crawling with the enemy, and with only a few hours of darkness in which to disappear. That alone was a chilling proposition, but there was no way around it.

On 20 March Lees and Farran sent a short radio message to Florence, seeking final clearance for the attack. 'Staff HQ of 14 Army – FARRAN agrees to use SAS to lead the attack . . .' In response, 15 Army Group radioed back a green light, while cautioning that the exact timing should be coordinated with their own plans. 'Confirm we attack . . .' Farran cabled a reply. 'First wave 20 British, second wave 30 Russians, third wave 40 Italians. All on foot. Plans irrevocable now.'

But it was at this very moment that the enemy decided to strike.

A German patrol crossed the river to the north-east, which marked the border of the Secchia valley. As a long line of grey-uniformed troops snaked into the partisans' territory, Farran fretted. The inevitable day of reckoning had come, but were the forces that he and Lees had armed, trained and encouraged up for the fight?

Now would prove it, one way or the other.

Chapter 13

Worryingly, the initial resistance proved hopelessly short-lived. The Green Flames positioned at the valley's entranceway fled, leaving the route of advance wide open. Mounted upon their two highly contrasting steeds – one large and powerful, the other doing a fine impression of a Welsh hill pony – Lees and Farran rode out to meet the enemy onslaught.

The heavily armed German troops advanced up the road, confident that the partisans would fall back before them. Instead, they stumbled into the murderous fire of a well dug-in Browning heavy machine gun. While Don Carlo's Green Flames may have taken to their heels, Parachutist Wooding and his ten-man Garibaldini unit had not. They'd been charged to hold the northern gateway to the valley, and hold it they would.

In a vicious day-long exchange of fire the Germans quickly learned there was no easy way through. The road, at least, was closed to them. When they tried to outflank Wooding's position, they ran into pockets of Green Flames, dug-in on the high ground. Upon witnessing how Wooding and his Garibaldini had stood firm, the Green Flames' backbone had been miraculously stiffened.

The ferocity of the resistance seemed to convince the German commander that this route of advance would prove too costly. By nightfall, the enemy patrol had withdrawn across the Secchia river, making for the safety of the plains beyond. Lees and Farran didn't doubt that they would be back, and in greater numbers, which made it all the more critical to proceed with the HQ assault. Any delay could scupper their plans utterly.

Florence headquarters had also got word of the enemy action. BLO Jim Davies had radioed through an alert about a *rastrellamento*. Lees and Farran received warnings, coupled with pleas that they not make life 'too difficult' for the neighbouring missions. Lees replied that their positions in the Secchia valley would hold, and anyway there was a war to be fought.

When Florence kept on repeating their *rastrellamento* warnings, the two commanders finally cracked. Farran and Lees drafted a terse, two-word reply: 'Rastrellamento balls'. Farrimond encoded it and sent it via the radio, knowing that it would not make them any the more popular at headquarters.

Farran's presence at Secchio had unchained Lees from the control of SOE Florence, just as Charles Macintosh had feared it would, and the SAS major's hotline to senior US and British commanders was deeply resented. 'Florence hated that,' Lees remarked, recognising that it made both him and Farran 'very unpopular'. But they were there to fight and sod the consequences.

In March 1945 US General Mark Clark had broadcast a special message to the partisans, making it crystal clear what he expected of them. 'Your bands, which contain only the finest examples of Italian soldiers, proved by their ability to resist the enemy through the hard winter, should now be . . . ready at a moment's notice to undertake the tasks which are ahead. Quality is what is necessary . . . compact highly disciplined and trained groups for efficient action . . .' In the Allied Battalion, Lees and Farran had honed just such an elite fighting group and they were poised to strike a killer blow.

On the night of 23/24 March David 'The Mad Piper' Kirkpatrick was the final figure to plummet into the darkness above the Secchia valley, to join Tombola. As with so many who had dropped before him, he'd never parachuted into action. With his safe arrival that made forty-two SAS and attached deployed on Tombola, Major Farran included.

No fading violet, Kirkpatrick had jumped in full piper's regalia, bagpipes and kilt included. Those on the ground – the Italians at least – thought that a woman was being sent in to join them. Fortunately, Farran was on hand to explain why a young man dressed in a 'skirt' had dropped from the sky. As part of that explanation, he got Kirkpatrick to pipe 'Highland Laddie' – the then-marching song for all British highland regiments – over the Swell Crimson DZ.

As the haunting, lyrical tones echoed across the snows, Farran felt a chill run up his spine. Silhouetted by the burning light of the marker flares flickering across the slopes to either side, the erect form of the piper, wreathed in smoke, appeared like some ghostly figure of ancient myth or legend. Farran was doubly excited by the partisans' reaction. They clapped and yelled for joy, keeping time to the lilting tune. They were still singing patriotic songs at the tops of their voices, as Farran led Kirkpatrick off to their church base.

Upon arrival at Tapignola, he asked the obvious question, it being early morning. 'Are you hungry, piper?'

'Aye, sir, I'm very hungry,' Kirkpatrick replied.

'What about some fried bacon and eggs?'

'Yes, sir, I'd like that very much.' Fresh bacon and eggs were a rare wartime treat.

Farran's grand flourish – getting a piper dropped in – proved a massive hit. Those gathered at the church decided to dance an Eightsome, a lively Scottish reel for eight dancers, as Kirkpatrick struck up the tune. He wanted to donate his parachute to the elderly lady who made him welcome in her Tapignola home. She had her eye on it, to make a silk wedding dress for her grand-daughter.

'Sir, is it all right for me to give her my parachute for looking after us?' he asked.

Farran said he could. It was the least they could do.

That evening back in Secchio, Farran gazed across the valley as the unmistakeable tones of 'The Retreat' echoed across from the church. Kirkpatrick had played it without any prompting, for it was the job of a piper to do so at the end of each day. Farran and Mike Lees marvelled as the stirring notes of the pipes rolled up and down the hills. It had to be audible for miles around on a still evening such as this, including to the enemy.

It was somehow both thrilling and daunting. The two commanders signalled back with their torches, acknowledging that they had heard Kirkpatrick, and that all was good with the world. But as they prepared to set forth from the Secchia valley, disaster struck. Mike Lees, always a whirlwind of action and a veritable human dynamo, was struck down. The iconic figurehead of the Reggiani partisans was hit by a debilitating bout of malaria, something he'd first contracted when on operations in Yugoslavia.

It was the summer of 1943 when Lees had been tasked with an urgent mission – the destruction of a railway that the Germans were using to resupply their forces lying to the south of Yugoslavia, in Greece. In the final stages of executing a recce of the target, Lees had been hit by heavy fever. Racked by nausea, pain and hallucinations, he'd stubbornly completed the days-long march, only to collapse at the end. Diagnosed with malaria, he was treated by an old crone, or a 'wise woman of the mountains' as the locals called her.

That 'wise woman' readied a mixture of herbs, roots, animal entrails and spices, laced with the strongest rakia (a locally-brewed fruit brandy). Lees was ordered to drink the concoction. It was dark green, thick and heady, with a bitter aftertaste. Having done so, he'd fallen into a deep sleep. The following morning he'd awoken with his body aching all over, but with a clear head. The fever had passed, and Lees put it down to a combination of natural remedies and powerful witchcraft.

But now, almost eighteen months later, the malaria had come back with a vengeance. Lees felt the first worrying symptoms as he, Farran, Gordon, Kiss and fellow commanders toasted their imminent departure for the raid. Farran had called for Kirkpatrick, telling him: 'Use this night, piper, as if it's a night you play to your officers in your own battalion.' It was a tradition in the Highland Light Infantry that every Friday, the piper would play tunes of his choice in the officers' mess, over dinner.

But as Kirkpatrick proceeded to play, Lees had felt increasingly weak and feverish. Taking a leaf out of the old crone's book, he'd dosed himself with a mixture of grappa and quinine, an extract of tree bark used to treat malaria. Even so, by the time the attack force was readying itself for departure the following morning, he was looking distinctly unwell. Attempts were made to persuade him against going, but to no avail.

'I tried to stop Mike,' remarked Gordon, his Black Owls commander, 'but he was a very proud man and very courageous.'

Farran had little more success. 'I was worried about Lees, for all my pleasure at his company. He had developed a fever . . . but refused to be left behind. He dosed himself frequently with quinine, but I did not like the unnatural drops of sweat on his forehead . . . His face was grave and pallid beneath the sweat. And he was unusually quiet.'

If anything, Bert Farrimond, Lees' radio operator, was even more concerned. As Lees bade a fond farewell to his Secchio crew – Farrimond and Lieutenant Smith would remain behind, manning the headquarters – the tough Lancastrian shook him gravely by the hand.

'Good luck, sir,' he told Lees. 'Don't stick your neck out too much, will you.'

Lees feigned good spirits. 'Don't worry, I've too much to live for.'

Lees turned to leave, but Farrimond reached out a hand to stop him. 'Can't I come with you, sir?'

Lees was surprised. Farrimond was a solid, pragmatic, salt-of-the-earth type and this was very out of character. 'Of course not, you've got to stay here to work the set.'

'I know that,' Farrimond countered, 'but I've had a feeling all morning that something's going to happen and I'd like to come.'

Lees forced laughter. 'Don't be a bloody fool. You'll be seeing ghosts next.'

With that he joined Farran and the advance party, and set off for Tapignola. Lees led a core of Black Owls, who would help spearhead the assault. Norice and Argentina, two of the finest Stafettas, marched alongside them, as did their commander, Kiss. The sun beat down as Farran moved abreast of Lees, the latter mopping the sweat from his brow. Strictly speaking, Lees was an SOE agent sent to liaise with the partisans, and Farran could have insisted he remain behind. But ever since he'd dropped in, Lees had hungered to hit the Botteghe HQ. He'd fought tooth and nail to make it happen, and in truth this was Mike Lees' mission. It was right and fitting to have him along, fevered though he was.

They descended the valley and climbed to Tapignola, where Farran spoke a few last words to those disappointed fighters who were being left behind. Jock Easton was among them, but someone had to command the defences – for no one doubted the blowback that would come. Here in the Secchia valley they would truly reap the whirlwind, of that they felt certain.

Having formed up with the twenty-four SAS, twenty Garibaldini and a similar number of Black Owls, Farran set a route north, heading for the rendezvous with Modena and his Russians. But even as they moved off, trouble was brewing once more at their Florence headquarters – as unforeseen and unsuspected as it would prove utterly infuriating.

Charles Macintosh held a meeting with US Colonel Riepe. The date for the Allied spring offensive to punch through the Gothic Line had been set: it would be unleashed between 1 and 5 April 1945. In light of this, a decision was made at high level to postpone Lees and Farran's operation, so it could coincide with that date – something that was easy enough to declare at headquarters, but perhaps a little harder to effect in the field.

'An isolated attack on a Corps HQ would alert the Germans to security needs of all HQs near partisan areas,' Macintosh reasoned, 'and, at the worst, might give them some idea of our future plans.' The fear was that the Germans would be forewarned of Allied intentions and thus forearmed.

Upon learning of this change of timescale, if not of heart, Walker-Brown interceded with General Clark himself, pleading that the raid be allowed to continue as planned. 'I forcibly put over that partisan morale, having been wound up to fever pitch could only be unwound at substantial risk to the success of the operation,' he remarked. For once, General Clark was not swayed by such sentiments.

A decision was taken to stand down the HQ raid and a message to that effect was radioed through to Farrimond. 'Signal No. 141 . . . to ENVELOPE . . . For ROY and MIKE . . . You will destroy this signal and ciphers after reading and guarantee security. News stolen from Colonel's desk means that you have only to wait one week after target date . . . and your plan is on with six jeeps. Your scheme will then be correctly timed for maximum effort . . . Will give you exact dates and details soonest.'

The signal embodied a carrot and stick approach. The carrot was the offer of 'six jeeps' to be dropped into the Secchia valley, which would mean that the HQ raid could be a quick in-and-out, vehicle-mounted affair. The stick was the need to coordinate the attack with the coming Gothic Line offensive, although the exact start date couldn't be radioed through, for fear of it leaking to the enemy. The 'news stolen from Colonel's desk' referred to intelligence that SOE had acquired regarding movements of senior German officers.

At Secchio, the message was received and decoded by a morose Farrimond. He sent a plainly worded reply: he was unable to deliver the missive because 'the party had started down towards the foothills'. Macintosh responded by *ordering* a postponement of the attack, and by copying his orders to Major Jim Davies, the neighbouring BLO.

'Please confirm you have proof subject received our orders to postpone attack,' he telegraphed, his suspicions of Lees and

Farran deepening. 'If not can you still send STAFETTA stating that these are 15 Army orders.'

Major Davies decided to take personal responsibility for getting the message into Lees and Farran's hands. He set off for Secchio himself, alternately bicycling and marching on foot as the terrain allowed. But of course, by the time he reached there Lees and Farran were long gone. Only one option remained. He'd have to send a courier dashing after the two commanders, in the hope of catching them before they slipped out of the hills.

Lees and Farran, meanwhile, were forging ahead. They approached the Secchia river, and the bridge that Wooding and his Garibaldini had defended so assiduously just a few days before. As they crossed it, Farran gave the order to Kirkpatrick: he was to play his pipes as the men stomped onwards through the dust and the spring sunshine. Lees, silent and sweat-soaked, strode ahead, as the ranks of fighters broke into song. Rendered to the notes of a rousing German marching tune, the words had been composed by the SAS themselves, capturing the dark humour of the time.

> *We're reckless parachutists,*
> *At least that's what we're told,*
> *But when action station's sounded,*
> *Then we don't feel quite so bold.*
> *We're the boys who ride the slip stream,*
> *We're the heroes of the sky,*
> *But we all know deep inside us,*
> *It's an awful way to die.*
> *Stand to the door, stand to the door,*
> *And my poor old knees are trembling,*
> *Up off the floor, up off the floor,*

And I'm seeing scores of gremlins.
Red light on! Green light on!
Out through the door we go,
F-f-fighting for breath, b-b-battered near to death,
Drifting down to earth below.
We're the boys who ride the slip stream,
We're the boys who jump for fame.
If our parachutes don't open,
Then we get there just the same.
There's a big court of inquiry,
And the packer gets the sack,
But all the juries in creation,
Can't fetch that poor chap back.

A hard climb from the river took the party to Valestra, the village rendezvous with Modena and his Russians. With former ballroom dancer Serjeant Guscott arranging clean straw to be laid in a barn as a billet for the men, Farran and Lees took stock. Resting on the village green, and with the evening sun illuminating the scene, they wondered vaguely at the line of villagers trudging up the main street, with bundles piled high on their shoulders. Their steps appeared hurried – harried almost – as they moved back the way the raiders had come.

It struck Farran that they looked almost like *refugees*. He sat up, suddenly more alert and ordered Riccomini to investigate. He was back within minutes. The news was not good. The Germans had launched another sweep towards the Secchia valley and were but a few miles distant, hence the fleeing villagers. Partisans had taken up positions in the northern limits of Valestra village, in preparation for what they feared was coming.

Wearily, Farran followed Riccomini to a high point, where figures were scattered among the rocks. Occasionally, one fired a burst into the distance, but the enemy were hopelessly out of range. Farran ordered the shooting to stop. He surveyed the far terrain through binoculars. A thin line of grey troops was advancing with purpose towards a small village set atop a ridge-line. Occasionally, he heard the distinctive *tack-pung* of a Mauser rifle firing.

Farran ordered more sentries set. This was the last thing they needed – to tire some among their force of raiders just prior to the HQ attack. But worse would be the enemy surprising them here, under cover of darkness. He returned to the village and was just in time to spy Modena's Russians arriving. Modena had marched them at a furious pace to get here, so they would need at least a full night's rest to recover.

The best chance of slipping through the line of advancing enemy troops would be to march that very night, before they closed in. But with so many among their force so fatigued, no such thing was going to be possible. With sentries set, Farran bedded down as best he could in the open on the village green.

'There were so many restless nights like that behind the lines,' Farran remarked of the moment. 'The strain on the nerves caused by constant watchfulness was the most tiring thing of all.'

With dawn there was both good news and bad. The Germans had advanced no further. Indeed, their chief aim seemed to be rounding up villagers for forced labour. That was the good news. The bad was that Lees' malaria had worsened. As Norice brought Farran a breakfast of a fried egg sandwich and a steaming mug of tea, Lees seemed to have little appetite at all.

Farran munched away, surveying his 'motley crew of ruffians'.

A group of SAS leaned against a nearby wall, trading war stories with the Garibaldini and wisecracks with the Stafettas. The Garibaldini were as tough a bunch of pirates as Farran had ever laid eyes on. Their uniforms were torn and stained, their boots similarly cracked, their faces pinched and weather-beaten. The red stars on their caps complemented the sprinkling of SAS red berets, intermingled with the colourful splash of the dresses worn by the girls.

But what struck Farran most were the smiles and grins and thumbs-ups he received from all who caught his eye. Their morale was peaking, as they sensed that this was their moment; that soon they would strike a daring and decisive blow. As Farran well appreciated, you couldn't order such an irregular force into action: you had to inspire and move them to fight. It was all about carefully timed theatre, leadership and inspiration, and right now he reckoned they'd got it spot on.

A figure approached him, a little nervously. It was one of the political commissar Eros's deputies. Should they proceed with the raid? he ventured. Or was now not the time to join the defence of the valley, as a major *rastrellamento* seemed to be in the offing? Farran knew that any such change of plan would be disastrous. For one thing, they were never going to alight upon such a fateful or determined moment as this again. For another, it was vital to prove that the partisans could carry out a plan of action regardless of counter moves by the enemy.

He decided to answer the man's query by making a general address. He called in the sentries. All gathered at the village green, straw from night quarters clinging to their clothing, the British unshaven and unkempt after days living rough in oxen stables. Modena's Russians kept to themselves, forming a phalanx of Slavic solidity. For sure, they were a force to be reckoned with. The SAS and the Italians milled about freely, mixing easily. The vibes were good. Very good. Now was not the moment to delay.

With a sweating Lees at his side, Farran laid out his plan of action, explaining why no delay could be countenanced. Each sentence was translated into Italian, plus German for Modena, and for Hans and the handful of other deserters from the Wehrmacht. Stage one of the operation would commence at dusk. It involved Hans ferrying the entire force north, using the one navigable road. He would do so in relays, using a truck he'd recently hijacked from the enemy.

Once the truck-leg was done, they would press ahead on foot, sticking to minor tracks and skirting enemy positions. Farran would lead the way, accompanied by a pair of SAS scouts and an Italian guide. Behind would come the rest of the force, divided into three columns. One would be led by the young Lieutenant Harvey, and consist of ten SAS plus their Garibaldini. The second would be led by Lieutenant Riccomini and Mike Lees, with ten SAS and twenty Black Owls. The third would be led by Major Modena, and would consist entirely of his Russians.

There would be no smoking or talking allowed, and the march would need to be executed double quick, if they were to reach their planned lying-up point by daybreak. If the lead figures stumbled into any trouble they would throw themselves flat on the deck, at which all behind would follow suit. Battle would only be joined if those at the head of the column opened fire on the enemy. The absolute priority was to slip through undetected.

Upon reaching their isolated farmstead destination they would lie low all day and move off after sunset, aiming to hit the Botteghe

HQ an hour before midnight. They'd creep in to the patch of woodland adjacent to the target, whereupon each column would move off – the Russians to block the road, Harvey's column to hit Villa Calvi, and Lees and Riccomini's to assault Villa Rossi. They'd withdraw on Farran's signal and scramble for the mountains.

In view of the momentous nature of their target, the objections of Eros's deputy seemed to evaporate. Who could not be caught up in the spirit of the moment? Seizing the initiative, Kirkpatrick broke out his pipes and began to play an Eightsome. As young men grabbed girls and twirled around excitedly, Farran knew now was the time. If he could only keep them in such a mood for a further forty-eight hours, nothing in the world could stop them.

As the dancing and clapping continued a diminutive figure elbowed his way through the crowd, making a beeline for Farran and Lees. It was a courier, and he had a slip of paper clutched in his young hand. Farran read it with a growing sense of shock and bewilderment. It was a curt message from Florence headquarters, which had been forwarded via a runner from Jim Davies. He read it three times over in utter disbelief: in essence, their mission had been cancelled. They were to stand their force down.

Countless times on previous missions Farran had found himself cursing distant staff officers, who had 'not the remotest idea of what was involved in a guerrilla attack . . . These people seemed unable to realise that assault by irregulars cannot be coordinated to a definite time table . . . they can only be carried out successfully by seizing opportunities when the time is ripe.'

Quietly fuming, he handed the slip of paper to Lees with a suitable disparaging remark. The big SOE officer seemed almost too fevered to pay it any heed. He glanced at the message, grunted, but Farran couldn't be sure if it had really even registered. Whatever action they chose to take it would be at Farran's bidding, the decision lying on his shoulders.

He pondered what they should do. The Stafettas had confirmed that there appeared to be little suspicion at the Botteghe HQ that an attack might be imminent. No extra or unusual defences had been set. But how long would that last? Once the enemy had learned that a sizeable raiding force had reached as far as the fringes of the plains, they were bound to be suspicious. What were its intentions, they'd ask themselves? What was the intended target?

As for the partisans, they would surely lose faith in the intent of Farran, Lees et al., if ordered to stand down. They would conclude that the British commanders, similar to their own, liked to talk the talk, but that was as far as it went. Having worked the partisans up into the kind of fighting frenzy that was required, Farran doubted if he could do so again, and certainly not following such a signal let-down.

By rights, he shouldn't even be here, leading this force of magnificent desperadoes. He'd jumped from the Dakota against orders. Yet he sensed he was going to have to do something similar again now. Far less physically daunting, the ramifications were incalculably more serious. It was one thing leaping from an aircraft when told not to; quite another laying waste to an entire German Army HQ entirely against orders.

Even so, Farran made his decision: he would act as if the message had never been received. As he knew well, a postponement was only one step away from a cancellation, and surely any attack was better than no attack at all. He shared his thoughts with Lees, while making one thing crystal clear: the responsibility for this sleight of hand – this necessary subterfuge – would be his, and his alone. Lees – dosed up and battling his fever – seemed almost beyond caring.

All that day they lay low in Valestra village. Now and again sporadic rifle fire echoed from the valley beyond, where German troops were in action. That was the very terrain they would have to slip through, come nightfall. With dusk, a battered ten-tonne former German Army truck rolled into the village. It was an incongruous sight, especially with blond, blue-eyed Hans at the wheel.

Lees had sworn that the deserter was utterly reliable. As the first contingent of raiders piled aboard the truck, Farran guessed he was about to find out. For the next hour or so Hans plied the route back and forth, his furthest reach limited by a road bridge that had been demolished by the partisans in an earlier action. Each trip proceeded without incident, Hans proving Lees' faith in him entirely justified. It was late evening on 26 March 1945 when the last fighters were ferried to the point of no return, where they would have to ford the river on foot.

There was one eventuality that Farran hadn't foreseen: Major Davies had asked for confirmation from his runner that the message had been delivered; this he had now received and had radioed back same to headquarters. In Florence there was a disquieting disconnect. On the one hand, Davies had guaranteed their order to cancel the raid had been delivered. On the other, there was a wall of silence emanating from the two maverick commanders, Farran and Lees.

Farrimond was bombarded with further messages, demanding confirmation that the attack had been cancelled. He argued that he could do nothing more. Tempers in Florence seemed close to breaking point. Finally, an extraordinary order was telegraphed to Farrimond, relieving Lees of his command. In a bizarre irony,

Mike Lees' replacement, who was already being made ready, was SOE Captain John W. Lees (no relation), formerly of the Manchester Regiment, a regular infantry unit.

But again Farrimond was unable to deliver the message, for by now Mike Lees and Roy Farran were beyond all reach. Of course, Farrimond was trying to shield his CO from such bothersome meddling, as he saw it. Lees would later write of his radio operator that he was 'Tough, unswervingly loyal and, like his Boss, outspokenly intolerant and contemptuous of poseurs. He never once let me down.' Farrimond, Lees and Farran were birds of a feather. They had little time for the 'pen-pushing map boys in Florence', as they disparagingly called them.

Yet in truth, right at that moment Lees would almost have welcomed a stand-down. 'Had I received an order delaying the operation I would have been mightily relieved, because I was very ill at the time and in no shape to march or to fight,' he would write. 'I strongly believed . . . that I was set up by . . . HQ in Florence. At the very least I was being used as a scapegoat . . . I was too aggressive for them by half.'

At their Secchio base, another key figure was being drawn into the furore over the stand-down order – Fritz Snapper, Reserve Lieutenant of the Royal Dutch Army and chief of the partisans' courier service. He was of a mind with Farrimond. 'Postponement would not only have been detrimental to the prestige of the BLO and SAS officers, but also to partisan morale which was very sensitive,' he reported of the incident. 'Major FARRAN and Capt LEES decided they must proceed with the attack even if it was against orders.'

Thus the dividing lines were drawn: between those chairborne at headquarters, and those soldiering at the hard end of operations.

Chapter 14

It was 0100 hours by the time most of the raiding party had forded the river. One of the last to do so was Lieutenant Harvey, marching at the head of the third column. They had navigated 'extremely rugged country, up mountains of considerable height and across rivers . . . flooded from the thawing snows.'

In an amusing if tricky moment, young Harvey's braces broke just as he was part way across the icy waters. 'This small occurrence caused me considerable discomfort, which I had to endure for some 24 hours, before I could make some makeshift arrangement to see me through.' No one wanted their trousers falling down in the midst of what was coming.

Once over the river, the column formed up as one. With Farran at its head the raiders moved off into the darkness. Before them, constantly quartering the ground back and forth, went the SAS scouts and their Italian guide. The noise they were all making seemed dangerously loud. Weapons clattered against kit; rocks set loose by footfalls tumbled into the river below; boots crunched on loose, friable earth.

Farran paused, glancing back at the dark line of men snaking south, the last figures silhouetted on a ridge against the moonlight. He had never once commanded a force as large as this – one hundred raiders – heading deep into enemy territory. It seemed impossible that they wouldn't be detected. He sent a whispered order to be passed from man to man, urging greater silence. The quiet of that still night seemed to magnify any sound.

'Marching at night through enemy country is an eerie experience at the best of times,' Farran remarked. 'But when it is with a long line of one hundred men, all completely silent apart from involuntary noise, the strain on one's nerves is indescribable . . . causing us to pause in dread of discovery.'

The column marched across a valley, fording another tributary of the Secchia. A narrow track wound ahead, its path washed by the silvery-blue of the moon, twisting and turning around a series of high rocky outcrops before reaching an isolated farmstead. As Farran approached, a dog started barking. A figure came to the door, swinging a lamp this way and that. Farran froze, the long line of men behind doing likewise.

Finally, cursing the dog for awakening him, the farmer slammed shut the door. Beyond the farmhouse lay the first major chokepoint, where Farran feared they might hit trouble. They had to cross the main Carpineti to Valestra road, which threaded east–west through the foothills. The highway barred their route: the target, the Botteghe HQ, lay some fifteen kilometres beyond it, across equally rugged country.

A small village, Casa de' Pazzi, lay astride the road and it was known to be garrisoned by German troops. Farran's plan was to make a detour around it, so avoiding any danger. But after two hours' punishing march, it became clear that their best laid plans had gone awry. One of his scouts, darting backwards and forwards in his canvas-soled shoes, encountered some kind of a settlement. It seemed they'd stumbled into the edge of the village. Farran dropped flat to the earth, crawling in close with Lees and the others. It wasn't long before the guide admitted that in the thick darkness he had miscalculated the way. They were already among the outskirts of Casa de' Pazzi.

Two choices lay open to Farran. One – to retrace their steps, which would entail a major detour. It was approaching four o'clock in the morning, with just two more hours until first light. There just wasn't the time. They'd have to plump for option two, deeply unattractive though it might be: to press on through the enemy position. Amid angry stage-whispers a second guide took over, berating his colleague for leading them into such danger.

He steered the men towards a scree slope that stretched beyond the southern limits of the village, which itself was carved into a dramatic hillside. With the black, blocky silhouettes of the nearest buildings just above them, the column of raiders began to creep along the precipitous drop. As Farran and Lees inched across the treacherous bed of loose rocks, they could hear voices drifting down to them. It stood to reason that only sentries – or insomniacs – would be awake at this hour.

No matter how one tiptoed, it was impossible to move without dislodging the odd stone, which careered down the slope in an ear-splitting clatter. A dog barked. Another and another took up the hue and cry. The column of raiders pressed on, at every step fearing discovery – at which moment their much-vaunted mission would become a debacle, SAS and partisans fighting a battle for a village that was of little strategic value.

As Farran was painfully aware, to disobey orders and succeed was one thing, but to do so and fail would be quite another. He figured they were about halfway across when the lead scout hissed a warning. He'd heard the distinctive *clatch-clatch* of steel on steel, as from somewhere a rifle bolt was rammed home and a weapon primed. Farran dropped flat, those behind following suit, as they clung to the loose, rocky terrain, struggling to anchor themselves and to keep still.

For ten minutes they remained motionless, ears straining for any further sounds. None came. Eventually, Farran signalled them on. They reached the far side and climbed towards the road itself. There Farran called a halt, as the scouts checked the way across. They indicated the coast was clear, and Farran and Lees flitted over, figures scurrying after them like so many frightened rabbits.

Farran urged everyone on, scrambling ever upwards through jumbled rocks and moving further away from the danger. Finally, the lead scouts slipped between a pair of giant boulders, into the shelter of a wide bowl of grassy land. There, Farran called the first halt of the night. They'd been on the move for eight hours, for the most part of which they'd been assailed by fear and tension. It was both nerve-racking and hugely wearying.

SAS and partisans alike threw themselves onto the long grass. One of the guides found a source of water. One by one they drank their fill. That done, Farran lay back on the soft turf and stared at the sky, resplendent above them in all its starlit radiance. He felt a nudge at his elbow. He glanced over, to find Norice the grey-eyed-Stafetta sitting cross-legged beside him.

Wordlessly, she handed him a hard-boiled egg, freshly peeled, together with a slice of bread. Farran smiled his thanks. He couldn't help but admire her in the fine light thrown off by stars and moon. With a tumble of thick dark hair fringing her features, she looked mysterious; magical; bewitching. Her muscled brown legs were complimented by white ski socks and ski boots, perfect kit for trekking through the mountains. She seemed barely touched by fatigue after the long night's march, whereas Farran felt whacked.

He forced himself to his feet. *'Andiamo,'* he signalled, the whisper being passed around from figure to figure: let's go.

All around tired men and women lumbered to their feet. Farran's eyes searched out the distinctive figure of Lees. The big SOE officer had barely spoken a word. For hours he'd stumbled along in a grim-faced silence, gripped by fever. Farran was worried if he'd even finish the march, let alone be able to play any part in the coming assault.

Twice he'd urged Lees to turn back, but both times he'd uttered a refusal, stubborn until the last. Instead, he'd somehow forced his legs to keep powering him forwards. Farran hoped to persuade Lees to remain at the farmstead, which was their intended lying-up point prior to the attack, but he wasn't exactly hopeful.

The way ahead led through hard, rocky terrain, scattered with thick clumps of trees clinging to wherever their roots could gain a grip. The mountain path wound up and down endlessly, taking them ever closer to the plains. There was less danger here in the foothills; less chance of discovery. Accordingly, the scouts ranged further ahead, alert to any threat, while the column of raiders straggled out for a good mile or so.

Farran could barely believe it when the first blush of dawn lightened the sky to the east. They were behind schedule, being a good few miles short of the farmstead. As good fortune would have it, a thick blanket of mist cloaked the surrounding terrain. They were winding their way into more open, flat meadowlands, which were mostly devoid of any cover, making the dawn mists a total life-saver.

Thankfully, the mist proved persistent, stubbornly refusing to burn off in the early morning sun. It hovered some three feet above the ground, shrouding his force from view. For once Farran indulged the hope that the gods were smiling upon them.

He glanced behind. The wisps of thick, wet mist conveniently distorted the shapes of those who followed. It was a godsend, for they were too tired to indulge in any great cunning or deception.

As the sun rose higher and the heat intensified the mist started to clear. With huge relief Farran climbed a slight rise, to spy the form of a brick-built farmstead perched atop a ridgeline, protruding from the mist like an island in the sky. That, he knew, was the aptly-named Casa del Lupo – House of the Wolf – their lying-up point for the hours of daylight. Their target lay just three miles beyond it as the crow flies.

He drove himself on, summoning hidden reserves of energy. When he judged they were close enough, he passed word down the line for Lieutenant Riccomini to come forward, along with ten SAS. He was ordered to push ahead and recce the House of the Wolf, while the rest of the column lay flat in the grass, shrouded by the last lingering wisps of mist. Riccomini was to move cautiously and to take his time, Farran cautioned. On no account was anyone to be allowed to escape from the farmstead – German or Italian.

Farran watched intently as the SAS flitted forwards, throwing a cordon around the place. That done, figures slipped through the front gateway and stole inside. Farran tensed for the sound of gunshots, but none came. After a minute or so he was waved forwards. It turned out that the only people present were the old farmer and his wife.

Mike Lees knew this place well: he'd visited it before, when carrying out his original recce of the Botteghe HQ. But none of them had ever been to this place attired as they were now – in full British battledress and bedecked with all the accoutrements of war, including a distinctive M1 bazooka, complete with rockets.

The bazooka – a man-portable, recoilless anti-tank rocket-launcher – had been included in one of the last air-drops. According to press reports, the American-made M1 'packed the wallop of a 155mm cannon'. It was a gross exaggeration, and early versions proved highly unreliable. More recent models were supposedly much improved, and Farran didn't doubt that it would make mincemeat out of the front doors of the villa targets, as they blasted an initial entry-way.

As the raiders filed silently in, Farran surveyed the farmstead. It was ideal for their purposes. The buildings formed four sides of a square, arranged around a central courtyard. The one narrow entrance faced south, so away from the direction of their target. The walls were thick and fortress-like, and indeed the place had very likely been designed to defend against mountain bandits in times gone by.

Farran allotted each of the three columns a stretch of the barns as a billet, and a flank of the farmstead to defend, in the event of trouble. Sleep was permitted, but sentries were to be posted, peeping cautiously from the upper windows, so as to keep out of sight. If anyone was seen coming to the farm, they were to be allowed to enter, after which the exit would be sealed shut. Whether German or Italian, they would be held captive until the mission was over.

Farran and Lees set up base in the kitchen. At first the farmer and his wife appeared terrified at the sudden arrival of so many rough-looking men-at-arms. But once they realised this was no raid, they become fawning and friendly. As the woman of the house rustled up breakfast, the farmer produced a bottle of grappa. He poured a round of shots, relating how German soldiers often paid them visits in search of eggs. Farran sent out word to double the watchfulness of the sentries.

The farmer seemed unable to comprehend that they were British. He insisted they had to be Germans, proudly relating how his son had served in North Africa and was now an officer in a Black Brigade unit. He produced photographs of a young man in Italian Army uniform, standing before a row of light tanks. A simple, rural type, the farmer seemed incapable of grasping that the force now billeted at his farmstead was fighting for the other side.

Fearing that one of the Garibaldini would overhear his pro-Fascist boasts and cut his throat, Farran told the farmer to put away his photos. Though puzzled and confused, the old man had let the grappa get the better of him. He insisted on relating a final story of how the dashing young man in the Italian Army uniform was actually the son of the village priest and not his at all, after which he roared with laughter, slapping Farran conspiratorially on the back.

Lees, meanwhile, seemed oblivious to all. He sat at the kitchen table head in hands, looking desperately sick. As the morning progressed and he swigged grappa and downed quinine pills, he seemed barely able to keep conscious. But still he refused to lie down, arguing that it would only make him feel worse. 'I dared not rest', Lees remarked of this moment. 'I knew that if I lay down now I should not be fit to go on again.'

Finally, Farran broached the subject that was foremost on his mind – that Lees was clearly too ill to continue.

'I'll be all right,' Lees mumbled. 'I'll be all right.' Meanwhile beads of perspiration pricked his forehead and trickled down his temples.

At midday Farran despatched Norice and Argentina on a final recce of the target. Their mission was to make doubly certain that the movement of the Allied Battalion hadn't been detected and the enemy's defences strengthened. Pulling off their battledress tunics and discarding their pistols, the young women set out as if they didn't have a care in the world, cracking jokes about how they would arrange dates with the German soldiers. Farran was hugely impressed. They had as much courage as any of their male counterparts.

Shortly after they'd left, two cowering Italians were herded into the kitchen. They came from a neighbouring farm, and while denying they knew of the presence of Farran and his men, in the same breath they claimed to have come here to warn of an approaching German patrol. They reported that the enemy were searching all neighbouring farms for partisans. Farran was used to such widely exaggerated rumour. While he didn't entirely believe them, he did warn Riccomini to alert his sentries to be on the lookout.

Farran ordered that the new arrivals be placed under guard in the shade of the courtyard. They would need to remain there all day and all night, he explained, but were free to depart come morning. They objected that they would be missed and that they had livestock to feed, but Farran couldn't help that. A little later three more farmers drifted in to Casa del Lupo, with similar stories – that German patrols were on the search.

It was worrying and Farran asked Lees what he made of the reports. After all, he had far more experience in these parts. Lees muttered something about the unreliability of the locals and that it was far safer to remain hidden. Farran agreed. If they sent out teams to search for the enemy, they'd risk blundering into those enemy patrols.

Farran's main concern was becoming the Stafettas. They'd been gone for a worryingly long time, and if they'd been captured that would blow the mission wide open. As a local BLO had recently reported, the fate of a Stafetta captured by the 'fiendish S.D.' – the *Sicherheitsdienst*, or the intelligence service of the SS – had been both horrific and hugely damaging. 'One of the girls [was] caught . . . [and] interrogated 26 times in 14 days. Given electric shocks and arrived back in a frightfully bruised state. Of course she spilt all she knew.'

As the sun set in a blaze of golden light, Farran became increasingly unsettled. He gazed out of the farmstead, searching for signs of the two missing women. To the south snow-capped peaks glowed red in the sun's last rays. A thousand feet lower the snow petered out, the mountains being fringed with a dark necklace of trees interspersed with isolated farmsteads. Lower still were villages, vineyards and olive groves, reaching out into the plains. In each of the cowsheds near him rough men were sleeping, their weapons and ammo piled in the mangers, the air thick with the scent of warm dung. But no mission could be launched from here, if Norice and Argentina failed to return.

Finally, a pair of figures sauntered out of the gathering dark. They had been delayed by over-attentive Germans, Norice explained, her grey eyes sparkling mischievously. She had wandered right through the enemy HQ, and produced a German cigarette from the bosom of her blouse, as evidence. She poured out information in a flood of Italian, punctuated by peals of laughter. The only significant new development was that a unit of anti-aircraft guns had been set up, to the east of the crossroads. That was hardly of any great significance.

Having congratulated the two women, Farran delivered his bombshell. They were not to be allowed to accompany the raiders, but would remain at the farmstead. Norice and Argentina were furious. They turned their wrath on Lees, berating him in wild outbursts of Italian. Though Lees understood, he was too far gone to care much. As they screamed and stamped and wept, Lees told Gordon to take them outside to cool off. His face was noticeably flushed and he appeared close to delirious.

Farran made one last attempt to persuade Lees to remain behind. The big man shook his head in wordless refusal. He knew fully well that the 'Malaria germ contracted in Yugoslavia . . . was active again, raising my temperature and sapping the strength that I would need . . .' Regardless, he steeled himself to continue, setting aside any thoughts of the long march back again: 'Sufficient only to see this attack a success and I should be content.'

With nightfall the mist returned. Farran had managed to grab a short sleep in the farmer's bed and he felt reasonably rested. It was time to issue final orders, over the fine meal that the farmer's wife had prepared – salami, spaghetti and bread, plus wine. As a fire roared in the hearth and Farran briefed the key figures – SAS, SOE and partisans alike – there was a distinctly last supper feel to the gathering.

'We move off at ten-thirty,' he announced, with his back to the blazing fireplace. 'We should reach Botteghe around midnight. We march in three parallel columns: the Russians, the Garibaldini and the *Gufo Nero*. You all know your roles when we get there. Any questions?'

Farran glanced around the gathering – Russians, Italians, Spanish, Germans and British united in one cause. He could just imagine how, three miles away, the German general and senior commanders would be sitting down to supper in Villa Rossi's magnificent dining hall. In Villa Calvi, staff would be locking away files and sending a last flurry of messages, believing a good supper and rest beckoned. Little did any of them know . . . Outside, guards would pace the perimeter, stamping their feet to drive out the chill. Stamping as the Nazis had done all over Europe, treading on the citizens of so many countries until even their friends, the Italians, rose up against them.

Racked with fever though he was, Lees likewise felt a surge of pride – pride that tonight would be the moment when 'Italy found her soul'; pride that tonight the spirit of resistance would rise up and strike a decisive blow.

Farran felt moved to make a final exhortation. 'Remember, the Corps HQ controls the whole of the front from Bologna to the coast. Its destruction will save thousands of Allied lives . . .' He glanced at the distinctive figure of Hans, dressed in full German uniform. 'If we are challenged, Hans will answer in German, and if we meet a patrol or the alarm is given, move straight in and attack. Is that understood?'

'*Capito*' – understood – the chorus of replies came back in Italian.

The raiders were ordered to muster in the darkness outside. The night was as black as pitch. Farran executed a last-minute inspection, just to ensure all had sufficiently darkened their faces, smearing them with soot. That done, Lees – seeming to have summoned hidden reserves of energy – did a final round of checks.

'Gordon, *pronto*?' he asked his *Gufo Nero* leader.

'*Pronto, Capitano.*' Ready, captain.

'Modena, *vy gotovi*?' Are you ready, in Russian.

'*Da, Gospodine Kapitan.*' Yes, dear captain.

'*Êtes-vous prêt*, Roberto?' French – for after years in the French

Foreign Legion, French was a second language for the Spaniard, Lance Corporal Robert Bruce.

'Oui, monsieur le capitaine.' Yes, captain.

With that, the long column of raiders marched out of the House of the Wolf, to war.

Chapter 15

With one of the local farmers acting as their guide they passed over some meadowland, there being little sound but the brush of boots through wet grass. The moon had risen and it glowed an eerie blueish-white through the low-lying banks of mist. They pressed on, crested a rise and suddenly the plains stretched before them as far as the eye could see.

Farran was amazed. The foothills stopped so abruptly, terminating in a vast and dark flatland, which seemed broken only by the moonlight glinting off the mighty River Po – a sliver of twisting silver snaking through the blackness. As Farran's eyes adjusted to the scene he spotted the odd pinprick of light – presumably a farmstead or home too remote for Italy's wartime blackout to have been fully enforced.

He glanced in the direction where he knew the Botteghe HQ had to lie: all there was dark and enveloped in a thick, brooding silence. It seemed impossible that soon it was to be torn asunder by the thunder of battle. Treading softly, Farran began to descend, slipping carefully into the black abyss. Once he glanced back: the last figures were stark on the skyline, seemingly elongated into giants by the weird distorting effect of mist and moonlight. Bizarrely, it reminded him of bushes warped by the intense heat of the Sahara, from his earliest missions in the war.

They neared the one major road that they had to cross, and the guide whispered a farewell, hurrying back the way they had come. The SAS scouts crept onwards. Bent double they scurried back and forth, checking that the route ahead was clear. At their signal, Farran led his men to the cover of a ditch, which ran along the nearside of the highway, ordering them to fan out on either side. On his word they broke cover and dashed across, but blundered into a thick hedge on the far side.

As men dived beneath it and wriggled through, weapons and kit banged and clanked alarmingly. To Farran if sounded as if a herd of elephants was on the rampage. He lay in the thick grass on the far side of the hedge, taking a moment to catch his breath. Beside him was Kirkpatrick, the piper, and his faithful 'aide' Bruno, the boy-partisan. Word filtered back that all one hundred of his fighters had made it across safely.

Ahead a farmhouse gleamed white in the moonlight. Farran recognised it from the aerial photos: it was his marker point from which to navigate the last few hundred yards to target. From now on that responsibility would be his, and his alone. He would steer a route across the night-dark terrain using a process known as 'pacing and bearing' – a simple technique that was the bread and butter of SAS operations. Taking a north bearing and setting his sights on a distinctive landmark lying due north, he would move off, counting his right footfalls.

From long experience he knew that ten such footfalls under a heavy pack amounted to some nine yards of terrain covered. By keeping to that northerly bearing, he'd need only to count out the paces and distance covered to know when to swing due east, for the target would then lie on their eastern flank. It sounded simple enough, but the mental effort involved in such pinpoint-accurate navigation, while remaining silent and alert for the enemy, was hugely draining.

He closed up the column, so no more than an arm's length separated each man. He couldn't afford to lose any now. They set forth, Farran moving stealthily at the very head of the snake. He tested his every footfall before putting down his full weight, his ears alert for the slightest noise or hint of danger. His heart leapt as a dog barked in a farm ahead and to his right. He crept onwards, making a slight detour around that and another farmstead, neither of which he could remember from the aerial photos.

There was the grunt of a heavy engine from the direction of the road they'd just crossed. Farran threw himself onto the dewy grass. Behind him a long line of figures did likewise. They lay still for several minutes, until the noise of the truck faded into silence. Moving with its headlamps blacked out, its progress was all but invisible to the naked eye. Farran clambered to his feet and signalled the off once more.

Shortly, they reached a ploughed field. The going worsened, thick loamy soil clinging to boots as one hundred heavily-armed raiders endeavoured to move silently across the rough, uneven ground. From pacing and bearing, Farran calculated they were close now – no more than a few hundred yards from the nearest enemy positions. He was terrified lest those on watch might hear the racket they were making, as they struggled across the rutted terrain.

All of a sudden he felt the ground give out beneath him. Moments later he'd stumbled face-first into a ditch. Most likely an irrigation channel, it had been invisible in the half-light. Passing a warning back down the line, he scrambled out and inched ahead, moving with ever more caution. Even so, when a second ditch yawned before him he was too late to prevent it from bringing him to his knees.

As he froze among the dank, muddy wetness of that second ditch, he heard a challenge ring out in German. For several seconds he tensed for the snarl of Mauser shots ringing past their heads in the darkness. Thankfully, none came. But it had taken more than an hour to cover a few hundred yards and they were falling behind schedule.

Farran felt a desperate urge to rush onwards, but he fought against the temptation. He crept resolutely on, moving with infinite care. His parachute smock snagged on a length of barbed wire. Carefully, silently, he untangled it and clambered over the fence, those behind whispering a warning to those who followed.

After his detailed studies of the aerial photos, the terrain here was etched in Farran's memory. He reckoned now was the time to swing east, to cover the final three hundred yards. If he'd got his sums right, they would reach the cover of the crescent-shaped woodland – which they'd nicknamed 'Half Moon Wood' – lying on the western flank of Villa Calvi. At that moment they'd be within spitting distance of the nerve-centre of the German 14th Army HQ.

Farran turned east and stole ahead more stealthily. A faint breath of wind seemed to part the mists for an instant, a beam of moonlight illuminating an utterly arresting sight. The distinctive form of Villa Calvi lay before them, no more than two hundred yards away, a ghostly white-walled mansion perched on a low hill and surrounded by a fringe of trees, and all seeming to float upon a sea of low-lying mist.

Not a light showed in any of the villa's windows, and Farran began to doubt if this really was their target. Were there any Germans present here at all? he wondered. The place looked utterly deserted. He felt a presence at his side. It was Lees, still somehow managing to master his fever.

'There it is, Roy,' he whispered, pointing out Villa Calvi, plus Villa Rossi beyond. There wasn't the vaguest hint of any light from that direction either.

Farran's eyes swung right, following Lees' outstretched arm as he indicated further landmarks: the telephone exchange, just to the south, with beyond that the guardrooms and the ranks of billets for the troops charged to protect the headquarters. Further south again lay the prison, plus the Spandau nests they had been warned about, but not a light was visible anywhere.

It was 0050 hours by now and all seemed so peaceful, so devoid of life. Both men found it distinctly unsettling. Had the enemy moved on? For days now that had been their greatest fear. Maybe all the delays and the insane flip-flopping in orders meant that they had reached the target, only for their prey to have flown?

'Doubts started to beset me now: could this be the right place . . . ?' Lees wondered. 'If this was the Botteghe headquarters, surely one of the many guards would have spotted us and opened fire?'

They had no choice but to continue, for that would prove it one way or the other. Farran gestured the column back into motion. Shortly, the first trees loomed stark and menacing before them. Moments later they'd slipped into the dark embrace of Half Moon Wood, Farran's navigation proving spot-on. Incredible as it might seem, he'd led his force of raiders to the heart of this German headquarters, seemingly undetected.

Under the cover of those trees Farran mustered his men. The

tension and adrenalin had been building for hours now. 'Fear, nerves, excitement, apprehension, worry, plans – all jumbled together to make me start at any noise,' he remarked. 'It would all be all right once we got going.'

Farran tried to speak, but the words froze in his throat. Finally, he managed to talk, but what he needed to say came out in a series of hoarse, barely-audible whispers. Were all present and correct? he asked. Somehow, it looked as if Modena and his Russians had disappeared. Lieutenant Harvey was there, with his SAS and Garibaldini, and Lieutenant Riccomini was there with his SAS and Black Owls, but the thirty Russian partisans were gone.

Farran felt a stab of alarm. The night was utterly still. The air itself seemed heavy and oppressive. He didn't for one moment doubt Modena's loyalty or his good intentions, but somehow they had lost a third of their force. He sent Kirkpatrick, the piper, to find them, with orders that they should form up their blocking group just to the south of the villas, from where they were to hose down any enemy movement.

The remaining figures bunched closer around Farran, tense and expectant, awaiting the final off. Kirkpatrick reappeared. There was no sign of Modena, he reported. Farran had to presume the battle-hardened Russian commander had split from the main force when it made sense to, making direct for their agreed position. It was a huge assumption to make and a massive risk to take, but time was against them now. They could afford no delay.

Farran grabbed Riccomini. 'Start time,' he hissed. 'You've got three minutes to get to Villa Rossi, so move fast. I'm sending in Harvey's force three minutes from now. Remember, the main German strength lies to the south, so it's from there you'll likely take fire. You've got twenty minutes on target, no more. If I fire the red flare before that, you're to withdraw. Understood?'

'Understood,' Riccomini confirmed.

Beside him stood Lees, massive and silent in the darkness. For an instant Farran wondered how he was coping, but it was too late for any such worries now. He signalled them to move. Riccomini led off, Lees lumbering after, with behind them ten SAS and Gordon with his Black Owls forming up the rear. They pushed ahead, weapons at the ready.

Most carried the Thompson sub-machine gun. Two decades old, it remained a favourite with irregular forces for a variety of reasons, many of which were reflected in the gun's nicknames: the 'Trench Sweeper', 'Trench Broom' or 'The Chopper'. The Thompson was of rugged design, had a high rate of fire, and its heavy .45-calibre cartridge delivered real punch. When fitted with a 30-round stick magazine, it was possible to sweep an entire enemy trench with bullets . . . or likewise the bedroom of an Italian villa.

As Farran watched that first raiding party leave, he wondered if Riccomini had noticed his very obvious fear – fear that had frozen his words in his throat. Farran had to hope that Ricky wasn't unduly affected by his CO's windiness. He counted out the seconds in his head, as the darkness and silence crowded close, as deep and still as the grave. He shivered, whether from the growing chill or from fear, he wasn't quite certain.

Farran cocked his carbine, trying to shake off the malaise that had gripped him. He signalled for young Lieutenant Harvey and they eased their way further into the woodland, following a narrow path that pointed the way to the perimeter of Villa Calvi. A short distance along it a thin strand of wire barred their way. It seemed to serve no defensive purpose, for it was easily stepped over. Farran was about to do just that when one of the Garibaldini stopped him.

He pointed to a sign nailed to a tree above the wire. Etched in red were the words: 'ACHTUNG. MINEN'.

Farran froze. The wire marked the border of a minefield, but there was no time to detour around it, for the three minutes were running. Without a word being spoken young Lieutenant Harvey stepped over the wire and pushed up the path, the SAS swarming after. The Garibaldini hesitated for a moment, before Farran urged them to follow, especially as there had been no explosions. Unbeknown to Farran, Harvey hadn't even seen the warning.

'A last "Good luck" from Roy Farran . . .' Harvey remarked of this moment, 'and we stepped over a low wire, crossed a largish patch, and then over another low fence. I thought this a peculiar arrangement, but then the penny dropped . . . Good heavens, surely I had not led my men over a minefield! . . . Then to my horror I saw the words . . . "Beware Mines." Well, we'd crossed it without mishap; the problem of how we'd get back could be solved later. There was going to be a lot of action in the next hour and a hard and fast plan would be doomed to failure.'

With Harvey and his men creeping ever closer to Villa Calvi, Farran forced himself to move, making for the road, with Kirkpatrick at his side. As they emerged from the cover of the trees, Farran tumbled into a dark slit trench. It was his third fall of the night, and it proved the most debilitating. In the process of trying to clamber out he lost his grip on his carbine. Kirkpatrick jumped in to retrieve it, handing it back to the SAS major, who had more than enough on his mind right now.

They pushed on, reaching the road leading to the villas, setting

'Wild Man' Lees – arm around horse – was already in the field, along with his radio operator, Bert Farrimond, (standing on his left), priest and partisan commander Don Carlo (astride horse), and fellow SOE agent Major Ernest Wilcockson (on Lees' right). Lees welcomed Farran and his SAS with open arms.

Having parachuted in against orders on a mission codenamed Operation Tombola, Farran linked up with Lees, billeting his forty-strong SAS at a derelict church. The enemy had executed the priest for supporting the partisans, so there was no more fitting place from which to plot revenge.

Lees had established his base at the remote village of Secchio, just a few kilometres to the rear of the Gothic Line. From there he called in weapons drops to arm the partisans, and raised a force of female agents – his 'Stafettas' – to spy out choice German targets.

Spanish SAS veteran Franscisco Jeronimo with female recruits. The 'Stafettas' were armed and would fight if necessary, but their real power lay in using their seduction skills to lure enemy troops into giving away crucial secrets.

In the Italian mountains bands of partisans were trained by SOE to use heavy machine guns and mortars, which were parachuted in by fleets of American DC3 'Dakota' cargo aircraft.

Some partisan bands, like this one led by Major Bill 'Mac' Mckenna, were charged to safeguard key targets like hydro-electric dams from enemy sabotage.

SOE Major Bernard 'John' Barton was scheduled to join Lees and Farran, charged to hunt down a top German general, inspiring Lees and Farran to target senior enemy commanders.

Lees sought intelligence on an enemy HQ that Field Marshal Kesselring was known to frequent. Dressed in local garb to recce the target, he discovered that the HQ – seat of the German 14th Army and situated in two fortress-like villas – controlled a vast stretch of the Gothic Line, commanding some 100,000 enemy troops.

Farran and Lees raised a force to hit the German HQ. It consisted of SAS, Italian partisans, Russian fighters who had fled enemy captivity and a smattering of German deserters. They rode in captured vehicles, Union Jacks roped over the roofs to safeguard them from marauding Allied warplanes.

On 26 March 1945 the raiders set out to destroy the HQ and kill the senior officers. Farran and Lees decided to ignore last-minute orders to stand down: it was impossible to command such guerrilla forces to a strict timescale, and they would never get another chance.

The raiders struck at night, having penetrated fearsome defences. Taking the enemy by surprise they torched the HQ villas, killing some sixty enemy and wreaking havoc on the 14 Army's command and communications.

Francis William Mulvey, an SAS veteran, was one of those wounded in action during the 14 Army HQ raid.

Days later, the Allied assault on the Gothic Line was launched, but the fighting proved ferocious with the enemy giving no quarter.

With Lees badly wounded, Farran's SAS launched all-out warfare, striking hard and fast from their mountain bases. During one such daring raid SAS Spaniard Justo Balerdi – battle name Robert Bruce – (centre photo, with cigarette), was shot in the head and killed.

Using mortars and a 75mm Howitzer nicknamed Molto Stanco – 'very tired', seen here in a photo with the Italian SAS detachment – the SAS shelled enemy lines, convincing German commanders that Allied forces had broken through and forcing them to abandon their positions.

By the third week of April 1945 the Gothic Line was broken. As northern Italy fell, the SAS staged victory parades with their partisan brothers-in-arms.

Post-war Roy Farran (in SAS beret) and Mike Lees paid regular visits to commemorate the partisan actions. WWII SAS veteran Jack Mann (in glasses) stands on Farran's immediate right.

Lest we forget. A reunion at Villa Rossi, former sight of the 14th Army HQ, with SAS veteran Lt. David Eyton-Jones far right. The plaque behind lists those SAS and others who died in the raid.

up temporary camp in the cover of some bushes. It was from there, sandwiched between the two targets, that Farran would orchestrate the battle. This was also the rendezvous (RV) point at which all would gather to execute their escape. He prepared his Very pistol and its flares, and nodded at Kirkpatrick to ready his bagpipes. He counted down the seconds in his head to the three-minute mark. Now was almost time . . .

Lieutenant Harvey, meanwhile, led his column of men towards the ornate, pillared gateway of Villa Calvi, keeping off the gravel drive as much as possible, which scrunched alarmingly underfoot. They slipped through as silently as wraiths and Harvey set his outer cordon, leaving his Bren-gunners within the fringes of the woods, their barrels menacing the building from all sides. He whispered final instructions: they were to shoot dead anyone who appeared at the windows or tried to use any of the doors.

There was to be one exception: the front door should be left unmolested. Harvey intended to blast it open with the bazooka, as the sleeping villa's rude awakening. Bren-gunners set, he led his men onto the wide expanse of manicured lawns that stretched up to the villa itself. It was incredible, but they had yet to encounter any resistance.

He gathered his force of men-at-arms – ten SAS, plus twenty Garibaldini – in a tight knot on the lawn. They were set a few dozen yards back from the massive wooden doorway and poised to storm through. Still there had been no cry of alarm or sign of discovery. Acting on instinct, Harvey darted across the close-cropped grass to try the door. He reached out to the massive iron-handle, but sure enough it was securely locked and bolted.

He hurried back to his men and readied the bazooka. It had a maximum effective range of a little more than a hundred yards –

but that was more than enough for its shaped rocket charge to tear across the lawn and rip the door into blasted wooden splinters, at which moment Harvey would lead his men forward at the charge.

They levelled the tube, held their breath and prepared to let rip. But there was a soft thud from the bazooka's firing mechanism and nothing more. The M1's rocket rounds were notoriously unreliable, and sure enough it had misfired. Hurriedly, fumbling in the dim moonlight, they armed it with a second round and again tried to fire. Again, it was a dud.

'No result – damn, now bad luck was with us . . .' Harvey recorded of the moment. 'We gathered around to try to determine the cause of the failure. Then I heard the unmistakeable crunching of boots on gravel . . . and then the deep guttural voices. Germans!'

They were in danger of getting caught in the open of the villa's grounds. Ordering his men to lie flat and motionless, Harvey dashed back the few yards to the gateway, taking cover behind one of its massive stone pillars. He spied the enemy patrol almost immediately. Four Germans were marching up the road towards where he was concealed, looking purposeful and determined. This was no mundane sentry duty, that was for certain.

Harvey waited until they were barely a dozen yards away. He needed to kill them all outright, so that none might escape. Then he stepped out of cover, Bren levelled at the hip, and pressed the trigger, unleashing a whirlwind of rounds. The sudden noise of that long and deafening blast tore apart the stillness of the night, like a clap of thunder and lightning.

'It was essential that this was all done at point blank range,' Harvey reported, 'to ensure that they were killed immediately, for those shots would set the whole area off . . . I could not afford to have wounded Germans on the road while I engaged myself in getting into the house.'

Breaking into the villa would require busting through that massive wooden doorway, and there was no time to get the bazooka working. Leaving four bloodied figures sprawled on the gravel, Harvey turned on his heel and ran, sprinting across the lawn and yelling for the others to follow. As they neared the cover of the villa's grand porch, the first yells of alarm were heard from a window high above, followed almost instantly by a long burst of fire.

It was answered by the rasping of a Bren, as above them glass shattered and voices screamed in shock and agony. Even as Harvey levelled his weapon at the door-lock and pulled the trigger, the fire from above intensified. One of his men – SAS Parachutist Mulvey – tumbled over, hit in the knee. From the shadows at the lawn's edge muzzles spat fire, as Harvey's Bren-gunners tore into the enemy figures now crowding the villa's windows, .303-inch rounds blasting splinters out of masonry and shattering wooden frames.

Directly below, Harvey was desperate to break into the building. 'I gave the lock a final burst,' he reported, 'pushed in the door, threw in a few hand grenades and ran into the dark interior.'

Those grenades had detonated inside Villa Calvi's fine entranceway, the deafening explosions echoing throughout the building and telegraphing that the impossible was seemingly happening – a hostile force had broken into the 14th Army's headquarters, apparently all but undetected.

Harvey dashed further inside, the Villa's hallway shrouded in darkness and wreathed in grenade smoke. 'There were scuffling noises and bullets started to fly,' he reported. 'The din was deafening in the enclosed space. I must see the lie of the room, so, holding my torch at arm's-length so as not to attract fire to myself, I switched it on and had a quick look around. The firing increased. They could see me, so I dived under a table . . . My sergeant opened up as I went to ground and killed the chief offender.'

SAS Sergeant Godwin let rip over Harvey's shoulder with his Thompson sub-machine gun, cutting the enemy fighter down. An instant later Harvey was back on his feet, sprinting for the staircase just ahead. Outside, someone must have got the bazooka working. There was the roar of the weapon firing, and moments later the rocket charge tore through an upper floor window and detonated, devastating fire and shrapnel punching through the rooms like a whirlwind.

Back at his roadside position, Farran had heard Harvey's first sustained burst of Bren fire with mixed emotions. Coming from the direction of Villa Calvi, it had sounded as if an entire magazine had been unleashed, the operator keeping his finger on the trigger without pause. Farran could only imagine that Harvey and his men were in action, and he felt a stab of excitement that the first fire had been British, as he had dearly hoped it would be.

But at the same time there was silence from the direction of Villa Rossi. Where were Riccomini, Lees and their men and why hadn't battle there also been joined? Villa Rossi's defenders would be waking up to the assault, and within seconds they would be at their defensive positions.

Harvey's burst was like a signal for all hell to let loose. A deafening barrage erupted from the ground just a hundred yards to the south of Farran's position, where the roadway ran past the

HQ's telephone exchange. From the muzzles sparking in the darkness, Farran knew that it had to be Modena and his Russians, as his line of thirty fighters let rip. True to form, Modena wasn't holding back: Farran could see streams of red tracer ricocheting off the walls of the telephone building and beyond that a cluster of guardrooms and billets.

Taken by utter surprise in the heart of their fortress, and hit hard in the depths of night, the enemy had to be wondering what on earth was happening. Which reminded Farran – his piper needed to play. He needed to stamp an indelible British signature on the battle, to deter against reprisals, plus he needed to stiffen the resolve of those charged to fight their way into the headquarters buildings, intent on wreaking bloody mayhem and murder.

Farran turned to Kirkpatrick, ordering him to play the marching song for all British highland regiments. All of a sudden the haunting tones of 'Highland Laddie' cut the night, the defiant skirl of the pipes rising above the snarl of battle. It was utterly spine-tingling. By way of answer, a ragged cheer went up from the Bren-gunners at Villa Calvi, but the enemy seemed equally keen to respond.

A burst of fire tore apart the air above Farran and Kirkpatrick's heads, targeting the unmistakeable tones of the pipes. It came uncomfortably close and it had the distinctive snarl of a Spandau. As further rounds ripped into their position, Farran grabbed his piper and bundled him into the nearby ditch.

'Keep playing,' he cried above the roar of battle. 'You're my secret weapon!'

Chapter 16

Kirkpatrick resumed his piping from a sitting position in the bottom of the trench, seemingly unfazed by the rounds that were snarling past. The bold notes of the pipes drew the enemy fire like nothing else. One round even nicked his bass drone, the longest pipe that creates the harmonising bass tone, and which protruded above both his head and the level of the ditch.

For a second or so Farran wondered whether he should move up to join Lieutenant Harvey at Villa Calvi, but someone had to man the RV point and signal their withdrawal. Instead, he dived into the trench to join his piper, cursing himself for not having held Harvey back for a few moments longer, to allow the Villa Rossi assault force time to reach their attack positions.

As if to underscore Farran's worries, the eerie wail of an air-raid siren started up. Low and barely audible at first, it wound up in pitch and volume, until the high-pitched scream echoed across the battlefield for a full dozen seconds, before dropping off to a low wail, and cranking up again. On and on it went, blaring out its oscillating warning. By now General Hauk and his senior staff would be fully awake, and preparing to fight back. The alarm had been well and truly raised at Villa Rossi, and Farran wondered what on earth could have delayed Riccomini and Lees.

In truth, Lieutenant Riccomini and Lees' approach had been somewhat more measured and stealthy than that of Lieutenant

Harvey at Villa Calvi. They'd crouched in a roadside ditch surveying Villa Rossi's boundary railings and the best route of approach, when Harvey's long burst of Sten fire had ripped the night apart. In response there had been a guttural yell, followed by a single shot ringing through the darkness, as a nearby sentry raised the alarm.

Riccomini reacted instantly. With Thompson sub-machine gun levelled at the shoulder, he unleashed a long series of bursts through the railings, blasting down the sentries one after the other. With four cut down, he was on his feet, yelling for his men to follow as he rushed the villa's gateway. The time for stealth was long past: this had become a full-frontal assault, guns-blazing, and the enemy knew it.

As Lees, Gordon and his Black Owls joined 'Ricky' and his SAS brethren sprinting for the gateway, so the first bursts of answering fire licked out of Villa Rossi's windows and the ghostly howl of the air-raid siren wound up to an ear-splitting crescendo. But as if to answer it, the wild skirl of the bagpipes rose up from behind them, spurring the raiders on. A wild cheer swept the ranks of the charging figures, SAS and partisans alike.

Lees – his fever momentarily forgotten – pounded through the gateway, as rounds cut around his head, ricocheting angrily off the massive stone pillars. On the left hand was inscribed the word 'VILLA' and on the right 'ROSSI', with each word surrounded by ornate stone carvings. Lees swerved left, and there, ten yards before him, was the expanse of Villa Rossi itself, rising four storeys to the highest towers.

A figure lunged out of the bushes to his right, barely an arm's length away. He saw a Mauser rifle raised, club-like, to strike. Before the sentry could swing it around to bludgeon his skull open, Lees fired, the muzzle of his Sten practically jabbing into the German's ribs. The blast forced the man backwards. He collapsed onto the lawn, face contorted in agony. Lees charged on, Gordon close at his heels and the Black Owls racing after.

Up ahead Riccomini scanned the target, desperately seeking a way in, while avoiding the line of fire from the upper windows. The high-arched front entrance was barred by a massive wooden door, strengthened with a cross-hatching of thick beams. Instead, Riccomini headed for a ground-floor window at which the slatted wooden shutters seemed to have been left mercifully open. Tommy gun spitting fire, he blasted in the glass and dived through, landing in a heap and rolling to his feet again.

Further figures vaulted in after, the SAS raiders dashing ahead and raking the ground floor with savage volleys of .45-calibre fire. Lees, meanwhile, made a beeline for the villa's front doorway. Using his bulk and his strength to force a way in, he barged it open, only to find himself momentarily blinded. Behind the closed doors and barred wooden shutters, the stone-flagged hallway proved surprisingly bright-lit. That he hadn't been expecting.

'Alarm was given by a hooter on the roof', the official SAS report recorded, 'and all the lights were switched on. The British ran through machine-gun fire, through the main gate . . . After fierce fighting the ground floor was taken, but the Germans resisted furiously from the upper floors . . .' How 'furious' that resistance would prove Lees was about to discover.

To left and right he could hear the crash of breaking furniture and the tearing rasp of gunfire. A pair of German soldiers, caught by surprise, surrendered instantly. But Lees had thoughts only for one thing: finding his way to the upper floor and dealing with a sleep-befuddled General Friedrich-Wilhelm Hauk and his senior staff. He dashed through the hallway, yelling for Gordon and the others to follow.

The hall opened onto a vast downstairs lounge, scattered with ornate furniture. There was still no sign of the staircase. Racking his brains for what the Stafettas and German deserter plus the POW had told him of the villa's layout, he took a sharp turn left, twisted left again, and suddenly found himself at the foot of a wide staircase, with a deep stairwell reaching into the shadowed depths below. It stretched above in a switchback fashion, the stone steps flanked with intricately carved wooden balustrades.

With barely a second's pause Lees began to pound his way up the steps, his Sten levelled at the hip. He powered onwards, all symptoms of his fever subsumed by the rush of adrenalin that had flooded his system. The landing above was ill-lit, so it was hard for Lees to make out who might be lurking there. Even so he sensed movement and the first hints of an enemy primed to meet fire with fire. He let rip with his Sten, as he raced up the staircase towards his quarry.

Back at Farran's roadside trench position Kirkpatrick piped on. High above them a blinding light suddenly blazed through the darkness. Farran recognised it instantly as a star shell – an artillery round that bursts to release a flare, which floats to earth beneath a parachute. It hung in the dark heavens, transforming the ground below into a harsh fluorescent-blue, the illumination creating a near-approximation of daylight.

Via the blinding light Farran could see how Modena's Russians were holding firm, pouring intense fire into the enemy positions beyond. 'The Russians returned fire very accurately and their ring was never broken . . .' the official SAS report recorded. 'Several enemy machine guns were silenced and heavy casualties were inflicted, especially in the area of the telephone exchange.'

Even so, Farran reckoned that a half-dozen or more MG42 Spandaus – Hitler's Buzzsaw – were now in action, the same weapon as had pinned him down during their exfiltration from the Châtillon garrison attack, months earlier, in France. As then, the German gunners were spraying the area with a fearsome volume of fire, which seemed to sweep right up to the villas' very walls.

At Villa Calvi, Lieutenant Harvey made a dash for the staircase, with Sergeant Godwin at his shoulder, both men hell-bent on winning the high-ground. 'We rushed the staircase, but the Germans were firing over the balustrade from above,' Harvey reported. Repeated attempts were made to reach the landing, but each was driven back in a rain of fire. 'It would be impossible to get past the hail of bullets,' Harvey concluded. 'We had just not enough men for that sort of thing.'

As if to underscore his worries, one of the villa's defenders tossed a grenade down the stairs. It came to rest between Harvey, Sergeant Godwin and one other SAS man, a Corporal Layburn. It was the latter who was closest to the blast. The explosion blew him off his feet, and he ended up lying on the flagstone floor in a pool of his own blood. Layburn was seriously wounded, and Harvey ordered him carried outside, to join the other casualties. Hopefully, their superlative medic, the Operation Galia veteran Jock Milne, would be able to stabilise him.

Harvey resolved to consolidate their hold on the ground floor and the stairs, so as to keep the enemy bottled in above. Via the Brens and the bazooka firing through the windows, they could still wreak havoc up there, while making sure the all-important ground floor remained theirs. One by one the key stations of the 14th Army's nerve centre fell to the attackers, as SAS and Garibaldini fought side by side, and Harvey and Sergeant Godwin held back the enemy at the staircase.

The 14th Army's map room, the registry and the W/T room were overrun in savage hand-to-hand combat, as figures fought and died amid the bloody chaos and confusion. Chilling screams rent the air. Some, from the floors above, had a distinctly female ring to them, but there was little time to worry about that now. Finally, the operations room itself was taken, and with it a distinctive figure fell victim to the assaulters.

'There was furious fighting,' the SAS report recorded of this moment, 'during which Colonel Lemelsen, the Chief of Staff, was killed.' Lemelsen, General Hauk's right-hand man, had been cornered in the ops room and gunned down.

It was now that the nineteen-year-old Lieutenant Harvey took a momentous decision. Time was running out and they needed a means to finish the job. 'No enemy remained alive on this floor,' he reported; 'outside our Bren gunners were continuing their good work, and many Germans were killed when they tried to shoot from the windows or run out the back door.'

But it was impossible to take the entire villa in the twenty minutes allotted. Instead, he decided to raze it, using fire. Harvey gave the order. Working frantically, his men grabbed heaps of 14th Army papers, maps, cypher and code books, piling them up in the map room, the registry and the operations room itself. They threw on broken furniture and added explosives, just to make sure the bonfires would go with a real bang and truly take hold.

As a final flourish, Harvey sent one of his men to search the villa outhouses for some petrol. He was back shortly brandishing a can. They sloshed it liberally over the piles of combustibles, as gunfire echoed from the upper floor, the surviving Germans fighting to prevent what they feared was coming, and the Brens hammered answering fire through shattered windows. Harvey and his men beat back several attempts to storm down the staircase, as the mountains of combustibles were set afire. Flames danced up the curtains and flashed across the debris-strewn floors, a thick pall of smoke rolling through the villa, billowing up the staircase and choking all.

Even as the fire at Villa Calvi took hold, Lees charged higher up Villa Rossi's spiral staircase, intent on reaching General Hauk's sleeping quarters. But as he dashed across a lower landing and climbed towards a second, he heard a cry of warning from behind. Before he could react a flash cut through the shadows above, and instantaneously a bolt of agony pulsed through his chest. Moments later he tumbled backwards, feeling his head crack against the floor.

Lees had rolled partly down the staircase before coming to a halt. It seemed as if something inordinately heavy lay across his legs, pinning him down. He felt along his body, realising there was someone lying across him, unmoving. His hand came away grasping a red beret, but it was drenched in blood. Lees tried to remember who had been with him on the staircase and could only think that it was Gordon, the commander of his Black Owls.

He started yelling now, urging those below to redouble their efforts to storm the upper floors. He pushed the body off his legs, as the roar of tommy guns from below grew into a deafening crescendo. Over all, he fancied he could hear the evocative tones of Kirkpatrick's bagpipes. They seemed to be saying: 'Get up, get up, why are you lying there,' Lees recalled. 'Why was I lying there? I felt no pain. There seemed nothing wrong.'

He clambered to his feet but collapsed again almost as quickly. His left leg was dangling limp and unresponsive. No matter how he tried to focus, the leg would not respond to anything that his mind told it to do. Savage fire was traded back and forth, as heavy boots thundered up the stairs once more. The distinctive form of Lieutenant Riccomini led the charge, with Serjeant Guscott close behind.

They dashed past Lees, racing for the upper landing. Riccomini had all but made it, tommy gun blazing, when a round caught him in the head, felling him instantly. It was obvious by the way that he had fallen that he'd been killed outright. Serjeant Guscott bent to drag his body clear, but then, enraged at the SAS lieutenant's loss, he turned and charged back up the staircase once more.

Guscott reached the landing beside the fallen Lees, yelling for others to follow. But as he turned back to the charge a burst from above tore into him, and a second Operation Galia veteran was cut down, dying where he fell. Both men had volunteered for this mission, though their Galia heroics had by rights earned them well-deserved leave. For their dedication and their courage on the Villa Rossi staircase, Lieutenant Riccomini and Serjeant Guscott had paid the ultimate price.

As for Mike Lees, his very life hung in the balance. Heavily wounded and unable to move, he was trapped between the guns of his own side and those of the enemy. The German defenders seemed emboldened by their kills. It was their turn to attempt to rush the staircase. As jackboots thundered down the polished stone steps, their charge was met by a hail of fire from below. Three of their number were cut down, falling in a torn and bloodied heap beside the bodies of Riccomini and Guscott, and with that their counter-attack faltered and died.

It was clear to all now – attackers and defenders – that the battle for the staircase had reached a stalemate. With all three of their commanders cut down – SAS, SOE and Black Owls – the Villa Rossi raiding force had been left bereft of a leader. Their half of the mission, at least, was turning into something of a disaster.

At Villa Calvi, the flames crackled and roared deafeningly and a series of explosions rocked the ground floor. Moments later, Harvey gave the order to withdraw. As they raced for the exit, his thirty-odd fighters little realised what awaited outside. They crowded through the blasted entranceway, which was billowing thick smoke, only to find themselves under attack from several directions.

'Despite our determined and accurate gunfire,' Harvey reported, of his Bren-gunners, 'grenades from above were being thrown onto the lawn and we had to run the gauntlet. Germans were now in the road where I had killed the sentries and they were firing towards the house. Our exit fully silhouetted against the fire was not easy and how we managed to get out without further casualties I do not know.'

Suffering only the two wounded, Harvey ordered his force to turn their guns on the villa. Figures were trying to drop from upper windows or dash out of the doors, as the fire and smoke took savage hold. 'We kept up our fire outside as more and more of the trapped enemy in the house tried to get out,' Harvey reported. Finally, having checked his watch and realising they had run well over their allotted time, he ordered his men to fall back. Having hit and hit hard, it was time to run.

At his position by the roadside, Farran was growing anxious. He kept fingering his Very pistol, wondering whether to fire the signal to end the attack. The twenty minutes was long past, but by the ferocity of the firing the battle for the villas was still underway. It was then that he noticed the red glow of flames licking high around the roof of Villa Calvi, lighting up the night sky. There at least the raiders seemed to have done their work.

Beside him, Kirkpatrick's bagpipes wailed, but they were in danger of being drowned out by the cacophony of enemy fire. A barrage of mortars tore into Half Moon Wood, crashing into the southern fringes of Villa Calvi's grounds and sending shrapnel winging through the trees. That was the terrain over which Harvey and his men were scheduled to withdraw. It was one thing launching such an attack against orders, and getting away with few losses. It would be quite another if his force was devastated, most being captured or killed.

One or two figures hurried through the trees, making for Farran's position. They were Russian and Italian stragglers – the first of those starting a spontaneous retreat. Soon, German reinforcements would break through Modena's cordon, Farran reasoned, for the battle-hardened Russians had to be running seriously short of ammo. If he and his men were to stand any chance of escape, now was the time to sound the retreat.

Farran raised his Very pistol and fired three red flares in rapid succession – the signal to withdraw. The first reaction was a spray of Spandau fire, as the ever-alert German gunners targeted his position. No doubt about it – it was time to get the hell out of there.

*

At Villa Rossi, Mike Lees began to crawl. While his leg was incapable of supporting his weight, it seemed to work as far as the knee, which meant he could inch along on all fours. Apart from the dead, he found himself alone on the bloodied staircase. Now, with his strength ebbing with every effort, he made a desperate bid to drag himself down, with the aim of making for the villa's exit. It would take a truly Herculean effort to get there, and then what? But he wasn't dead yet and God knows he wasn't the type to give in. He made the ground floor of the villa and, gritting his teeth, forced himself to keep crawling.

Kershaw, the former Olympic bobsleigher, had taken charge here on the ground floor. He remembered the final words that Farran had spoken to him, back at the Casa del Lupo: *If we cannot force a way in . . . surround them, burn them down and see that no one escapes.* While Private Raphael Ramos, the fearless Spanish Civil War veteran and French Foreign Legionnaire, kept the Germans bottled in upstairs, he and a group of fellow SAS tore down curtains, grabbed soft furnishings and wooden chairs and piled them in a heap in the kitchen.

It was centrally located, and it looked as if it would burn ferociously, once the mountain of combustibles had been ignited. They had been here, fighting for their very lives for well over thirty minutes now. As Kershaw set a match to the pile, fanning it into a roaring furnace of flame, he yelled to the others to prepare to evacuate. If they could burn General Hauk and his surviving fellow officers to death, that would be fitting revenge for the three commanders they had lost on the Villa Rossi staircase – Riccomini, Gordon and Mike Lees.

On duty at the stairs, Ramos reckoned he'd accounted for

six German officers, as they'd made repeated attempts to storm their way down and reclaim the villa's ground floor. With thick smoke billowing through the rooms he finally turned to leave, firing one last burst up the bullet-pocked stairway. As he went to depart he all but tumbled over a figure on the floor. It was Mike Lees, doggedly crawling on his bullet-torn legs and making for the villa's entrance.

Ramos reached to help the wounded SOE officer, as a third figure joined them. It was Siciliano, one of Lees' Black Owls, who began yelling excitedly above the din of battle.

'*Capitano! Capitano!* Come away!' he told Lees. 'We could not get up the stairs. We are going to burn the place down.'

'Who's that?' Lees croaked a reply.

'Siciliano. We are going to burn the place down!'

'Plus it's Ramos,' the Spaniard added. 'We've got to get you out of here.'

Ramos and Siciliano draped Lees around their shoulders, hauled the wounded captain to his feet and hustled him towards the villa's smoke-enshrouded doorway. As waves of pain and nausea swept over him, Lees began alternately to hop and to be half-carried outside. They emerged from the burning villa to be met by 'heavy machine gun fire', enemy soldiers crowding the windows above them.

Leaving Lees in cover, Ramos dashed back inside to deter any who might attempt to shoot them down. Only once the flames and smoke took irrevocable hold, making any attempt to reach the ground floor impossible, did Ramos leave. With Siciliano's help he took up the thirteen-stone form of Lees, and the trio made a dash for the cover of the nearby woodland. It was the thick smoke billowing from the windows that saved them. As they stumbled for the trees, heavy bursts of fire ricocheted around their ears, but the shots went wide of the mark.

They limped into cover, miraculously dodging enemy fire and laden down with the injured Lees. The area remained 'alive with angry Germans', and behind them a lone figure was cut down. Typically one of the last to break fire, SAS Corporal Sammy Bolden was caught in a furious fusillade of bullets and grenades unleashed from the villa's upper floor as the enemy fought to the bitter end. Veteran of Operation Cartoon, the daring Commando raid off Norway's coast, Bolden was another to fall victim to the lack of time allotted to the Villa Rossi assault.

With Lees in tow, Ramos and Siciliano retraced their steps towards the rendezvous point, as behind them the firing at last died down to sporadic bursts. The three paused so they could catch their breath. Siciliano turned back towards the two villas. 'Look, look, they are burning!' he exclaimed, excitedly.

Lees glanced where the man indicated: a halo of angry red lit up a wide swathe of sky. Villa Calvi appeared like a raging inferno; Villa Rossi too was wreathed in thick smoke and flames. In spite of his injuries, Lees felt a flood of relief. Against all odds it seemed that they had accomplished what they had come here to do.

'We must hurry, *Capitano*,' Siciliano urged.

He was right: the time to flee was now. But Lees felt overcome by a crushing sense of hopelessness. 'I'll never crawl thirty miles back to the mountains and they can't drag me that far,' he told himself. He felt so weak and faint he didn't particularly care what happened to him any more.

He turned to Siciliano and Ramos. 'Leave me here, my friends . . . I must stay and take my chances with the Germans.'

The men shook their heads, emphatically. 'To be tortured? Never!'

Siciliano and Ramos managed to attract the attention of another SAS man, a giant of a red-headed Irishman called Patrick 'Pat' Burke. Together the three began to hurry Lees' bloodied form through the last of the trees, as they sought out Farran and the rest of the party.

But by the time they reached the RV point, the SAS commander and his raiders were nowhere to be seen.

Chapter 17

At Villa Calvi Lieutenant Harvey had decided to do the unexpected and dispense with the immediate RV. 'As our troops got thinner on the ground the Germans would soon be rushing about unhindered and here we were, still in the middle of the hornet's nest . . . I decided to head in the opposite direction . . . this would probably deceive the enemy, who would try to cut us off on the direct route back to the mountains. We were extremely tired and the extra miles I was inflicting on my men was not an easy decision . . .'

Harvey pushed north through the darkness, before turning west, giving the burning HQ as wide a berth as possible. 'We walked straight through an enemy post unchallenged and cut the telephone wires,' he reported. 'I got a severe shock while cutting the wires strung along a hedge. One was a power line!' By severing lines of communication, they would spread more confusion among the enemy, which could only boost their chances of escape.

But Harvey's task was far from easy. His thirty-odd battle-worn men were laden down with injured – Parachutist Mulvey, shot in the knee, and Corporal Layburn, suffering from his grenade wounds. Harvey decided the 'risk to the remainder of us was too great', if they attempted to flee with both men. Mulvey, whose knee had been shattered, was the least mobile. It made sense to leave him. 'Having explained this to my men, a couple of them volunteered to stay . . .' Harvey recorded, '[in order that] this small party could hide up and make its way back more easily . . .'

Harvey's report, written sometime after the raids, makes it all sound so simple and straightforward. In truth, this must have been one of the most fraught decisions for a commander to have to make – to leave three of his men behind, one severely wounded – let alone for an inexperienced lieutenant of just nineteen years, engaged on his first combat mission.

Harvey advised the three stay-behinds to hide up during daylight, to move only at night and to live off the land as they edged their way towards the safety of the mountains. With that agreed, the main force departed, heading for the fallback RV point – Casa del Lupo, the House of the Wolf – the wounded Parachutist Mulvey being left in the care of his two fellows.

At his roadside position just south of the burning villas, Farran had waited and waited. He'd delayed for as long as he dared, but there had been no sign of either the wounded Lees or those who were supposedly helping him to safety. Lees had been strapped to a discarded ladder to form a makeshift stretcher, or so Farran had been told, but he and his bearers failed to materialise. Finally, as the sky blazed an angry crimson, Farran gave the signal for the off.

Lieutenant Harvey and the Villa Calvi raiding party were nowhere to be seen, but it made sense they were making their own way to the fall-back RV. Likewise Modena and his Russians. It was the badly wounded Lees who worried Farran. Regardless, he took up position at the head of what remained of his raiding party and set a course due west, making for the Crostollo river, a tributary of the Po. They'd trekked in moving up the Crostollo's eastern bank. To execute their escape, he planned to cross the river, before turning south towards Casa del Lupo.

It was 0225 hours on 27 March 1945 when they hurried away from the 14th Army HQ. A raid scheduled to last twenty minutes had morphed into a ninety-minute epic. As Farran well knew, time was set against them now – they had precious few remaining hours of darkness in which to execute their flight into the safety of the hills.

Behind them, star shells burst like a firework display across the night sky, illuminating a scene of utter devastation. 'It was a satisfying sight,' Farran wrote. 'If only we could regain the safety of the mountains, the raid could be marked up as at least a partial success.'

Indeed, Farran had received reports that General Hauk himself had died during the fighting at Villa Rossi. That, plus the utter inferno of devastation wreaked at Villa Calvi – the 14th Army's operational HQ – was approaching the knock-out blow that he and Lees had hungered for.

The withdrawal turned into something of a helter-skelter dash. Parties split up into smaller groups as they raced for the river. By something close to a miracle they managed to link up at the crossing point, after which Farran formed up his column. Though they were plagued by a crushing fatigue, he couldn't countenance the slightest pause. Already the sky to the east was lightening, and convoys of German trucks could be heard racing along the road ahead of them – reinforcements, making for the headquarters.

Sporadic bursts of fire echoed from the direction of the burning villas. Either there were remnants of Modena's Russians still in action, or the Germans were shooting at ghosts. The progress of Farran's weary column proved frustrating slow, and he was desperate to cross the road before first light. From that direction came the steely clatter of tank tracks, forcing the ragged line of men to go to ground. They lay low for several minutes, as the rattle faded into silence.

Farran drove his men onwards. In his haste, he made an error of navigation. It was only the eagle-eyed gaze of one of his men that saved them. He pointed out a warning sign – they'd almost stumbled into an anti-aircraft battery. To skirt around it, they were forced to execute another exhausting detour. Finally, they reached the road. Choosing a moment when it seemed deserted of traffic, Farran urged his men across. Figures flitted over in the half-light, dirtied and bent double like so many scurrying rats.

Moments later, they hit the slope that ascended to the first ridgeline, upon which perched the fall back RV – Casa del Lupo. The farmer hardly seemed overjoyed at the raiders' return. After the night's dramatic pyrotechnics, he'd finally grasped that the mystery force weren't Germans, after all. He was scared stiff at their reappearance and begged them to leave as soon as possible. Farran needed little urging – they couldn't afford to tarry.

Lieutenant Harvey's force straggled into the RV, and together the surviving commanders got a quick heads-up as to the cost of the battle and the fate of the missing. While the British losses – two dead, three wounded – were extraordinarily light, considering the carnage they had wrought, Farran took the news particularly badly. It was the death of Lieutenant Riccomini that hit him hardest, 'one of the bravest chaps that ever lived.'

'It was his second operation in three months,' Farran would write of Riccomini's loss, 'and by rights he should have been resting in safety ... Another grave loss was Serjeant Guscott, who marched across the mountains . . . to join me.' Guscott had made the epic sixty-mile journey on foot through 'awful country' to join the SAS raiders. 'It is strange how the best men are always the first to die. Perhaps we others are not good enough.'

But for now, there were several dozen of those 'others' whom Farran somehow had to spirit to safety. Modena's Russians arrived, minus half a dozen of their number. Those six had been captured in fierce fighting, and few doubted what dark fate now awaited them. Along with the absent Mike Lees, Gordon, the Black Owls commander, was also missing. But the news on Gordon at least seemed somewhat promising: wounded on the Villa Rossi stair-case alongside Lees, he'd been dragged out and carried away from the burning villa by his Black Owls.

Farran had no idea where those two wounded commanders might be. Lees and Gordon – plus their stretcher-bearers – were missing, fate unknown. They would have to fend for themselves. He was incapable of offering any kind of assistance, not least until he made the safety of the Secchia valley, which lay over forty kilometres due south of their present position. It would be a far greater distance, of course, using the convoluted series of paths and tracks that Farran intended to follow.

The sun rose, flooding the expanse of rumpled foothills before them with a fierce light, and making their onward journey an even more daunting proposition. Near by, the byres in which the men had slept the previous day beckoned enticingly, but Farran was having none of it. Within a matter of minutes he had formed up his ragged band for the off.

'The strain of the fighting and the carrying of the wounded men was telling on us all,' reported Lieutenant Harvey, 'but we had to keep going. It was daylight now and we had to get as many miles between us and the scene of the action in the shortest possible time. The odds against us in the attack on the Headquarters had been great . . . and the enemy would surely send a very large force after us . . . We could ill-afford in our present state to fight them. We had lost one-third of our force killed and wounded . . .' And missing, of course.

Harvey found a decrepit old mule in one of the barns. That would have to do for the wounded Corporal Layburn. After Farran had dressed Layburn's wounds with bandages, they roped him tightly to the saddle. He was far more badly injured than most had imagined, when he'd stumbled doggedly from the scene of the attack. Caught in the grenade blast at the foot of the Villa Calvi staircase, Layburn's legs had been peppered with shrapnel.

Once strapped into the saddle they hung limply down. Despite the bandaging, they oozed blood. But the most amazing thing was that the wounded corporal had yet to cry out, despite the agony of his injuries. Farran ordered the off, making it clear there could be no more halts.

At first spirits were remarkably high. A soft mist cloaked the ground, which should aid in their escape. Stories were whispered back and forth down the line of march, as men recounted the wildest of tales of the night's action. The best seemed to be that of a certain German officer who had been chased onto the lawn of the Villa Rossi, dressed only in his pyjamas. Thin cotton had done little to stop bullets.

But as the day progressed the sky clouded over and a thin rain began to fall. It made the path underfoot muddy and treacherous. Here and there villagers hurried past, looking distinctly harried. They all spoke of the same thing – the countryside thereabouts was crawling with vengeful Germans. Their patrols were everywhere, the locals reported, and all roads were blocked. This time Farran didn't doubt their word. It was exactly as he had expected.

'We were too short of ammunition and our weapons had fallen too often in the mud for us to look for a fight,' he remarked. Their only hope of escape lay in slipping through undetected. As the raiders trudged onwards, voices charged with the thrill of battle fell silent. Farran kept them marching through the rain, and they straggled out on the path behind. Like the others, he began to swallow Benzedrine tablets as if they were boiled sweets.

Before long, the old mule carrying Layburn had to be abandoned. Half-blind, it kept stumbling in the mud, causing the wounded man to slip sideways. Eventually it collapsed, trapping Layburn. Men whose limbs were leaden with fatigue fashioned a makeshift stretcher from cut branches strung with parachute blouses. With one man on each corner they hoisted the injured Layburn and began to carry him, stretcher poles balanced on their shoulders.

The stretcher-bearers were so tired they repeatedly collapsed to their knees in the mud. Despite his old injuries, Farran took his turn at this exhausting task. Eventually, Layburn asked to be left behind. None would hear of it. They marched blindly, reeling forwards as if on a drunken sally home from the pub. Farran was painfully aware of their predicament: if they met a German patrol of any strength they were virtually incapable of resistance.

Bearing weapons caked thick with mud from repeated falls, they dispensed with scouts even. No one had the energy to dash from ridgetop to ridgetop ahead of the party. Farran led them over a main highway without a pause, not even bothering to check if it was clear of the enemy. Somehow they made it across. They trudged through the centre of a village, making no attempt at any kind of concealment. Locals stared at their harrowed, muddied faces in open astonishment.

Meanwhile, a few dozen kilometres to their rear two other parties of desperate fugitives slipped into precarious hiding. One was made up of the two men from Lieutenant Harvey's force, bearing the injured SAS Parachutist Mulvey between them. An Irishman, an underage Mulvey had actually falsified his date of birth, so as to qualify for recruitment into the British military. Now, as a baleful sun rose high over the plains of the Po, he and his escorts darted into an isolated farmstead, begging shelter and aid.

They were blessed with good fortune. As luck would have it, the family were resolute supporters of the resistance. On the kitchen table Mulvey had his shattered knee bathed and dressed, whereupon the three men were shown to a place of hiding. Wads of cash were thrust into the farmer's hands, as a token of their gratitude. He seemed grateful, though money would do little to save him and his family, should the Germans come calling.

A patrol of German soldiers had arrived at the Albinea church that morning, bearing three bodies – those of Lieutenant Riccomini, Serjeant Guscott and Corporal Bolden. The priest was ordered to organise a grave-digging party. He chose a spot in the north-eastern corner of the cemetery, which overlooked the direction of the two villas, which even now were wreathed in thick smoke. That the dead were 'Commandos' was seen as being proof that this had been a British-led raid, which was good for the locals, for it militated against reprisals.

If anything, Mike Lees found himself in the most perilous situation of all of the raid's survivors. His journey that morning had been an utter nightmare. Strapped on the ladder, Siciliano,

Ramos and Burke had hurried him through open terrain, desperately seeking refuge. With the enemy headquarters just two miles behind them they had collapsed exhaustedly at a farmstead. There Lees learned that the wounded Gordon – his Black Owls commander – was with them. Gordon's leg was broken, so both he and Lees were stretcher cases, and there seemed little hope that they might escape a vengeful enemy.

The party pressed on, the inferno of the burning villas red and angry at their backs. Three hours later the stretcher-bearers stumbled into a barn. It formed part of a farm that was owned by 'friends', Lees was told; rock-solid allies of the resistance. As Ramos and Burke went to close the massive barn doors, Lees raised himself weakly on one elbow. In the distance the sky was burnished red where the 14th Army HQ blazed. How on earth could they stay here, he wondered, in plain sight of the target they had so audaciously attacked?

Lees didn't have long to ponder the question. He and Gordon were carried to a bed of straw and laid down to rest. Their escorts built a pile of bales around their place of hiding, until it would appear from the outside to be a solid stack of hay. At least, that was their intention. An old farmer woman lived there alone, and only she would know where they were hidden. She had been sworn to absolute secrecy.

Ramos, Burke and Siciliano, plus the other stretcher-bearers, prepared to depart. They had to try to make it back to the Secchia valley, and they were leaving Lees and Gordon in the hands of the very capable local resistance. One of the partisans reassured Lees that his sister, who lived in a nearby town, would come to visit within the next few hours. She was a nurse and she would be able to tend to his, and Gordon's, wounds.

Lees had one last request, before the three departed. He got Burke to scribble down a note to Farran, dictating what he wanted to say. Riddled with gunshot wounds, incapable of movement, bereft of proper medical attention, and marooned in the heart of enemy territory, he knew his chances were slim. Now, he figured, was the time to tell it like it was.

'Dear Old Roy – I think we pulled it off fairly well,' Lees began. 'I got my dose with Gordon and Sgt. Guscott being slap-happy and trying to get upstairs in Villa Rossi. Wounded in . . . left leg and right shoulder. Gordon got a smashed leg. Guscott dead. These two English boys carried me away, with the help of the Garibaldini.' By 'these two English boys' he meant Burke and Ramos, an Irishman and a Spaniard – both honorary Brits in the SAS.

'I hope the show was a success,' he continued. 'I am at Rivalta near Canali, hiding up and hoping not to be caught . . . Look after the show for me as I will be laid up for a long time . . . and tell Charles Macintosh to fuck himself.' The sentiments directed at Macintosh reflected the level of Lees' anger at Florence head-quarters. Though not privy to all of their machinations, he was convinced they had had it in for him. In effect, this was his death's-bed revenge.

Lees ended the missive asking Farran to get a letter through to his wife, Gwen, 'saying I am OK.' The letter was signed '(Written as dictated for Capt Lees) (Pat Burke)'.

Burke folded the sheet of paper into his pocket, and with that he, Ramos, Siciliano and the others hurried out of the barn, swinging the doors shut behind them, and leaving the stricken forms of Mike Lees and Glauco Monducci – Gordon – in pitch darkness. As exhaustion, trauma and blood loss got the better of them – not to mention Lees' malaria – the two men drifted into an exhausted sleep.

Their last waking thoughts were whether anyone would ever come to find them.

Chapter 18

By the time they stumbled into the final approach to Valestra, the village from which they'd set out, Farran and his party's endurance was at its very end. They had been marching for over twenty hours with barely a break, but even so Farran decided a little show was in order, to mark their muddied, bloodied return. That they had evaded capture was little short of a miracle, for which he could only think to give thanks.

He ordered his ragged line to form up into columns, three abreast, with those carrying the injured Layburn taking up the lead. As they approached the village, Farran told his piper to play. Though he was utterly wrecked, Kirkpatrick summoned the strength to blow life into his bagpipes. Women came to their doorways, drawn by the music, and they cheered. Crowds of excited children began to scamper along, marking the column's progress.

To left and right, exhausted men did their best to pick up sore and leaden feet and march in time to the piping. Shoulders were thrust higher and backs straightened, as the men realised they had made it through the enemy lines to the Secchia valley, their place of refuge. Farran hoped that the pursuing Germans might hear the notes of the bagpipes, and take them for defiant proof that the British raiders had reached a point beyond their easy reach.

After leading the Valestra victory parade, Farran's legs gave up on him completely. From somewhere a horse was found to carry him the last few miles. It was midnight by the time the raiders marched into Tapignola, making their way to their church quarters. They were met with a tumultuous reception, but most were far too gone to care.

'The men bedded down in the cattle shed and the wounded were given attention,' Lieutenant Harvey reported. 'I too snatched a couple of hours sleep, my first since the few we had had . . . before setting out . . .' While there were few medical facilities at Tapignola, SAS doctor Jock Milne transformed the church's hallowed grounds into a makeshift hospital. So professional was the care the injured were to receive there, that when eventually they had the bullets and shrapnel removed from their wounds, there were to be few if any complications.

Utterly spent, Farran was put to bed in the house of a local schoolmistress, who happened to be away. All in all, they had marched for twenty-two hours to escape the enemy dragnet, and, bar the halt at Casa del Lupo, they'd been on the go for fully two days. Counting the cost of the raid, the losses were incredibly light . . . so far: two British dead, two missing presumed dead, three wounded (two of whom – Mulvey and Mike Lees – were missing); three Italians wounded (one missing) and six Russians captured (and presumably summarily executed), plus two wounded. At first Farran believed General Hauk himself had been killed, but recent reports were equivocal. Even so, Colonel Lemelsen, his Chief of Staff, was dead, as were countless others of his officers and men.

They'd turned Villa Calvi into a gutted ruin, and Villa Rossi was also badly fire-damaged. More importantly, the entire nerve centre of the 14th Army – maps, registry and operations room – had been eviscerated. As Farran would report, 'Villa Calvi was completely destroyed along with the greatest part of the Head-quarters' papers, files and maps.' The enemy must have realised they were far from safe anywhere. Incredibly, the convoys of trucks arriving at Botteghe the morning after the assault weren't just bringing in reinforcements: they were also there to evacuate whatever remained of the headquarters.

Farran fully expected a reaction of utmost savagery, to answer the daring and audacity of the raid. But first, back on the plains of the Po, Mike Lees and Gordon had visitors.

Even as Farran had fallen into an exhausted sleep in the school-mistress's bed, so Lees had heard the creak of midnight hinges, as the door to their barn was swung ajar. Voices whispered softly in Italian, as bales of hay were prised aside. By the light of a lantern Lees spied the farmer woman with two pretty young Italian ladies at her side. The taller of the two stepped forwards.

'I am Gianni's sister,' she introduced herself, Gianni being the partisan leader whom Lees held in such high esteem. 'My friend and I have come to stay with you . . . You will have more visitors tonight. Antonio is bringing a doctor.'

Lees asked the obvious question: 'Who's Antonio?'

'He's the leader of the resistance in this area.'

She turned to ask for hot water. Minutes later the old farmer lady was back, hefting a huge and smoke-blackened kettle. Together, the two young women set about readying Lees and Gordon for the doctor. Lees heard the Black Owls commander groaning in agony, as they cut his trousers off him. He had been shot on the staircase at the same time as Lees, a bullet shattering his leg.

One of the women turned to Lees. 'Where are you wounded?'

'I don't know; I can't feel or move my leg below the knee,' he explained.

Having ripped up his trousers – they were stiff with congealed blood – she still couldn't find any injury. Eventually, she discovered a bullet hole in Lees' hip, and another in the back of his leg, just above the knee. He wondered what that might mean. Another round had passed clean through his chest, with a fourth hitting his left arm and a final one passing through the calf of his right leg.

'As they worked tenderly and efficiently cleansing and bandaging the wounds, I reflected how lucky I was still to be alive,' Lees observed, with signature understatement. The doctor arrived. He'd clearly been brought there against his will, and he kept muttering darkly as he inspected the two men's wounds. With the help of the young women he managed to improvise a rough wooden splint for Gordon's leg.

But after studying Lees' injuries, the doctor confirmed what he had most been fearing. 'The nerve has been hit.'

'How long until it gets better?' Lees asked. He needed to be well enough to walk and to escape.

The doctor shrugged. 'Who knows? I can do nothing. You should be in hospital.'

Lees hardly needed a medical doctor to tell him that. He felt his hand tighten around the revolver hidden beneath his blanket. The nearest Allied lines were over fifty miles away and the plains were crawling with the enemy, so where exactly did the doctor suggest he find a hospital? His mind flipped to thoughts of Gwen, the woman he'd only recently married. Thank God she didn't know of his plight. Most likely, she would be asleep right now, dreaming of their future together, but that future had never felt so far away.

The doctor left. He was right: Lees did need to get to hospital. The question was, how? It was then that Antonio, the local resistance leader, showed himself. He'd not wanted the doctor to see him, or at least not in his present role. He was small and wiry and dressed in a thick leather coat, but the most remarkable thing about him was his weapon: he had a big German Spandau slung across his chest, which quite simply dwarfed him.

Having introduced himself, he gave it to Lees straight. 'The Germans are searching everywhere for you. You must move tomorrow. It's not safe to stay here.'

'But how can we do that?' Lees asked.

Antonio shrugged, unconcernedly. 'Ah, we will find a way. We can do nothing at night. There is a curfew and patrols everywhere following your attack.'

'So how did it go?' Lees couldn't help but be curious.

Antonio's face creased into a smile. Ambulances had been buzzing to and fro for twenty-four hours, he explained, ferrying the wounded to the hospital in Reggio. At the town's cemetery, ranks of fresh graves had been dug. Villa Calvi was a gutted wreck, and Villa Rossi was fire-scorched and deserted. As for the Germans, they seemed both terrified and furious in equal measure.

Antonio pulled out a cutting from a local Fascist paper and handed it to Lees. 'Last night a strong force of bandits attacked the garrison stationed at Botteghe,' the report said. 'After fierce fighting they withdrew, having suffered heavy losses. It is believed these brigands were British and some damage was done.'

Apart from the disinformation it contained, one other thing did make Lees smile: Farran's piping of 'Highland Laddie' had clearly done the trick. A British signature had been stamped indelibly on the 14th Army HQ raid, and there had been no mention in the article of any reprisals.

'Did we kill the general?' Lees asked, popping the question foremost in his mind.

'I don't know,' Antonio answered. 'Many officers were killed, and he has not been seen since.'

With that Antonio left, promising to return later with a plan for how they might move the two wounded men. Instinctively, Lees liked the resistance leader. He seemed a straight-talker and remarkably unfazed by their present predicament. Once Antonio was gone, the young women injected Lees and Gordon with morphine, to help ease the pain. That done they closed the bales of hay around them, leaving them to sleep.

Sometime later Lees was shaken awake. A hand closed around his mouth, as a voice hissed close on his ear: 'Don't make a sound.' It was one of the nurses.

Beside him, Gordon had his back propped against some bales and his pistol gripped in hand. Outside, Lees could hear a woman wailing in distress.

'Fascists,' the nurse murmured. '*Brigate Nere*. They are searching everywhere.'

The *Brigate Nere* were known for their bloodthirsty brutality. If they were discovered, he and Gordon would have no choice but to go down fighting. Lees struggled onto his one good knee, readying his pistol. Neither man would want to be taken alive.

He gestured to the rear of the barn, eyeing the nurses worriedly. 'For God's sake, slip away now, while you still have a chance.'

The nearest one smiled. 'We are partisans too, and you are in *my* charge,' she said with emphasis, revealing the tiny revolver she had hidden in the palm of her hand. 'Lie down,' she added, 'and keep quiet and still.'

The old woman's voice sounded nearer now. 'There is nothing there, I swear! It is only a barn.'

Then the sound of a blow and the wailing started again. The door crashed open, light flooding in. For several long seconds there was silence, as the Black Brigade militiamen scrutinised the barn's interior. Then the door crashed closed and the voices died away.

The nurse beside Lees was crying softly. 'Thank God,' she muttered, 'but we must get you away today.'

It was early on the morning of 28 March when the *Brigate Nere* had searched Lees and Gordon's place of hiding. In the Secchia valley, Roy Farran had just woken from the mother of all sleeps. Following a hurried breakfast he had a first, urgent task to perform: he needed to break cover. Heaven only knew what would happen, once he broadcast news of the past forty-eight hours, but delaying could only make matters worse for all, especially Mike Lees.

He penned a short, succinct message, stripped of any of the high emotion of the moment, and had his radio operator send it. '51 Corps HQ attacked night of 26/27. Fair success. Heavy casualties. Fierce resistance. 40 German dead, one villa blown up, other partially destroyed. LEES wounded.'

Lord only knew what would result. Had Farran done enough to avoid the repercussions that the message might provoke? He just didn't know. More to the point, he had bigger things to worry about just now. His friend and fellow commander was wounded and at the mercy of the enemy, plus shortly the Secchia valley was bound to have visitors. Unwelcome ones.

'I expected the German reaction to our impudence would not be long delayed,' Farran wrote. 'And I was right.'

Farran's first priority was to muster the valley's defenders. That morning, he despatched Lieutenant Harvey back to the all-important Cisa Box, their final redoubt, boasting their 75mm howitzer, Molto Stanco. Runners were sent to the defensive positions scattered around the perimeter, carrying the same warning: they were to expect the enemy to come in strength and driven on by anger at the success of the Botteghe raid.

That morning Farran received the first worrying reports. Four columns of German troops were pushing towards the mouth of the Secchia valley, boasting some four hundred troops. They came equipped with mortars, two field guns and horse-drawn transport, which was not such an unusual form of carriage for German infantry moving through such terrain.

Facing them Farran had Lieutenant Mike Eld, a man hand-picked to hold this position. But Eld commanded a perilously thin line. Dug in on high ground overlooking the Secchia river, he had ten fellow SAS, armed with one mortar, one Vickers heavy machine gun and several Brens. On paper, it was something of a David versus Goliath confrontation, but thankfully Eld's tiny force was stiffened by the brigade of Garibaldini led by Gianni, the finest partisans in the entire valley, Farran believed.

As with Eld and his SAS, the Garibaldini had dug trenches along the ridgeline. So long as the river was in spring flood – swollen by meltwaters – their positions should hold against a full-frontal attack. The Germans advanced to the river's northern bank, from where savage battle was joined. Mortar barrages and machine-gun volleys scorched back and forth across the Secchia's boiling waters, as Eld targeted the enemy's chief point of vulnerability – their horse-drawn transport.

Lieutenant Eld had been busy while his commander was away, raiding the Botteghe headquarters. Repeatedly, he'd crossed the Secchia and paced out the distances to key targets, noting them down for future reference. As a result, as soon as a horse-drawn gun-carriage was spotted, Eld could call out distance and bearing to his mortar team and the shells would rain down. It must have been utterly unnerving for the enemy, who were blessed with no such foresight.

Typically, Eld had set upon some highly imaginative means to wrong-foot the enemy, and to make his tiny force seem far more numerous than it was. He got his men to open up with the Vickers machine gun, via pre-established lines. The Vickers was peculiarly suited to being fired in a parabolic trajectory, so effectively lobbing rounds over long range and from behind cover. In that way enemy troops were hit by savage bursts of highly-accurate fire, with little idea whence it came. It left the impression that multiple such weapons were in action.

Eld had signs posted along the riverbank warning of minefields. To give substance to such – imaginary – barriers, he had his men detonate charges of dynamite along the river, using timer-pencils (time-delay fuses). By such means, they had charges going off at all times of the day and night. Eld got the better of the first bruising exchanges of fire, but Farran remained concerned. His chief fear was that his front-line forces would run out of mortar and machine-gun rounds, for resupply by air was always an issue.

Accordingly, he mounted up his diminutive pony – the black stallion Jock Easton had procured for him – and rode out to the front-line. There he linked up with Gianni, the Garibaldini commander, who offered to guide him onwards, cautioning that they should continue on foot. Leaving his horse behind, Farran pushed ahead, as the rattle of machine-gun fire and the boom of exploding mortars grew ever louder. With Gianni warning him to keep his head down, they clambered into a trench, which led to the ridge top position.

Eld seemed delighted to have visitors. Having given Farran a quick tour of his positions, he asked for news of the raid and especially any casualties. Farran told him what he knew. Jock Milne, the medic, was working wonders at his Tapignola church-cum-hospital. That morning, the wounded Mulvey had arrived, after a hair-raising flight through enemy-held terrain and a miraculous escape. Jock Milne had already got to work stabilising his injuries. Mike Lees and Gordon were badly hurt, and they had been hidden under the very noses of the enemy. Farran was working on a plan to try to pluck them to safety.

Though saddened at the news of the loss of Riccomini and Guscott, who were hugely popular members of the SAS, Eld and his men were boosted by the success of the raid. As Farran scanned the enemy positions through his field glasses, Eld explained that he feared the Germans were there to stay. He'd landed a barrage of mortar bombs in the midst of a horse-drawn column and machine-gunned groups of infantry, but the grey-uniformed troops kept coming.

Eld reckoned they were establishing some kind of a forward base, in preparation for the big push. From what he observed, Farran had to agree. He ordered a show of strength, directing a pin point accurate mortar barrage that blasted into one of the enemy's positions, scattering their troops. But the Germans answered quickly and in kind, their field guns belching smoke and flame, 88mm shells tearing into the ridgeline and sending the defenders diving for cover.

Faced with such firepower Eld's force were outgunned, and as the enemy built its strength, they were heavily outnumbered. But whatever it might take, the enemy had to be prevented from crossing the Secchia, for the river was the Allied Battalion's crucial defensive line. If that was breached, the forces of the enemy could sweep into the valley all but unhindered.

With the Germans' initial build-up 'the position was becoming serious,' Farran concluded, 'and I was even more worried when I received reports of the arrival of enemy reinforcements.' He didn't doubt that more and fierce action was coming.

Sure enough, on 1 April – Easter Sunday – 1945, the German battalions would launch their drive across the river, aiming to tear deep into the valley, and they would catch its defenders by surprise. Farran had twice disobeyed orders to poke a stick into the hornet's nest deeper and harder than any special forces had ever done before.

The enemy would come seeking vengeance at a fittingly ominous juncture – April Fool's Day.

Chapter 19

At Florence headquarters, Farran's radio message had landed like a bombshell. Upon learning that the raid on the 14th Army HQ had gone ahead regardless, there was utter consternation from all quarters bar one – veteran Operation Galia commander, Bob Walker-Brown.

'My reaction was at first one of absolute admiration,' Walker-Brown declared, upon learning of the news, 'but I was prepared for . . . a fairly sizeable rocket from Headquarters . . . In the event I found little difficulty in presenting the senior staff officers with the facts of life at the Partisan sharp end.'

Walker-Brown hailed the raid as being one of the SAS's 'most heroic actions and brave and effective attacks'. He made it clear that it would never have happened had they been forced to stand down. 'There's no doubt in my mind that had Roy Farran accepted a go-slow order, that operation would . . . have disintegrated.' But his was sadly a lonely voice in the wilderness.

Senior Allied commanders bemoaned the growing tendency of partisan leaders all along the front to take matters into their own hands, stressing that they had absolutely 'no authority to defy the central command'. In their eyes the raid on the 14th Army headquarters was even worse, for in this case, it was Allied commanders who had chosen to disobey orders. It hardly set the kind of example they sought.

Of the Botteghe raid, SOE's Charles Macintosh would conclude: 'It was all a great pity since, had it been ten days later, the attack on the Corps HQ would have brought a major contribution to the all-out effort, and the brave men who participated would have received greater recognition.'

Far from receiving 'great recognition', the top brass proposed that Farran be court-martialled for his flagrant breach of orders. It was only when US Colonel Riepe pointed out that the SAS commander had to be given free rein to defend the Secchia valley, that such sentiments were shelved. Shelved but not forgotten. Retribution for his insubordination could wait – that was if he survived the coming showdown.

As for the badly wounded Lees, his punishment was already being meted out. Even as he'd suffered his terrible injuries, so his replacement BLO, his namesake, John Lees, was being readied to parachute into the Secchia valley. While Mike Lees lay trapped on the plains of the Po, fighting for his life and surrounded by the enemy, John Lees was taking over his field of command – just as war red in tooth and claw was coming to the valley.

After his visit to Lieutenant Eld's front-line positions, Farran was back at his Secchio base by 31 March, where he got busy hatching a plot to rescue Mike Lees. It was to be as audacious and daring as anything that he had ever conceived. During the weeks that he'd spent in Florence agitating for a mission, Farran had stumbled across some highly unusual characters in the shadowy employ of the SOE. One was the Italian fighter ace Flight Lieutenant Furio Lauri, recently installed at Florence's Rosignano Airbase.

The tales of Furio Lauri's exploits were legion – most notably a series of breathtaking rescues of downed Allied airmen from behind enemy lines. In the most recent, in February 1945 Lieu-tenant James of the 12th (US) Air Force had been forced to eject from his stricken fighter plane. As he'd bailed out he'd collided with the tail of his own aircraft, further smashing up his leg upon landing.

He'd ejected over the plain of the Po, near the city of Parma, some fifty kilometres north-west of the Secchia valley. Rescued by the resistance, it was arranged via radio to lift him out for urgent medical attention. The mission would be flown by Lauri in his Fieseler Storch, the spotter aircraft that he could practically land on a sixpence.

From Rosignano Lauri had taken off in the long-legged ungainly-looking plane and flown across the Gothic Line. He'd reached the tiny airstrip only to find it menaced by strong cross-winds. He'd landed anyway, but in the process had damaged the Storch's spindly landing gear and its single propeller. The aircraft was stranded, as was Lauri and the wounded American pilot. Worse still, the Storch made a hugely visible target.

Lauri ordered the aircraft to be wheeled behind a barn and cov-ered in brushwood, so as to conceal it. The village carpenter and blacksmith began to fashion replacement landing gear, using the parts of an old bicycle, the bodged-together repairs being bolted to the airframe. But attempts to craft a replacement propeller from wood proved beyond them. Instead, Charles Macintosh, back at the SOE's Florence headquarters, managed to persuade a senior Allied commander to loan him the propeller from his own Storch, which was used to fly air-liaison missions.

The propeller was carefully wrapped and loaded into a Mitchell B-25's bomb bay. It was parachuted into the stranded pilot, where-upon it was bolted onto the Storch. Furio Lauri duly took to the air, the wounded Lieutenant James riding shotgun. At Rosignano Airbase a team of press reporters and senior US commanders awaited the heroes' return. Upon touchdown, Lieutenant James gave his first interview to US Armed Forces Radio as he was being stretchered to a waiting ambulance, a proud Furio Lauri walking beside him.

Farran concluded that what Lauri had done for Lieutenant James he could also do for Mike Lees. But there were enormous challenges. First, they'd need somehow to spirit Lees out of the hornet's nest of enemy forces now crawling over the plains. Second, they'd need to get him – and possibly Gordon, depending on the extent of his injuries – to a usable airstrip. And third, Farran would need to persuade the SOE top brass to pull out all the stops, for without them no such mission was going to be possible.

SOE headquarters already had an inkling as to how serious were Mike Lees' injuries. On 31 March they'd received the first official casualty report telegraphed from the field. It read: 'Capt. Michael Lees. Wounded on 26 March 1945. 3 Bullets left thigh.' Highly inaccurate, it did nevertheless record that Lees had been shot multiple times, while doing little to reflect how truly desperate was his predicament.

Aware of Lees' recent, distinctly 'undiplomatic' letters and missives, Farran sent a short radio message to Macintosh, in an effort to build bridges. 'From ROY to CHARLES. Sorry to hear LEES in disgrace owing to his rude signals . . .' It was followed by Farran's desperate plea for help. 'MIKE's condition critical. Operation essential. Carrying to PALANZANO . . . Warn HOLLAND and lay on Torch pick up . . . Ack when laid on.'

Major Charles Holland was one of the neighbouring BLOs.

His territory lay closest to Lees' hideout, and he was known to possess a tiny but usable airstrip situated near the village of Palanzano. 'Torch' was code for the Storch – Furio Lauri's distinctive, do-anything aircraft, with its unrivalled short take-off and landing capabilities.

Farran sent that plea for help early on the morning of 1 April 1945, the very day that he was to learn of the enemy's potentially catastrophic breakthrough in the Secchia valley. But first, Mike Lees was to have unexpected visitors.

At his hideout Lees was oblivious to all but his and Gordon's dire fate. Right now, their very survival hung by the slenderest of threads. Thankfully, in Spandau-toting Antonio they had an ally beyond compare. It was dawn when a horse-drawn cart turned up at the old woman's farmstead, piled high with manure. Nothing so remarkable about that. But this cart contained a false bottom – a compartment constructed beneath the thick and oozing load.

Lees and Gordon were helped aboard, dark liquid seeping from the dung above and soaking into their bandages and hair. Despite the extreme discomfort – not to mention the deleterious effect a good dousing in manure-juice might have on their wounds – the carriage proved a stroke of genius. For twelve agonising kilometres they jolted along tracks thick with enemy forces, but no one seemed particularly keen to search the cart and its pungent cargo too thoroughly.

In this way they were brought to a safe house on the outskirts of Reggio Emilia – well out of the dragnet cast by an enraged enemy. By now Lees' leg appeared to be paralysed, and he was so weak from his injuries that he could barely move. But at the safe house Antonio had worked miracles. Resistance fighters armed with machine guns stood watch in neighbouring buildings, forming a cordon around their place of hiding. There the nurses were installed on permanent duty, and a motor car made ready in the courtyard, in case they had to make a rapid getaway.

Fresh dressings, medicines and morphine had been readied, all stolen from a local hospital. Their host, a short and sturdy farmer very much in Antonio's mould, seemed utterly unperturbed at their presence and the untold dangers it brought. He busied himself preparing fine meals, washed down with choice bottles of wine. Gordon's father, who lived locally, even paid a visit, bearing gifts of soap, toothbrushes and shaving gear.

A second doctor came to inspect the wounded men. Gordon's leg was troubling him, and it turned out not to have been set properly. When that doctor, a Dr Chiesi, had finished dealing with it, he turned his attentions to Lees. He proved to be a very different kettle of fish to his predecessor: he cared passionately for the cause of the resistance and showed little fear of the enemy.

By the time he had finished inspecting Lees' wounds, Dr Chiesi's expression was grim. 'The nerve in your leg is severed,' he announced, gravely. 'If it is not repaired within ten days it will die completely.'

'What exactly does that mean?' Lees pressed.

'That unless you have an operation, you may never again be able to work that leg properly. You might walk about in irons, but it would never again be normal.'

Lees blanched. 'Well, I can't get to a hospital, as you know. Can you operate on me here?'

The doctor gestured at their surroundings. 'It would be impossible. There is no proper light, no equipment, and you would need to lie absolutely still. No, I could not do it. Here, it is impossible, I am afraid.'

Once the doctor was gone, Lees reflected upon his predicament: ten days to save his leg. Even if he were able to walk, it was impossible. Two days to the Secchia valley, maybe more; from there, a four-day trek to cross the Gothic Line and from there the march to Florence. Paralysed and unable even to stand, it was beyond hopeless. Much that Lees might rack his brains, he could think of no alternatives.

Shortly after the doctor's visit a courier arrived. It was a Stafetta, but due to Antonio's intense security she had had the devil of a time tracking down their place of hiding. She brought Lees' mail from home – delivered in a recent resupply drop – plus a note from Roy Farran. Lees ran his eager eyes over the letters from his sweetheart, Gwen. New spirit and determination ebbed into him as he read those words. He had to get out of there, for her as much as anything. Then he tore open the letter from Farran.

Dear Mike . . . You don't know how sorry we all are about
your rotten luck and will do everything we can to help
you escape. Gianni has volunteered to take his whole
Garibaldini brigade to bring you back from the plains . . .
The couriers have also volunteered to take you through
the lines if you could stand the journey. Alternatively, base
have wirelessed to say that if we can prepare a landing
ground they will send a light aircraft to fly you out. We
can do nothing, however, 'til we know where you are and
if you are fit to move.

Lees crunched some numbers. If he sent the courier back today, she would take two days to reach Secchio. One day for Gianni to prepare his partisans and they could be here in forty-eight hours.

Possibly. Moving slowly on a stretcher, Lees' ten days to save his leg would be up almost before he'd been spirited back to Secchio. More to the point, if the Garibaldini came in force and in the open on the plains, the enemy – roused to wrath by the Botteghe raid – would pounce. It wasn't even worth contemplating.

But a light aircraft putting down at an airstrip . . . Lees had heard the tales of Furio Lauri's exploits. The nearest safe strip was in BLO Holland's territory, which neighboured their own. He grabbed a map. Ten miles across the plains then twenty over the foothills – there lay the strip. But how on earth was he to complete such a journey?

Farran signed off his note, stressing that the Botteghe raid had been 'a good night's work and we are preparing for plenty more. The Partisans are in fine fettle. I only wish you were here to lead them. Bert is prostrated; he wanders around Secchio murmuring, "I knew it would happen. I warned the silly bastard!"' This was a reference to Bert Farrimond, Lees' radio operator, whose premonition that something bad would happen had seemingly come to pass.

That evening Antonio came to visit. Lees explained his predicament and asked if there was anything he could suggest. Antonio thought for a moment, before a wicked gleam came into his eye.

'I can't promise, but I have an idea,' he ventured.

'What is it?' Lees pushed, eagerly.

Antonio smiled, enigmatically. 'I will say nothing more. But tomorrow, I will return.' With that he was gone.

As Lees' longed-for escape seemed just a little more tangible, so Roy Farran was about to embark upon a ferocious battle for survival himself – and for all in the Secchia valley.

The runner woke him at three o'clock on the morning of 1 April 1945, bearing alarming news. German troops had launched a surprise attack, advancing in force at night and crossing the all-important River Secchia. They'd opted to bypass Lieutenant Eld's positions, striking instead at the line supposedly held by Don Carlo and his Green Flames. Resistance had crumbled, especially since Don Carlo's brother had been killed in the fighting, which resulted in the warrior-priest himself losing heart.

'If the reports were correct,' Farran concluded, 'the Germans were already deep into our valley,' and Lieutenant Eld's forces were 'threatened with encirclement'. Knowing how fragile the partisans' morale tended to be, he worried that 'the slightest pressure would put them to flight'. He was hardly surprised when the first reports filtered in of partisan units taking to the hills.

The move by the enemy was unexpected, swift and astute. They'd struck by the Secchia valley's weakest point, and the 'only solution that might save our base was to drive the Germans back across the river', Farran reasoned. He sent a runner to Eld, with orders to hold his positions at all costs. A second runner was despatched to Tapignola, to warn those based at the church to ready themselves for immediate battle. Jock Easton was told to take the Allied Battalion and march north to reinforce Eld's positions, in an effort to stabilise the front-line.

Meanwhile, Farran would meet the enemy head-on, in an effort to 'halt the German advance before our entire position in the valley crumbled'. A third runner was sent to Modena, to muster his Russians. Farran desperately needed their help spearheading the full-frontal counter-attack that he was contemplating. Orders given and plan of battle sorted, he set out on his tiny black steed, Whoa Mahomet, to lead his men into battle.

As the dawn sky brightened, Farran spied the disturbing evidence of how far the enemy had broken through: hundreds of refugees were on the move, driving herds of cattle and sheep deeper into the hills. The entire valley was awash with figures like swarms of ants, which was so unusual at such an hour. Here and there he spied the distinctive forms of groups of armed fighters, as bands of partisans headed for whatever refuge they could find. The German drive was in danger of becoming an out-and-out rout.

Shortly, Farran ran into the first group of Green Flames fleeing in the opposite direction – away from the advancing enemy. They told alarming stories of their commander being inconsolable at the loss of his brother, and of the Germans advancing in unassailable strength. The shock and surprise of the night attack had served only to fuel such fears.

Farran pressed on, dispensing with his trusty steed as the noise of battle drew closer. Finally, he reached a low ridge where the Green Flames' rearguard were in contact with the enemy. Twenty-odd veterans lay behind the cover of a hillock, facing the enemy's foremost units – German machine-gunners positioned on a hill about two hundred yards away. These men had been fighting for hours now, in a desperate effort to stabilise a chaotic retreat and with no effective command: they were overjoyed to see the familiar figure of the SAS major.

Farran belly-crawled the last few yards to join them. Via his field glasses he studied the enemy lines for a few long moments, before rolling over to question one of the partisans. An instant later a fierce burst of fire tore into the terrain where he'd just been lying, spattering Farran in grit. Had Farran needed a reminder of how desperate the present situation was, he'd just got it. He estimated the enemy had pushed three hundred troops across the river, facing which he presently had some twenty men.

'The situation was extremely dangerous,' he concluded, but if they could halt the enemy here until dark, or until the Russians arrived, 'we still had a chance of saving the valley.' Those chances were about to get a boost from an entirely unexpected quarter.

Farran had been on the ridge for about an hour, trading fire with the enemy, when John Lees – Mike Lees' replacement BLO – arrived. Tall, dark and powerfully built, John Lees struck Farran as looking very much like the Black Owl fighters that he had inherited from his predecessor. He had brought twenty of those elite warriors with him, and as bullets tore around their heads Farran pointed out the nearest enemy positions.

John Lees appeared to be 'no man to run at the first whistle of bullets,' Farran concluded. He spread the Black Owls along the ridgeline, lending the valley's defenders a total force of forty. Equally important, he'd managed to bring two Bren guns and a good quantity of ammunition. Farran explained the key priority was to somehow make the enemy believe they were facing a far stronger force than they really were.

As the sun rose higher, signal flares continued to arc into the sky. Worryingly, they seemed to be aimed to the rear of Farran's line now, suggesting that the enemy were moving behind his position, executing an encirclement. From the north-west he could hear the echo of battle, indicating that Lieutenant's Eld's forces were in action. All across a wide front the enemy seemed to be advancing, and Farran could only hope that Jock Easton had reached Eld's positions in time.

It became roasting-hot on the ridgeline, but Farran could afford no retreat to any place promising shade. At the slightest sign of weakness he felt certain the enemy would be up and at them. Their positions here simply had to hold. For three hours they sweated in the heat, as machine-gun fire whipped along the ridgeline, bullets whining as they ricocheted off the hard, sun-baked earth. Farran could only hope that the enemy didn't mount a full-frontal charge, for his line was bound to crumble and break.

He kept loosing off shots with his carbine, aiming at the distinctive grey helmets of the German gunners. It seemed to take an age before he detected the pounding of approaching feet – boots thumping upon the rough track behind. The voices confirmed it: it was Modena and his Russians. Heedless of the bullets that whipped after him, Farran raced down the slope to meet them.

It turned out that the Russian commander had been one step ahead of Farran: as soon as he'd heard the sounds of fighting, he had got his men on the move. After a good amount of back-slapping, Farran explained the plan to Modena, using Lieutenant Stephens, his Austrian Jewish SAS man, as interpreter. Surprisingly, Modena seemed eager for what Farran suggested – a full frontal charge to drive the Germans out of their positions, after which they'd chase them back across the Secchia river. Dramatic and near-suicidal, it seemed to appeal to the Russian commander no end.

Modena suggested one refinement to the plan. His men had completed the forced march laden down with a three-inch mortar and rounds. They would begin the assault with a softening-up barrage. That agreed, Modena broke out a bottle of grappa, took a large swig, passed the bottle on and kissed his Italian girlfriend, before yelling out orders. His men listened intently, and almost before he'd finished they doubled up the hillside to join the ridge-line's defenders.

As Modena took charge of the mortar team, Farran paused to shake hands and wish him luck, before returning to his position in the centre of the line. After a few false starts, the Russian mortar crew seemed to find their range and began to scatter high-explosive shells among the German positions. As the mortar barrage grew to a crescendo, so the combined force of partisans and SAS began to pour fire into the enemy, scores of Brens, Stens and tommy guns hammering in the rounds, long tongues of burning tracer licking across the terrain.

With the Germans' heads well down, Farran clambered to his feet atop the ridge. Raising an arm above his head he gestured first to the right side and then to the left, urging all to rise up and follow. He was about to set off when he realised that not a soul had stirred from their positions, and as bullets cut the air to either side of him he dived back into cover. It was late-afternoon by now and if they didn't seize the initiative shortly, darkness would fall and it would be too late.

A few moments later Farran steeled himself once more, this time yelling for all to follow and dashing forwards several paces, so as to set an example. A handful of Russians got to their feet, but no more, and sustained bursts of enemy fire soon drove them scurrying back again. Farran lay in cover gasping for breath, wondering what to do. Maybe it might be a case of third time lucky. Or maybe the third time he raised his head from cover, he would get it blown off.

Shouting, yelling and berating all to find their courage, Farran sprang to his feet once more and began to dash down the slope. One by one the Russians rose behind him, cheering wildly. A ragged line formed up and began to sweep downhill, chaotically at first but gaining in shape and energy as more and more joined the surge. Farran sensed that this time he would carry the partisans with him. Sure enough the wild mob thickened, as scores of screaming fighters began to thunder towards the nearest enemy positions.

On Farran's right he could see Stephens in the vanguard, leading the surge. To his left, fittingly, was the distinctive figure of Modena, driving his men on. Once, twice, Farran stumbled on the rough ground, but the momentum was well and truly unstoppable by now. Incredibly, the Italians – moved by the dramatic spectacle and the stirring war-cries – began to outpace the more solidly built Russians. Soon, they were in the very vanguard of the charge. The line of bearded, unwashed wild-men, yelling curses in a colourful mixture of languages, swept towards the enemy, the Italians firing long bursts from the hip as they went.

As they closed on the enemy their line began to break before the barbarian horde. Along a broad front Farran saw red Very lights arc into the sky – presumably the signal for retreat. He was now lagging well behind the vanguard, but he witnessed one of the enemy's more-dramatic attempts to make a stand. Taking cover in a white-walled farmhouse, a group of German troops were overwhelmed as crazed partisans seemed to charge right through their bullets, unleashing long bursts of tracer as they ran.

An Italian partisan wielding a Bren led the final assault, the Russians close on his heels. He unleashed a torrent of fire at point-blank range through the windows, as moments later grey-uniformed figures stumbled out with their hands held high. The partisans took few prisoners – gunning down most of the enemy. The frenzied bloodlust that Farran had unleashed was beyond anyone's control, the Germans throwing down their weapons and fleeing.

Farran struggled on, trying his best to keep up. A wild young partisan, long dark hair flowing in the breeze, came up to him and pumped his hand enthusiastically. He had sweat pouring down his features. 'Maggiore McGinty,' he exclaimed, 'what a wonderful *Festa di Pasqua*' – Easter Festival. Good point, Farran thought: it was after all Easter Sunday.

With that the partisan ran off to join the melee, leaving Farran alone in the fading light. The enemy advance the previous night had been ordered and seemingly unstoppable; their retreat the following evening was a rout. As they tried to cross piecemeal back over the swollen Secchia they were gunned down by their pursuers, or they strayed unwittingly into the range of Lieutenant Eld's and Jock Easton's guns.

'By nightfall not a single enemy soldier remained alive on our side . . .' Farran remarked. 'It was an accomplishment that surprised me no less than the enemy . . . For the first time the Reggio partisans had outfought a German Battalion, completely defeating it.'

The Secchia would run red that night.

Chapter 20

As evening faded to darkness Farran found himself alone. The sporadic sounds of fighting drifted across to him – the final mopping-up operations. It was a starlit night and he was cold and beyond exhausted. He was forced to trudge his weary way back to Secchio, his horse being nowhere to be found. Now and again he stopped to drink from a muddy puddle, so desperate was he to quench his thirst.

As he stumbled along in the dark Farran ran into a familiar figure: it was Colonel Monti, the 'commander-in-chief' of the Reggio partisans. Immaculate as ever, he sat astride his big brown mare, wearing riding jodhpurs and with a smart crop in hand. Farran saluted, and Colonel Monti informed him that he was riding out to join the battle.

'*Mon colonel*, the Germans are utterly defeated,' Farran informed him, in his best schoolboy French, the only language that he and the colonel shared. 'We have driven them back across the river.'

Colonel Monti looked incredulous. He asked Farran to repeat himself, as if unable to grasp that it might be true, or perhaps fearing that he had misunderstood Farran's French.

'The Germans are beaten,' Farran told him, by way of the simplest explanation he could muster. 'It is a great victory.'

The colonel stared, wide-eyed with amazement, before whipping his steed around and cantering off towards the front. Farran could appreciate the colonel's consternation. The victory was unprecedented. It just went to show what irregular forces could achieve when given the right leadership and the self-belief that was so crucial to any battle.

Following the dramatic turn-around, Farran – together with John Lees – decided it was time to shout it from the rooftops. If the partisans could hear of their exploits earning widespread renown, it would stiffen their spirit for future sorties. And as Farran well knew, with Allied forces poised to punch through the Gothic Line, soon the partisans would be called upon to hit the enemy hard. Boosting their morale right now was critical.

John Lees sent a plea to Macintosh to that effect: 'Please ask PWB to broadcast on ITALIA COMBATTE a programme praising the REGGIO . . . formations. A mention of the counter-attack on Easter day when three coys of Germans were chased back over the R. SECCHIA . . . leaving 20 dead and 30 prisoners would do. I really want this as the MODENA AND PARMA DIVS have been mentioned, but never my lads.'

'PWB' was the Psychological Warfare Bureau, the Psychological Warfare Division by another name. The Modena and Parma divisions were neighbouring bands of partisans. Notably, while stressing the challenges of replacing such a towering figure as Mike Lees – 'It was difficult taking over without anybody who really understood the form' – John Lees was already referring to the partisans as 'my lads'. He'd got his feet well and truly under the table at Secchio and he'd led the spirited counter-attack from the front.

As for Mike Lees, he was about to begin a journey of epic proportions, one that would determine whether he would live or die.

*

The maverick SOE agent and his resistance leader guardian, Antonio, had set upon a plan of unprecedented audacity to spirit him away to the hills. Recognising that Mike Lees couldn't survive such a back-breaking journey hidden under a heap of manure, they'd decided to resort to a spot of inspired thievery and bluff.

Desperate times called for desperate measures, and in that spirit Antonio had got his men to hijack a German field ambulance. The first Lees knew of this was a visit by Antonio, shortly after dusk on 3 April. One glance at the man's face told Lees that he was bringing good news.

'You must be ready at dawn tomorrow morning,' Antonio announced. 'An ambulance will take you into the mountains, speeding you through the checkpoints.'

Lees was overjoyed. By his reckoning he had six days left to save his leg. If they could get the Storch in to the landing zone to rendezvous with the ambulance, he might just make it. To that effect he scribbled two notes for Antonio to deliver via courier. One was to Farran explaining their plans, and asking him to contact Florence and request the aircraft. The other was to Charles Holland, asking him to make ready the airstrip.

It was the early hours of the following morning when Lees awoke to footsteps on the stairs outside his room. As his hand went to his weapon, the door opened softly. A candle spluttered by his bedside, throwing the mystery visitor into faint light and shadow: to Lees, it looked suspiciously like a man dressed in the full grey of a German army uniform.

'Who is it?' Lees barked a challenge.

By way of answer there was a short, throaty laugh, as the figure pushed the peaked forage cap up from his forehead. 'Sir, your ambulance awaits!' he announced. It was Antonio.

Under the cover of darkness Lees and Gordon were loaded aboard the waiting vehicle – a square-bodied truck, iconic red cross symbols as tall as a man emblazoned across its roof and side. This was only stage one of the journey, Antonio warned. If they made it across the plains, blagging their way through the German checkpoints, they could get only so far into the hills. Eventually, Lees and Gordon would have to transfer into a bullock cart, for the going would be too difficult for the truck. Even so, as they set forth into the pre-dawn darkness Lees felt buoyed by a spirit of hope.

But even as that hijacked ambulance rumbled through the dark streets of Reggio Emilia, so an urgent cypher message was winging its way to London from SOE Florence headquarters. It made clear that even should Lees survive the coming journey and escape, he was about to face a witch-hunt . . . regardless.

'In a recent engagement Capt Michael LEES rpt LEES wounded in leg as a result of an attack made by him contrary to orders. It is thought possible he may have acted under orders issued by Major FARRAN of SAS, but matter will be fully investigated on his return. As LEES' condition said to be critical am attempting exfiltration by special Op on 5th, rpt 5th.'

Even if Lees' life and his leg could be saved, he was seemingly being rescued in part so that he could face the music. Farran, likewise, was far from exonerated, despite having rallied the defenders of the Secchia valley. There were others of Lees' brothers-in-arms who were facing dark troubles the likes of which none might have reasonably foreseen.

As Lees settled back in the ambulance for the ride of his life, so Paul Morton, the Canadian reporter with whom he had shared the Operation Flap mission, was also in the line of fire.

In early April 1945 a query arrived in London from SOE's New York office, which used the cover name of the Inter Services Research Bureau (ISRB). 'A newspaper correspondent called Paul Morton has been writing articles and making broadcasts ... describing his experiences after being dropped in occupied territory in Northern Italy. If he has in fact been employed as an agent, some of his statements are indiscreet ...'

A flurry of further messages arrived at the SOE's London headquarters, questioning Morton's 'indiscretions' and his credentials. 'I note from our records MORTON was employed in July, 1944, as an attached correspondent with MARYLAND. Will you kindly advise ... if he was, in fact, dropped in Italy and whether he was given any authority to write articles and make broadcasts ...'

Morton's problem was that he was now peddling an 'inconvenient truth' as many saw it – that the Italian partisans, communists included, were taking the fight to the enemy with spirit and panache. Even as the Italian resistance was being called upon to rise up and help sever the Gothic Line, fear of 'Reds' taking over meant that such exploits were to be downplayed. The schizophrenic flip-flopping of Allied policy – both to simultaneously support and subvert the Italian resistance – continued. Indeed, in April 1945 BLOs were still telegraphing from the field berating the lack of weaponry drops, due to the 'political winds of change' turning against them.

Those trying to garner support for the partisans were to be subjected to a witch-hunt. For Morton, it was to be of a signal savagery. Not content with spiking his stories, his ten-year stint as a reporter with the *Toronto Daily Star* came to a sudden end. Morton was sacked, with no credible explanation as to why. Quietly, secretly, a report had been written accusing Morton of making up his tales of operations behind the lines, branding him a liar and rendering him utterly unemployable. By April 1945 his reputation had been comprehensively mauled and lay in tatters.

Fortunately for Roy Farran, the fact that he was needed by Allied commanders, the Americans first and foremost, rendered him immune to such predations – for now. He was about to be called upon to rouse his Allied Battalion to spearhead an assault on Highway Twelve, one of the key resupply routes feeding the Gothic Line. In short, Farran, despite his rather flexible inter-pretation of orders, was seen as being indispensable. By contrast Mike Lees, badly wounded and out of action, was fair game.

Even as he fought for his very life, considerable efforts were being devoted to nailing him. A flurry of messages sought to prove that he had received the signal to stand down the Botteghe raid, and that it had been deliberately ignored. One read: 'A personal message was sent to Major FARRAN and Capt LEES advising them that the attack should be postponed ... Confir-mation that Capt LEES and Major FARRAN received this signal [to stand down] was given ... 26 Mr 45.'

Another provided London with a searing indictment of Lees' supposed record in the field. 'This officer gave considerable trouble from the time he was first infiltrated. He was resentful of all orders ... and his attitude towards these is typified by the extracts from letters written by him in the Field (attached as Appendix "B").'

Some of Lees' more colourful and forthright messages were appended to that report and they made for damaging reading. In short, the knives were out for him. Farran, meanwhile, received Lees' hand written message about his escape by hijacked German ambulance with a surge of hope: maybe his friend was about to be plucked to safety, after all?

At the same time – 5 April 1945 – Farran received urgent orders in the field. He was warned that the main Allied offensive to breech the Gothic Line had begun, but that it had run into ferocious resistance. He was urged to take his Allied Battalion and make all efforts to hit and harass enemy traffic on Highway Twelve, the main supply route for two German divisions manning the key section of the Gothic Line. There was no time to delay.

Thankfully, a fresh pair of hands had just been parachuted in to boost Farran's command. On 4 April 1945 Colonel Hardt's DC3s had flown yet another resupply mission over the Secchia valley. Along with the crates of mortars, heavy machine-gun rounds, grenades and ammunition, they'd parachuted in a distinctive figure – Karl Nurk, the Estonian big game hunter, irregular warfare veteran and fluent Russian speaker.

In recent months Nurk had been serving with the Special Boat Service, operating across the Aegean, the stretch of sea sandwiched between Greece and Turkey. But Farran's summons – that he needed Nurk as his bridge to the Russian partisans – had duly plucked him out of the Aegean and parachuted him into the skies over Secchio.

Farran was overjoyed. 'No longer would I have to rely on Lieutenant Stephens' interpretation of Modena's German.' Nurk 'had all the likeable qualities of the Russian émigré – recklessness, a taste for wine, women and song and a perpetual sense of drama . . . He immediately made great friends with Modena and on the first night I heard them singing Russian songs together at a very late hour.' Nurk wasn't a Russian émigré, of course. He was

Estonian and had fought *against* the Russians in the Winter War. But he was the bridge that Farran longed for.

There was another key reason that Farran had agitated to have a man like Nurk – a fellow major – join him, as he prepared to launch an all-out offensive against the enemy. Tellingly, with Mike Lees gone, command of the Allied Battalion had become something of a lonely occupation. Not any more. 'A born adventurer,' Farran wrote of Nurk, 'he was as gay as his reputation and equally fearless. I felt I had found a kindred spirit.'

Striking Highway Twelve was a daunting proposition, even as a classic hit-and-run exercise. But Farran had been called upon to do so much more. He was tasked with moving the Allied Battalion lock, stock and barrel onto the plains, to savage the enemy's supply lines. It was a herculean task, breaking down all of their defensive positions and mobilising their heaviest weaponry. Even Lieutenant Harvey's 75mm howitzer, Molto Stanco, was to be brought to join the hotchpotch convoy that was being assembled – led by Hans the German deserter's captured truck and scores of lumbering ox-carts.

By 7 April Farran intended to move to within striking distance of Highway Twelve, and to somehow hide by day and attack at night, when the road tended to be chock-full with German military traffic. But to get there, the column would have to cross 'appallingly rugged country, and would, therefore, be in no condition for an immediate attack. They had to be fresh for the actual raids,' Farran cautioned, 'because utmost care would be needed for the final approach . . .' Highway Twelve ran along the top of an exposed ridge and there were no convenient gullies or defiles from which to mount ambushes.

By removing the Allied Battalion Farran knew that he was

leaving the Secchia valley vulnerable. He was warned of such by Colonel Monti, who felt as if he were deserting them. In part to deflect any reprisals, Farran charged Kirkpatrick, his piper, to execute a last-minute tour of the villages, playing at every opportunity, so as to stamp the indelible signature of 'Britishness' on all that had transpired. Kirkpatrick's was to be a whistle-stop tour, and Farran was just about to have delivered the means to make it happen.

On the night of 5/6 April 1945, Farran invited the key resistance figures – Colonel Monti, Gianni, Don Carlo, Barba Nera, Eros – to watch a truly awesome display of Allied military might in action, all orchestrated by Scalabrino, his veteran drop-zone enforcer. In part, it was to reinforce in their minds that for Italy, the hour of liberation was now at hand. Now was the moment to rise up and seize back their country.

It was well past midnight by the time the drop zone – a round-topped hill, whose sides fell away to sharp gullies – was ready. Next to the Casa Balocchi DZ, this was the next-best field, and it lay close to the exit of the valley – the route by which Farran's Victory Column would head, to hit Highway Twelve. But that also put it well within sight of the nearest enemy positions.

As Farran and the resistance leaders stood waiting, wrapped up against the night chill, his veteran W/T operator, Corporal Cunningham, employed a radio-homing set to guide the incoming planes. Known as the 'Rebecca/Eureka transponding radar', it consisted of an airborne receiver and antenna system fitted to an aircraft, to detect a radio signal transmitting from the ground-based 'Eureka' unit. The Rebecca calculated the range and position of the Eureka, based upon the timings and direction of the signal.

Bang on schedule the faint throb of straining aero-engines

echoed through the dark skies. Farran yelled for the flares to be triggered and the signal fires lit. The ghostly silhouette of an aircraft roared overhead, but it wasn't the kind of warplane that Farran was expecting. For an instant he wondered whether to douse the signals, in case it was a marauding enemy night-fighter. But just as quickly it was gone again, the heavens reverting to a starlit stillness and silence.

For Farran the wait became nerve-racking. Was this crucial piece of theatre to end in an embarrassing no-show? Some fifteen minutes behind schedule the distinctive laboured throb of heavily laden aircraft filled the skies, as a flight swept in at a lower and more purposeful altitude. Farran ordered the flares lit again. Steering a path between the high peaks, the flight of aircraft emerged from the darkness carrying their highly unusual payloads.

As the first plane thundered in, the underside of its fuselage was illuminated in the flares' harsh glare. It was a Halifax heavy bomber, but crammed into its bomb-bay was the square bulk of a Willys MB jeep, the bomb doors held open to accommodate the bulky cargo. The Halifax turned sharply and came in for its drop-run, making a beeline for the hilltop DZ. Moments later the black silhouette plummeted from the aircraft and parachutes blossomed in the air above it, one suspended from each corner.

But one of the chutes failed to open properly. It bunched up like a sack of damp washing, crushed by the jeep's slipstream. The vehicle flipped crazily, the other chutes became entangled, and moments later there were a series of harsh ripping sounds as the parachute silk was torn asunder, leaving the jeep plummeting towards earth like some kind of giant demented bomb. Screeching like a banshee the vehicle streaked towards the watchers, careering into the centre of the DZ right in the midst of the signal fires.

Thankfully, no one was hurt, but when Farran turned to reassure his distinguished guests he found that they had fled. He managed to round them up again, and in short order a second jeep was dropped, this one behaving impeccably. It swung to earth gently, suspended on its four chutes, landing with a faint crash on its sprung carriage – a bespoke steel pan fitted with springs. Within moments the DZ crew had freed the jeep from the pan, fired it up and were roaring away to clear the ground for the next load.

Four jeeps were dropped, not including the first that had broken free and torn itself to smithereens. The last was released in broad daylight in full sight of the nearest German garrisons. The drop had done wonders to stiffen the nerves of the partisan leaders and it must have been morale-sapping in the extreme for the enemy. Masses of ammo accompanied the jeeps – chiefly mortar and howitzer rounds. With the vehicles to hand, Farran had a sense that they could mount the kind of fast, mobile shoot-and-scoot warfare a target like Highway Twelve called for. It hadn't escaped his notice that with such mobility and grunt they could tow Molto Stanco into battle, pretty much at will.

Farran's Victory Column began to take shape, as those commanding the valley's perimeter defences were called in. Parachutist Murphy was dragged back from his position in the shadow of Monte Pena; Parachutist Wooding and Corporal Larley returned from their frontier outposts; and finally, Lieutenant Eld was pulled back from his front-line defences. Modena's Russians marched into the muster point, as did the choicest Garibaldini and Green Flames units. The guns on the jeeps were cleaned and they were fuelled for action. Molto Stanco was delivered by Lieutenant Harvey, who had collapsed the Cisa Box, breaking the big gun down into its constituent parts. It was reassembled and hitched to a jeep.

A trailer was parachuted in, to be towed behind a jeep piled with howitzer shells. Scores of ox-carts were requisitioned by Barba Nera, and heaped high with provisions, kit and weaponry. Likewise, mules grumbled under heavy burdens. By his deadline – 7 April – Farran's Victory Column was all but ready, one jeep remaining to be dropped in. He left David Eyton-Jones – whose feet had still not fully recovered from his frost-bitten ascent of Monte Cusna – to take charge of the last jeep.

As Farran set out at the head of his Victory Column, it was to be Eyton-Jones who was to see the first action. Shortly after his jeep was parachuted in, a US warplane plummeted from the sky with its starboard engine on fire, crashing in sight of their position. In its wake three parachutists drifted to earth, landing in an open field in clear sight of both Eyton-Jones and the enemy.

The young SAS lieutenant didn't hesitate: he mounted up the newly arrived jeep to ride to their rescue. Even as he set out, a German Kubelwagen – a Volkswagen light military vehicle and the Germans' nearest equivalent to the jeep – raced towards the downed airmen from the opposite side. Knowing that his jeep boasted some serious firepower – a Browning and a pair of Vickers K machine guns – Eyton-Jones didn't baulk. Understandably, the US airmen found it hard to believe that either force racing towards them could be friendly. This far behind the lines surely they had to be Germans.

As Eyton-Jones slammed his jeep to a halt, three figures came out of hiding with their hands held high. Even as his jeep-mounted weapons menaced the Kubelwagen, Eyton-Jones urged them to climb aboard. 'I called over that I was British,' he recalled, 'and would they get into the jeep, as I could see a German car with troops heading towards them.' The American pilot seemed confused: 'Aw, gee, my navigator must have got it all wrong.' Eyton-Jones told him otherwise. 'I assured him his navigator was quite correct, they were in German-occupied territory.'

With all aboard, Eyton-Jones ferried the bewildered US airmen back to comparative safety. After celebrating their miraculous salvation, Eyton-Jones charged Fritz Snapper to smuggle the airmen back through the lines, with an escort of McGinty's Arrows to speed them on their way. That done, he formed up at the head of the supply column of bullock carts, and on Barba Nera's orders they got underway, heading for the plains.

Hours later they were reunited with Farran's advance party. The SAS major formed his forces up into four distinct units. The first, Sun Column, consisted of five SAS plus Modena's Russians – now swelled to one hundred fighting men. Sun Column was a potent outfit, and it was assigned to hit the section of Highway Twelve where it linked up with the Gothic Line and where battle was likely to be at its fiercest. Accordingly, it was the most heavily armed, boasting Molto Stanco, three mortars, a heavy Browning machine gun, plus fifteen Brens.

The second unit, Moon Column, was commanded by Jock Easton, and consisted of twenty-five SAS plus thirty of the finest Garibaldini. Equipped with two Vickers machine guns, three mortars and ten Brens, its job was to raid the mid-section of the highway, where it cut across the plains. Star Column came next, consisting of five SAS plus sixty mixed Italian partisans, armed with three mortars, one Browning and fifteen Brens. In Farran's mind, Star Column was the weakest of the three. It was tasked with striking Highway Twelve at its most vulnerable point, where the roadway ran out of the foothills.

Finally, there was Farran's own command, Eclipse Column, which consisted of four jeeps and ten SAS. It was configured as a fast, hit-and-run force, which would strike at the kind of heavily defended targets that would put the fear of God into the enemy. With Eclipse Column in particular Farran had one aim foremost in his mind: if he could strike fast enough and with suitable potency, he hoped to convince enemy commanders that Allied forces had broken through the Gothic Line, so prompting a hell-for-leather retreat.

As the Victory Column wound its way out of the foothills, Farran ran his eye along its length: it straggled for many miles. Whoa Mahommet had been found again, and he trotted his diminutive steed this way and that, feeling an immense sense of pride. What they had achieved here, seemingly from nothing, was little short of a miracle. Just weeks back the partisans had been demoralised and in disarray. Now, they were setting forth to drive out the enemy invaders.

The SAS members of the Victory Column seemed in particularly high spirits. Even though he lacked a horse, Major Karl Nurk seemed happy to stick close to the Stafettas. The men sang as they marched, and Kirkpatrick gave the occasional blast on his bagpipes, though he was apparently lacking in treacle with which to lubricate the bag (treacle preserves the skin, while allowing moisture to wick through). Farran's men, dusty, unshaven and wearing mud-spattered and ripped uniforms, gave a cheer from beneath their faded red berets.

'They were the cream of this rag-tag army,' Farran remarked, 'and

I loved every one of them . . . there were no finer troops than these.' After weeks of training with and fighting alongside the SAS, the Italian partisans were also in fine fettle, as were the Russians. Just how fine his motley force might prove Farran was about to discover, as they crossed the Secchia and moved deeper into bandit country.

It was evening by the time Barba Nera's entire one-hundred-strong bullock cart convoy had managed to ford the river, with Eyton-Jones and his jeep to the fore. Farran formed the force up as one defensive unit and they set up camp for the night. But having made contact with headquarters, there was worrying news. Cunningham delivered a long message, which had taken an age to decode. In essence they had been ordered to strike at Highway Twelve with no delay.

'Our orders were clear for once,' Farran remarked, 'and, having contravened instructions over the [HQ] attack . . . and my very presence on the wrong side of the lines, I did not dare delay our advance . . .' He called his commanders together, to deliver the unwelcome news. Tired as they were, they would have to push on through the gathering darkness, moving far beyond the territory they had covered when striking at the Botteghe HQ.

Though they faced a gruelling night march through uncharted terrain, spirits remained high. 'As we moved into unknown country, I felt the same excitement as I knew the men felt,' Farran remarked, 'and began to watch from every vantage point for signs of the enemy.'

From his own vantage point, Farran's fellow Botteghe raid commander was also watching anxiously. In his mountain-top position, Mike Lees searched the skies for a tiny, fragile-seeming aircraft, which might pluck him to safety.

Tantalisingly, the impossible promise of salvation beckoned.

Chapter 21

Just as he had hoped, Antonio's ruse with the German ambulance had worked wonders, spiriting Mike Lees – and Gordon – through checkpoint after checkpoint. Time and again they'd slowed at the approach to an enemy roadblock set up for the very purpose of trapping them, only for the German sentries to gesture in greeting and to wave them through. Never before had Lees so appreciated the advantages of making like the enemy.

An agonising journey three days by bullock cart had followed, as they'd crawled ever higher into the mountains. Over time it had become a blurred kaleidoscope of heat, pain, agony and semi-oblivion, as he and Gordon had lain on a bed of straw, groaning and crying out at every lurch and jolt. Pitched this way and that, Lees' pain-racked, fevered imagination had relived the last few months of operations, which had been 'some of the happiest of my life'.

He remembered his arrival in January 1945 and 'running like rabbits frightened by a stoat', as the partisans had broken before the German *rastrellamento*. The long weeks of preparation that had followed, 'building an army from a rabble'. The day in late February when those same partisans had driven the Black Brigade battalion across the Secchia, trapping them and leaving very few alive, 'confirming that my work had been worthwhile'.

Then there was the questioning of Hans, the German deserter, and the first intimations of the kind of target offered by the Botteghe headquarters. Following that, 'on the crest of a wave, the advent of the parachutists and our attack on Botteghe', and all that had transpired in the aftermath of the raid. 'I thought back over . . . the wild music of those pipes and the terrible moment when I could not walk, then those anxious days hiding out in the plains, for the first time in my life helpless and relying on others . . .'

Beginning with his mission with Major Temple and ending with his terrible injuries, it had been 'A long trail, always moving, always alert, attacking, escaping, but always preparing for that day . . . when, guided by a few British officers, the partisans all over Europe would rise against the enemy.' Any day now, Lees reflected, 'the partisans, strong and united, will advance from their strongholds to drive the Germans out.' He lamented how, 'on the eve of that day, crippled and useless, I had to withdraw from the game. Hard justice indeed . . . but the mountains are cruel though fair and a wounded man is no use to them.' Still he longed to be a part of this final uprising, 'praising, cursing and encouraging' to the last.

As it was, that was never going to happen. Instead, on the morning of 6 April 1945 Mike Lees lay on a stretcher on the edge of a tiny field seemingly sliced from the very side of the mountain above the village of Ranzano. Strung along either side of the tiny, postage-stamp-sized 'airstrip' was a line of silk parachutes – markers for the incoming pilot. The strip was no more than a hundred yards long by thirty broad, so not a great deal wider than the wingspan of the inbound aircraft.

Beside Lees squatted a familiar figure – the former schoolmaster, Corporal Phil Butler, who'd served as Lees' right-hand man in Secchio. Butler had trekked across the hills to aid in Lees' evacuation, as had Kiss, the commander of his Stafettas. Lees turned to the pair of them, as all eyes scanned the sky to the south, ears straining for the noise of a light aircraft at altitude.

'Any sign?' he queried.

Butler shrugged. 'No, but it can't be long. They're due soon after ten. Not long now and you'll be in liberated territory. How're you feeling?'

'The leg hurts like hell,' Lees replied, honestly. 'Otherwise, not too bad. If all goes well that'll be fixed by tonight. Give me a hand to sit up, will you?'

Butler put his arms around Lees' broad shoulders and helped him into a sitting position. It was a magnificent morning. All around them spring growth, verdant green, sparkled with dew. Further north the valley carved around towards the plains, which were thick with a heat haze. South lay the humped folds of Monte Cusna – *Uomo Morto*; Dead Man – rising to the glistening white snow-cap where Eyton-Jones and Kershaw had almost met their end.

To every side woodland echoed with birdsong, and here and there blazed a riot of colour – wild primrose and crocus patches breaking into bloom. Over the months that he had soldiered here, Lees had grown to love these mountains and their people. The clear air, the open spaces, the freedom and adventure – all would soon be a thing of the past, should the aircraft reach him and pluck him to safety. But at least he should survive, and keep his health.

A cry from Butler brought Lees' mind back to the moment. 'There it is,' he yelled.

Sure enough, seemingly impossibly high above Cusna, a tiny

black speck hung in the heavens, sunlight glinting off its wings beguilingly. So slowly it seemed hardly to be moving, that speck gained shape and substance. To either side Lees could make out the dart-like forms of two further aircraft – Mustangs, circling protectively around the tiny form of the Storch.

In broad daylight, at times dropping to tree top height to avoid enemy gun batteries, at others braving high passes close to the aircraft's service ceiling, Furio Lauri had nursed the aircraft thus far, and was now beginning his approach to what appeared to be an impossible landing. Gradually, the noise of the aircraft became audible, its single engine put-puttering like a lawnmower on a hot summer's day.

The fuselage appeared impossibly spindly and improbably fragile, sandwiched between two ridiculously large, oddly curved wings. It seemed more butterfly than warplane. It circled over the tiny strip, the pilot sizing up what lay below. Would he even risk a landing, Lees wondered. He could see the pilot's face gazing out of the cockpit, as he studied the approach and the terrain, a thick frown creasing his brow.

He passed over, wingtip practically kissing the grass as he banked and dipped below the height of the field, dropping from view. Lees wondered if he had decided it was not worth the risk. The ground was rough and the strip small, plus unpredictable cross winds sheered across these mountains. The Storch made several more approaches, but each was aborted as the pilot must have figured he couldn't quite land.

Finally, Lees heard the engine note change: from a murmur, it had become almost a roar, the noise echoing up from below and rebounding across the valley. Moments later the Storch reappeared, rearing up just a few feet above the end of the strip, where it seemed to hover motionless for a second, before touching down like a great bird. It rumbled to a bumpy halt in less than a fifth of the length of the strip, in an incredible feat of airmanship.

Eager hands lifted Lees up and rushed him to the waiting aircraft. Lauri sat at the controls, engine still running, as Lees was manhandled into the seat directly behind him. The cockpit was cramped and Lauri had to struggle to get the parachute strapped to Lees' body. Figures crowded the doorway – partisans wishing good luck and godspeed. Lees shouted a few words of farewell through the door.

'Bye-bye, Phil. My love to all and a kiss for Don Pedro's mother. And tell Bert not to bust himself.' By 'Bert' he meant Bert Farrimond, his ever-faithful radio operator.

Then, as the partisans took hold of the wings and lifted the tail, Lauri brought the engine up to full power, dropped his hand to signal release and the Storch began bumping across the strip. All too soon the aircraft dipped over the edge of the field and plummeted into the abyss. For a long moment Lees feared they were done for, before the wings began to gain lift and the nose lurched violently upwards, throwing Lees back into his seat.

Having averted disaster, the pilot set a course for Cusna and, beyond that, Florence. Major Charles Holland, the BLO who had organised this daring evacuation on the ground, would refer to that airstrip as Mike Lees' 'tennis lawn . . . The pick-up to evacuate Capt. Michael Lees took place on a flat 100 yd spur with a sheer drop on three sides. The STORCH had great difficulty landing but the take-off was perfect . . . LAURI deserves a medal for his landing . . . He made 5 attempts . . . each one more dangerous than the last.'

It was eleven o'clock in the morning on 6 April 1945, when the

Storch began the long climb to overfly the snow-bound heights of Cusna, the Mustangs buzzing and swooping protectively around it. As the aircraft droned ever onwards Lees settled back into his seat, trying to ignore the pain in his leg, and little realising the trouble that he was flying into.

Upon arrival at the Rosignano airbase, he was met by a junior SOE officer whom he didn't particularly recognise. Oddly, the man seemed acutely embarrassed and Lees didn't have a clue as to why. 'At that stage I had no knowledge that they were claiming that I had ignored orders,' he remarked. 'Indeed, at no stage was I ever told this directly to my face, although my subsequent treatment reflected their displeasure very clearly. They just handed me over to the medical services and left, washing their hands of me.'

Lees was admitted to a general military hospital, in Florence, before being transferred to a similar facility in Rome. His admission records noted the following: 'He was not admitted to any medical unit or formation during the period 26 March 45 – 6 Apr 45.' Of course, that was the time that he had languished, injured, hiding and running from the enemy on the plains of the Po. That amounted to eleven days, so longer than the ten that Dr Chiesi had given him to repair his severed nerves.

Still, Lees reached hospital hopeful that his leg might be saved. Unfortunately, he was placed in a general ward, with no one to agitate and lobby for the urgent and specialist treatment that his injuries required. Utterly exhausted from his back-breaking journey, plagued by multiple gunshot wounds that hadn't been properly treated and ailing from the recent bout of malaria, Lees was hardly in a fit state to fight for the kind of treatment that he so desperately required.

'So much for the ten days and the risks taken by the partisans to get me ... promptly out,' Lees concluded. Indeed, it wouldn't be for many weeks, and only due to his family pulling strings at the very highest level, that Lees would finally get the specialist treatment that his damaged nerves required. By then much of the damage was irreparable.

'The war came while I was still young and inexperienced in human nature,' Lees would write of this time. 'I was dumb enough to believe that everybody else was motivated by a simple and straightforward desire to get on with the war. I learned about the perfidy of men and organisations the hard way ... I was a tough guerrilla leader, but stupid to a degree in dealing with staff at Base; perhaps we didn't tick the same way.'

To what degree Lees and the staff didn't 'tick' was shortly to be demonstrated, as the witch-hunt gathered pace. But for now, he was languishing in a military hospital, largely forgotten, as 'his' partisans, commanded by Roy Farran, embarked upon their last great hurrah.

In the memory of Mike Lees, the Reggio partisans were to spread chaos and havoc behind the enemy's front, helping break the spirit of the Gothic Line defenders.

Chapter 22

From his ridgetop position Farran observed the helter-skelter of enemy traffic, which crammed Highway Twelve in a riot of disarray. For two weeks now he and his Victory Column had played their part in fomenting a collapse of the German defences across a wide swathe of the Gothic Line. Their actions had commenced in a mass battle against an entire German *panzerjäger* – tank-hunter – battalion.

Surprised in a village on the approaches to Highway Twelve, the Victory Column had won that ferocious firefight more by good luck than judgement. Karl Nurk had scored a lucky hit with an early shot on the howitzer. The commanders of the *panzerjäger* unit had set up headquarters in a farmhouse, but Nurk had spotted them and duly slotted a 75mm shell through the window. Meanwhile Lieutenant Harvey had used the Vickers machine guns from the high-ground to cut the enemy's ranks to shreds.

The German force – some 400 strong – had suffered a minimum of sixty dead, with many more injured. So enraged were the survivors that they had torched the village of Marinello during their retreat. It turned out that the *panzerjägers* had been endeavouring to open a new supply route to their front-line positions that would cut through the mountains, as the open expanse of Highway Twelve was proving too vulnerable to Allied airstrikes. Farran's Victory Column had stopped them in their tracks.

The battle had taken place on 10 April 1945 and many more had followed. With Lieutenant David Eyton-Jones' feet having mostly recovered from their frostbite, Farran had placed him in command of Star Column – the sixty Italian partisans, stiffened by five SAS. By 16 April all four columns – Sun, Moon, Star and Eclipse – were harassing and ambushing enemy traffic the length and breadth of Highway Twelve, but still there was no Allied breakthrough of the *Gotenstellung*.

Indeed, an 8 April assessment of enemy forces manning the Gothic Line, authored by Allied Forces Headquarters, concluded: 'They represent an as yet unbroken and coherent element of the Wehrmacht with a fine defensive record behind them. They . . . are in strong heavily defended positions which may cost the Anglo-Americans heavy losses to breach . . . Even if breached, they may be capable of sufficient power of recovery to confront the Allies with a series of delaying actions on successive river lines . . . They represent a considerable source of manpower should some form of desperate last stand materialise in the Austrian Alps.'

Eleven days into the assault on the Gothic Line, German units were still holding firm, in response to which Farran redoubled his efforts to fool the enemy into thinking that their front was crumbling. Rather than concentrating on sneaking close to Highway Twelve to launch ambushes, he ordered his columns to hold back in cover, mounting mortar, howitzer and heavy machine-gun attacks, targeting the enemy's garrisons and vehicle parks. In so doing he intended to give the impression that the Allies' heavy artillery and armour had broken through. If they could spread enough fear and panic, the lines should crumble.

In the first such exploit Farran himself took the jeep convoy –

Eclipse Column – deep into hostile terrain, with the howitzer in tow. From a high point they unleashed seventy 75mm shells onto the enemy garrison based in the town of Sassuolo. So carried away did Farran become that he even ordered the shelling of the town's military hospital. For once, the SAS commander was overruled by his men, who refused to do it. There was no need: the streets were awash with German army trucks and troops, fleeing this way and that in panic.

After the attack, Farran sent the Staffetas on their bicycles into town to check. Sure enough, they returned with news that the German commander had ordered an evacuation, fearing that the Allies had broken through. This, Farran realised, was the answer. It was hardly classic SAS tactics – which were up close and personal ambushes and raids – but it was exactly what the present circumstances called for. Fear of an Allied breakthrough was a weapon that they could wield to good effect, decimating enemy morale and causing them to flee. It was perfect.

Lieutenant Eld scored the next success, mortaring German positions from the foothills with similarly spectacular results. As more and more such attacks were executed, the only challenge for Farran was to keep his columns supplied with enough mortar, machine-gun and howitzer rounds. The Dakotas resorted to flying deep into enemy territory, dropping supplies to fields only recently secured by Farran and his men. With the jeeps to hand they could load up and motor out of there, before the enemy could cause any trouble.

Farran empowered his commanders – Eld, Harvey and Eyton-Jones first and foremost – to make nowhere safe for the enemy. 'The partisans captured a German soldier as he visited a farmhouse to buy eggs,' Eyton-Jones recounted of his next attack.

Under questioning, the captive revealed that there was a major German garrison in the nearby village of Montebonello, with a key sentry position atop the church tower. Eyton-Jones took a compass bearing on the tower, and that night they launched their attack, using a Browning heavy machine gun.

'We'd loaded belts of ammunition with tracer bullets and incendiary,' Eyton-Jones recounted. They opened fire, streams of tracer 'burning across the sky and swinging in arcs from the church tower to the village square. There must have been vehicles parked in the square, for very soon it was rocked with explosions. The barrel of the Browning was red hot when we loaded it back onto the mule . . .' The following morning the Stafettas reported German forces evacuating Montebonello.

Not to be outdone, Lieutenant Harvey launched a ferocious attack on Highway Twelve, leading the Moon Column with the unbridled aggression of youth. Harvey chose to ambush a convoy at night, where it was forced to navigate a U-shaped bend in the road. Opening fire from three sides, his forces tore apart trucks and horse-drawn carts, causing scores of casualties. Somewhat wild at heart, Harvey decided to stay to witness the bloody aftermath, as enemy troops turned on each other in the darkness and confusion.

'The enemy from each side of the U fired at each other,' he reported. 'When this started I ordered our withdrawal. I stayed on for fifteen minutes myself, fascinated by the mischief that I had started and which now had developed into quite a battle, each side thinking the other to be the ambushers.' Come morning, so shattered was their morale that 150 enemy soldiers sought to surrender to him – almost three times the number of fighters Harvey had in his Moon Column.

With Lieutenant Eld leading a series of jeep-mounted raids, Farran, an astute and driven commander, used the British successes to berate Modena and his Russians, urging them to greater efforts. Modena duly led an all-out assault on the German garrison at Lama Mocogno, a town that straddled Highway Twelve itself. In ferocious fighting they seized five hundred prisoners – five times the number of troops that Modena had in his command.

On 21 April Farran deployed Molto Stanco to unleash a barrage of 75mm shells onto Reggio Emilia itself, where an injured Lees had only recently been sheltered. The German commander reacted by ordering his entire force to evacuate that major garrison town, even sanctioning the blowing up and demolition of key positions as they pulled out.

'Within two hours of our attack, the enemy blew up the Post Office,' Farran reported. 'Various other demolitions were heard and it was reported that Fascists were levelling the town. We only realised later . . . that the timing of this attack had been so opportune.' What made it so timely was revealed the very next day, when Farran received reports that the German front was crumbling, their divisions falling into a mass retreat.

'There were only two crossings over the river Secchia left open to three German divisions (the 232, the 114 and the 334), which were withdrawing north-west towards the Po,' Farran reported. 'At midday we noticed an enormous column of lorries and carts and a few tanks head-to-tail crossing the ford . . . Our whole force, with the guns, took up position on the last foothills overlooking the plains . . .'

Farran ordered every available man, gun and vehicle into action. 'My plan was to throw everything at the Germans . . . For this was no time for caution; if we delayed, the opportunity would be lost forever.' Leaving the jeeps and guns parked in the lee of the ridge, Farran crept forward with Karl Nurk, keeping to hands and knees as they crested the high ground. An incredible sight met their gaze: as far as the eye could see columns of German troops and vehicles stretched northwards across the plain.

While the congestion was terrible everywhere, it was worst at the two chokepoints directly below – a bridge and a ford that crossed the Secchia. A dense column of troops, trucks and armour crawled towards those two crossings. Even closer, maybe a hundred feet below their position, a German infantry battalion lolled in the shade of some trees surrounding a farmhouse. They looked utterly spent. No sentries had been posted and no defensive positions set.

'The signs were unmistakable,' Farran remarked. 'This was a picture of a rout, of an army in full retreat. The Gothic Line was broken.'

Farran and Nurk crawled back to their men unnoticed by the enemy. Jock Easton was busy sighting the howitzer, drawing up ox-carts laden with shells. Leaving ten men to screen the gun from attack, Farran arranged the jeeps with their water-cooled Vickers heavy machine guns along the line of the ridge. The plan of attack was simple. Upon Farran's word Easton was to open fire with Molto Stanco, shelling the two crossing points, which were jam-packed with military vehicles.

The Vickers were to join the fray, pouring in fire, as were the mortars. The range was less than four hundred yards, making the densely packed convoys sitting targets. Positions set, Farran crawled back and slid into a convenient slit-trench that someone had dug into the forward slope of the ridge. He checked with

Easton, via his walkie-talkie radio-telephone, that he was ready with the howitzer.

That confirmed, Farran grabbed his binoculars and studied the sweep of the targets. Enemy forces crawled across the plain like a giant and restless colony of ants. Still he hesitated to give the order to open fire. The retreating forces were so numerous and so apparently well-armed, it seemed suicidal to give the word to attack. The Victory Column was outnumbered over a thousand to one, not to mention seriously outgunned.

'Almost any serious reaction by the enemy might mean annihilation of my force,' Farran reasoned, 'for the hills behind us were so open and so bare that escape would be impossible. This action we contemplated was far different from our customary guerrilla tactics of hit-and-run.'

Farran sensed the eyes of his men upon him, silently pleading for him to give the word. Not for the first time, he wondered if he had lost his nerve. It was then that he felt a figure wriggle into the trench beside him. It was Karl Nurk. Nurk shook Farran's elbow and pointed at the jumbled mass of German transport trying to negotiate the river crossings.

He grinned. 'Come on, let's go.'

By way of answer, Farran spoke into the radio handset. 'Jock, you ready?'

'Ready,' he replied, curtly.

Farran passed him the bearing off the map, telling him to fire one round at the river, range fifteen hundred yards. The crash of the gun split the air, the shell whistling over Farran and Nurk's heads, over those of the German infantry gathered at the farmhouse, and exploding on the river bank just to the north of the ford. Instantaneously, the Vickers opened fire, spraying the road directly below with long bursts of fire. A truck was hit, bursting into flames and slewing sideways, completely blocking the route.

The Brens and mortars joined in, tracer and incendiary rounds tearing into the enemy columns with devastating effect, mortar shells crumping among hordes of fleeing figures. Farran told Easton to drop his aim one hundred yards and a little east. His second shell burst just short in the river. Farran adjusted again, and the third shell was bang on. A truck towing a gun was blown onto its side in the middle of the river crossing. Further vehicles caught fire, throwing up thick and roiling clouds of smoke.

From below, the German infantry began to return fire, Mausers raking Farran's ridgetop position. His men answered with long bursts of Sten fire, which tore into the open terrain. At the river crossing carts were hit by the shellfire, their horses panicking horribly. A terrified horse-team dragged its cart off the road. Others were hit in the water. As those coming from behind tried to find a way past, they in turn became bogged in deep mud. The confusion and chaos were indescribable.

In no time a dozen trucks were aflame in the river, surrounded by overturned carts and struggling horses. Five were burning fiercely on the riverbank, with another six on the road below. The odd ping of a rifle shot kicked up dust on the rim of the trench, indicating to Farran that the enemy were still returning fire, but it was as nothing compared to the carnage being wrought. Eventually, a Spandau gunner began to plaster rounds all over Farran's trench position. No one had been hit yet, but it needed to be silenced.

Farran ordered some of the Garibaldini into the fray. These were very different men from those Farran had set out to train, at the start of Operation Tombola. Now, in a repeat of the wild dash that had driven the Germans out of the Secchia valley, they raced down the slope, no longer needing the SAS major to take the lead. After short-lived and sporadic resistance, the Germans threw down their arms.

Only with nightfall did Farran's ridgetop guns fall silent. They had fired 150 shells via the howitzer, but it was now too dark to aim and to shoot effectively. Across the terrain a pall of thick oily smoke testified to the utter devastation wrought. In the final hours, pathetic figures whose vehicles were on fire had scrambled up the slope, brandishing white handkerchiefs and with their hands raised. They sought someone, anyone, to whom to surrender. That night, Farran's camp was overwhelmed with would-be prisoners.

At dawn the flood of enemy vehicles had become a trickle. Farran took his jeep and motored down to Highway Twelve, to check out the lie of the land, barely daring to believe that the battle might be over. On the approach to Sassuolo he ran into Ken Harvey's Moon Column, battle wearied and dust-covered, but likewise jubilant. They handed Farran something of a novelty right then – packets of American chewing gum.

Up ahead the US 1st Armoured Division was advancing and the Germans were reported to be in retreat everywhere. Farran ordered his forces to regroup in Modena, the city that dominates the south side of the plains of the Po. There, his Sun, Moon, Star and Eclipse columns were reunited. The Americans had bypassed the city, their armoured legions racing after the retreating Germans. The streets echoed to the occasional gunshot, as liberating forces celebrated and chased away the last Fascist diehards.

Yet even here victory was to be bitter sweet. There was to be

343

a sting in the tail for Farran and his Allied Battalion. A formal victory parade was to take place in the city, immediately after which Farran and his men were ordered to disarm the Russians. Once that was done, they were to be loaded aboard transport so they could be 'repatriated' to the Soviet Union. Few doubted what fate would await the likes of Modena, if that order were carried out. Most were horrified at the very thought of it.

'I had not the moral courage for what seemed to us at the time to be such a cruel, unfair and premature act,' Farran remarked of the order. 'Those clever people in Florence could never understand the mutual trust between comrades-in-arms. We had fought together, some had died together, and now in the hour of our victory we were asked to take away their arms.' Worse still would be sending them back to the USSR to almost certain death.

'The Russians, I was sure, would feel themselves disgraced,' Farran remarked of the order, 'would feel that the British trusted them less than they trusted the Italians.' Farran couldn't contemplate openly defying his orders. There had been quite enough of that of late and he was fearful that he was going face a court martial. Still, there were ways and means to evade such impossible, inhuman instructions as these.

Someone got a warning to Modena. Along with his beautiful Italian mistress he disappeared. Eyton-Jones was one of those charged to load the Russians aboard waiting transport. He, like the others, had a simple means of 'obeying' his orders, while ensuring they proved utterly ineffectual. He opened the door on one side of the train carriage to load the Russians aboard, then unlocked the door on the opposite side to ensure they could escape.

'Few of them turned up,' he remarked happily, of his Russian comrades-in-arms, 'and their leader never came. A lot of them got onto one side of the train and got out of the other ... for they knew if they were going back to Russia, Stalin was going to kill them.'

The victory parade and the wild partying gave the SAS the perfect way to bid farewell to their partisan brothers-in-arms. The following day the main body of No. 3 Squadron formed up in convoy for the drive back to Florence. They left a rear party, commanded by Eyton-Jones, to ensure the squadron's fallen were properly buried in the graveyard at Albinea, close to their infamous raid at Botteghe. Riccomini, Guscott and Bolden were already there. Sadly, Lance Corporal Robert Bruce – Justo Balerdi, the Spanish Civil War veteran and French Foreign Legionnaire – had been killed in the final days of operations.

On the night of 20/21 April two SAS jeeps had ambushed a German position in what Farran described as a 'daring attack'. They'd targeted a German supply dump, racing in with machine guns blazing. Long bursts of tracer from the jeep's weapons had torn into a large truck and ammunition trailer, destroying them completely, and detonating a heap of anti-aircraft shells. An enemy vehicle was seized intact, and scores of prisoners taken, but at the height of the raid Balerdi had been hit in the head by a bullet and killed outright.

Eyton-Jones' final mission was to bury Balerdi alongside his fallen comrades Bolden, Guscott and Riccomini. Balerdi's Spanish SAS comrade, Private Raphael Ramos, asked if he might accompany Eyton-Jones, to help lay his 'brother' to rest. No one was sure if they were directly related, or just 'brothers-in-arms', but it was only fitting that a fellow Spaniard should help to bury him. So it was that Ramos joined Eyton-Jones for the journey back to the site of the bloody and portentous headquarters raid.

But first, they had to inter Balerdi's corpse. Locals had buried the Spaniard in a field, his body shrouded in a tarpaulin. Eyton-Jones and Ramos unearthed his remains from the shallow grave. 'His face was still locked in grim determination,' Eyton-Jones remarked of the fallen Spaniard, 'with eyes open and teeth barred.' Upon reaching the Albinea graveyard, Balerdi was laid to rest alongside his SAS comrades. The priest seemed nervous, for German troops were still roaming the area, but Eyton-Jones and Ramos were undeterred. They arranged for a stonemason to erect crosses over the graves, in part so Balerdi's family could locate their fallen son once the war was over.

Lieutenant Harvey sought permission from Farran to return to the Secchia valley, ostensibly to shut down their headquarters, but in truth to bid a last farewell. It was granted. 'With Jock Easton we went in a jeep and . . . returned to our old haunts . . .' Harvey recounted. 'Everywhere we were feted – the war was virtually over and the peasants, with whom we had lived for so long and had done so much for the cause of liberating their country, were free.'

The main body of the SAS force prepared to depart Modena. Jeeps were loaded with the wounded. Norice, the grey-eyed Stafetta, refused to leave them, while Farran lacked the heart to order her to stay. She rode on one of the jeeps, together with the two civilian cars, captured German Army trucks, and a German Army ambulance, which rounded off the bizarre convoy. The chief stress faced by Farran and his men had been the nervous strain of long weeks operating behind enemy lines. Consequently, they were in unusually high spirits, and they draped a captured Nazi swastika over the gun carriage that held Molto Stanco.

The odd, hotchpotch cavalcade must have made an astonishing sight, as it made its way back through the advancing Allied forces. Dusty, dirty, bearded, blood-stained and in many cases long-haired after months in the mountains, Farran's SAS stood in sharp contrast to the smart, gleaming, well-ordered columns of military might.

'They must have wondered who on earth we could be,' Farran remarked. 'We were the *"Battaglione Alleato"* . . . otherwise known as the *"Battaglione McGinty"*, whose motto was *"Chi osera vincera"* – Who dares wins.'

As the convoy wound its way into the highlands, passing through the Gothic Line defences, the devastation was clear: massive bomb craters pitted the blasted, denuded landscape, which in many places resembled the surface of the moon. This ghostly terrain – this valley of the shadow of death – was a testament to the ferocity of the main battle, and Farran's party fell quiet as they passed through.

During the journey the SAS major had time to contemplate all they had achieved and what troubles might now lie ahead. Over the past few weeks his Victory Column had shelled, machine-gunned and mortared nineteen towns and villages, targeting the German garrisons stationed there. At a conservative estimate Farran reckoned they'd accounted for some 300 enemy killed, with many more wounded, and hundreds taken prisoner. Scores of enemy vehicles had been destroyed.

But by far the greatest impact was the chaos, panic and insecurity such actions had caused among the enemy. Farran cited this in his official report, lauding 'the morale effect of so formidable and enterprising a force in the immediate rear of the enemy . . . There is little doubt that the actions fought considerably accelerated the panic and rout of some three to four German divisions.' That equated to as many as 100,000 men-at-arms.

Farran's casualty list was stunningly light. It included four SAS 'Killed', or 'Missing – believed killed' – Lieutenant Riccomini, Serjeant Guscott, Lance Corporal Bruce (the Spaniard, Justo Balerdi) and Corporal Bolden, plus six wounded. Then there were the nine Russians killed or missing in action, plus a handful of Italian casualties. It was a tiny toll, considering the damage caused to the enemy.

Of particular note, Farran stated, was the raid on the 14th Army headquarters: 'the success of this attack . . . had a great effect on the outcome of the final battle in Italy.' In its official regimental report on Tombola, the SAS would echo Farran's sentiments: 'A Staff Colonel and sixty other Germans were killed in fighting which resulted in the destruction of the main Headquarters . . .' That same report lauded 'Major McGinty, who by threats and persuasion was able to achieve cohesion and efficiency from so heterogenous a force.'

The real impact of the Botteghe raid would only become clear in the months that followed. During that long drive to Florence, Farran's mind was mostly occupied with thoughts of what fate might now hold in store for him. Once he reached Allied headquarters, was he to be thrown into a military gaol, facing charges and a court martial? That was his overriding fear.

'Fortunately, I did not receive a trial by court martial as I expected,' Farran would note, of his arrival back in liberated territory. Certainly, there were those in British high command who were determined to try him on two counts: parachuting behind the lines against orders and attacking the Botteghe HQ when ordered not to. But their intentions were frustrated, and largely due to the efforts of US Colonel Riepe, the commander of Allied special forces operations in Florence, plus a handful of other senior American figures.

Upon reaching Florence, Farran learned that the Americans were putting him forward for the US Legion of Merit – a high valour medal given for exceptional conduct in battle. It was to recognise the service that he and his SAS had provided in raising the Allied Battalion and wreaking havoc behind the lines, which had contributed greatly to the final Allied breakthrough. It was, as Farran pointed out, his 'ace in the hole', for 'I could hardly be court-martialled for something for which I had been decorated.'

The citation for his Legion of Merit recorded that Farran's operations on Tombola had 'materially assisted' the attacks of the United States military forces and contributed significantly to the success of Fifteenth Army Group and its breaking of the German defences in Italy.

But sadly, there was to be no eleventh-hour reprieve – or glory – for the chief architect of the Botteghe HQ raid, Mike Lees.

Epilogue

Lees, Farran and their ilk had played a crucial part in bringing victory and liberation to Italy. On 26 April the city of Milan was liberated by Italian partisans and on the 29th the entire 6,000-strong German 232nd Division was captured. Allied forces marched into Milan the same day, as Hitler committed suicide in his Berlin bunker. At noon on 2 May 1945 – so less than a week after Farran and his men had withdrawn from the field – hostilities ceased in Italy, almost a million German troops surrendering complete with their equipment. That same day the Red Army took Berlin. On 7 May the Germans' unconditional surrender had been signed and the war was over.

In *Daggers Drawn*, Mike Morgan's excellent history of the SAS in the Second World War, he rightly concludes of Operation Tombola: 'The exploits of this brave, motley band ... during the final weeks of the war were to go down in [SAS] regimental history.' No less than Lieutenant-Colonel Brian Franks, DSO, MC, commander of 2 SAS during the war years, would echo such sentiments, writing that 'the detachment of this Regiment played a big part towards bringing about the final surrender of the German armies in Italy.'

The fears expressed that the 'Reds' would somehow execute a violent and bloody communist takeover in Italy proved unfounded: with very few exceptions, in towns and villages across the country Committees of National Liberation were formed, which combined all political factions in a nationwide effort to bring the rule of law and good governance to the nation. They enjoyed widespread support and the backing of the populace.

In the run-up to the German surrender, SOE Florence had kept headquarters in London closely informed of the breakneck pace of developments. Codenamed 'Freeborn', their series of reports summarised the messages that had come flooding in from missions all across the front. One, despatched on 25 April, dealt with Macintosh's central area of operations. It read:

Owing rapid progress in Apennine Battle Zone, all missions controlled by Macintosh at 5th Special Force Unit now overrun after making solid contribution to Allied advance and having considerable success in anti-scorch measures. Following reported from sets (a) Carrara, no repeat no excesses by partisans and no evidence of purge or bloodbath (b) Bologna no repeat no disorder. Partisans being [?] used [?] as guards, electricity and water functioning 24 hours after fall.

Despite the odd, disjointed language, it revealed the spirit with which the partisans had seized back control of their country, belying the fears of those in Allied high command who worried there would be a communist-instigated 'purge or bloodbath'. Of course, hindsight is a fine thing and perhaps one could argue this wasn't to be known at the time. However, a simple listening to the BLOs – those on the ground embedded deep within partisan command and control – would have reflected how little they credited such fears.

Ironically, a telegraph sent by Sir Noel Charles, the British ambassador in Rome, to the Foreign Office, sums up the situation admirably. 'After successful patriot insurrections in Milan, Turin, Genoa and other northern towns and withdrawal of German and Fascist troops, law and order were preserved to a remarkable degree.' It was, of course, the Foreign Office that had stoked the fears of communist-leaning partisans – the dreaded 'reds' – seizing control in a violent, post-liberation overthrow.

Subsequently, the achievements of the Italian partisans were to be lauded by many. Colin McVean Gubbins, Chief of the SOE – who had lost his son on behind-the-lines operations in Italy – heaped praise upon their efforts. His words are worth quoting in full:

> The final effort of the Italian partisans, who numbered thousands, was timed to coincide with Alexander's attack on the vaunted Gothic Line in Northern Italy. They had been harrowing Kesselring's communications all winter, and now the time for the coup de grâce had come. They fought like demons, many British officers and NCOs alongside them, parachuted in to train and organise them and to provide arms and ammunition. Some 65,000 strong they seized Genoa, Milan, Turin and other towns as the Allies advanced, opening the way for the lightning thrust of Alexander's forces to the Alps and cutting off the ignominious surrender of Kesselring's entire Armies – total victory.

In his book *Echoes of Resistance: British Involvement with the Italian Partisans*, author Lawrence Lewis echoes such sentiments, while making special mention of the 14th Army HQ raid. He concludes: 'The [resistance] movement was far more important in the disruption it caused to German activities . . . For instance, the upset caused to the German communications by an attack such as that which wiped out the Albinea headquarters – possibly the most significant single action involving Partisans in the entire history of the Partisan movement . . . cannot be quantified by pure statistics.'

Indeed, documents retrieved from German archives suggest that following the Botteghe (Albinea) raid, the 14th Army headquarters was bereft of all communications for fifteen days – constituting the vital period when Allied forces launched their final assault on the Gothic Line. When the 14th Army eventually re-established its headquarters, the Germans chose to site it in an Italian village where it was vulnerable to, and was subsequently hit by, Allied warplanes, so speeding its final demise.

Foremost SOE assassin Major Barton did parachute into the region, on his Cisco Red II mission, charged with assassinating General Heinrich von Vietinghoff, but by the time of his arrival Lees was caught up in the Botteghe HQ raid. Barton went on to call in air-drops and to build up a fresh band of partisans, with a view to the coming offensive. His citation for his mission records that at one stage, 'Major Barton and his WT operator were surprised . . . in a house by a Fascist officer who . . . held them up at the point of an automatic. Major Barton, regardless of his own safety immediately leaped on the officer and succeeded in killing him. While retrieving his automatic . . . he found the house surrounded by Fascists, but with the aid of his wireless operator he succeeded in shooting his way out.' Barton and his partisans went on to play their own role in the liberation of northern Italy. After the war he moved to Africa, became a farmer and raised a family.

*

In having to try to balance the conflicting demands from London over support for the Italian resistance, SOE Florence's Major Charles Macintosh doubtless had been handed something of a poisoned chalice. He was a smallish cog in a far larger machine. However, that does not explain the antipathy he apparently felt and extended towards Mike Lees, nor the relentless witch-hunt that would follow Lees' evacuation from Italy.

In his official report on Tombola, Farran would explain his decision to proceed with the 14th Army HQ raid as follows: 'Unfortunately, I had already left on the long march to the plains when the cancellation was received on my wireless set in the mountains. In any case, having once committed a partisan force to such an attack an alteration in plan would have been disastrous to guerrilla morale in the whole area.'

Farran must have known he was treading on thin ice: the report is very carefully worded. Fortunately his American Legion of Merit served to exonerate him of all blame. The citation reads: 'After he himself had parachuted behind enemy lines, he assumed command of his nearest operational party and led it on many raids which inflicted casualties and damage on the hostile forces . . . Major Farran's effective leadership of both his special unit and Italian partisans contributed significantly to the success of the 15th Army Group.'

Making no mention of disobeying orders, the honour effectively quashed any arguments that Major Roy Farran, DSO, MC and two bars, should face any kind of disciplinary action. Farran, to his immense credit, was one of the few in command who chose to stand by Mike Lees.

*

Long after victory had been declared in Italy, Lees was finally flown to Britain, to a military hospital in Chester. On 25 May 1945, seven weeks after Lees had been rescued via pilot Furio Lauri's dramatic air mission, a letter arrived at SOE headquarters concerning his injuries. Lees had arrived back in the UK just a week before, to be treated for 'wounds received while a BLO in Northern Italy'. The letter noted the 'gravity of Capt. Lees' condition', and concerns that he might be hospitalised for some considerable time, during which the issue of his rank was playing on his mind.

Lees had been promised promotion to the rank of major in the field, which would have fitted his role and position as Secchio BLO, or so he claimed. In the letter, an appeal was raised to 'Col. Hewitt, Commander No. 1 Special Force', latterly the official name of the SOE mission in Florence. 'It is strongly urged that everything possible be done to regularise this officer's position,' the letter noted, 'and above all to remove the cause of his present anxiety, as it is feared that this may impede his recovery.'

Lees' appeal to Hewitt was perhaps understandable. After all, this was the man who, as one of SOE Maryland's senior commanders, had issued the glowing report following Lees' crossing of the lines in September 1944, bringing with him the two Italian resistance leaders. But his response to Lees' 25 May 1945 appeal from his Chester hospital bed utterly belied such sentiments. Lees' hopes for promotion were to prove naïve and misguided. Dated 12 June 1945, Hewitt's letter pulled no punches. 'At no time, either before his departure or during his time in the field, was the question of his promotion raised with me by him or anybody else,' he wrote of Lees. There was worse to come.

'From the day he was infiltrated until the day he was exfiltrated,'

Hewitt's letter continued, 'Captain Lees was troublesome, insubordinate, unreasonable, tactless, irresponsible, and highhanded. His activities culminated in an action against the enemy which, in spite of its gallantry, he had been expressly forbidden ... to undertake. In view of the wounds he received disciplinary action against Captain Lees was not taken.' Hewitt attached a report to his letter outlining 'this officer's conduct in the field.'

Hewitt's *volte face* was all the more surprising bearing in mind that Roy Farran, who had overseen any contravention of orders and in any case outranked a malaria-racked Lees, had been decorated for commanding the 'forbidden' Botteghe raid. Regardless, Lees, hospitalised and ailing, was about to be hung out to dry. By 15 June – three days after Hewitt's damning letter – the betrayal of Mike Lees was all but complete.

The issue had been raised to a higher level. In a letter marked 'Confidential – BY BAG', the following was written of Lees: 'From the day that Capt. Lees was infiltrated into Northern Italy until the day he was exfiltrated, he has been most unsatisfactory.' Lees' conduct was described as 'troublesome, insubordinate and irresponsible,' especially in his 'action against the enemy'. After stressing that there was 'no question of this officer being promoted', the letter concluded that Lees was 'not recommended for re-employment within this organisation'.

In short, by mid-June 1945 Lees had been refused promotion, his reputation had been traduced and he had been thrown out of SOE. There was worse to follow. Ten days later, a note marked 'PERSONAL AND CONFIDENTIAL' was circulated concerning Mike Lees, landing on the desk of the Queen's Own Dorset Yeomanry – Lees' parent regiment, in which the Lees family had long served – as well as that of other interested parties.

It read: 'You will, by now, have seen the various signals and reports that have been passed between this HQ and LONDON on the subject of Capt. M. LEES; and you will appreciate that much of his report is biased and, I am afraid, untruthful.' By 25 June 1945, Lees was being accused of being 'biased' and 'untruthful' – a liar – regarding his record in the field. The note continued: 'It would be a comfort to know that his case is now fully closed. He is lucky that we should remember his gallantry without taking official note of his shortcomings.'

Actually, to the contrary, official 'note of his shortcomings' was about to be made most emphatically.

Roy Farran, to his credit, fought against this bitter tide. On 25 June, the same date that the above note was authored – it is incidentally signed anonymously 'AM 2' – Farran authored a glowing citation for Mike Lees, in which he recommended him for the award of the Military Cross. It encapsulated with great eloquence Farran's view of the SOE officer and his achievements during the months that he served in the Secchia valley.

He organised his partisan division into an efficient guerrilla force and by his courageous example inspired the Italians to attacks on the enemy which they would not otherwise have performed. On March 4th he conceived a plan for attacking the German Corps H.Q. which controlled the whole . . . front from BOLOGNA to the sea. With great skill and courage he carried out a preliminary reconnaissance which revealed all the details of the H.Q.

The H.Q. was attacked with great success by a mixed force of British parachutists and partisans. Capt. Lees led his own band of partisans into the Corps Commander's villa with such dash that the ground floor and first landing on a spiral staircase were taken ... in spite of intense fire from the enemy. When his men hesitated in the face of such intense fire, with complete disregard for his own safety he stood on the staircase and waved them on, inspiring them to further efforts. Eventually he was seriously wounded, but continued to shout inspiring orders to his men ...

The citation went on to outline the convoluted and ingenious means by which Lees was evacuated from the field, before stressing the huge strategic value of the Botteghe HQ raid for 'the outcome of the final battle in Italy'. The raid's success was 'largely due to the gallantry, initiative and unequalled courage of Captain Lees', Farran concluded.

The MC recommendation was subsequently stamped 'Citation passed and approved by SOE.' After that, it was sent to 15 Army Group – the Allied command charged with the liberation of Italy – for final approval. There it apparently hit a brick wall. The official response came in a 25 July 1945 letter, marked 'Honours And Awards – CONFIDENTIAL'. It argued that in effect Roy Farran had no right to propose such an award.

'Captain LEES was not under command of 2 S.A.S. Regiment at the time nor was he working in support of that unit,' the letter stated. While admitting to the heroism and gallantry involved in the Botteghe raid, the letter continued: 'In the opinion of 15th Army Group the value of this operation depended on its timing, and Captain LEES with the SAS ... carried it out prematurely and recklessly in spite of the express orders.'

In short, it was case closed. Farran's best efforts had failed. Mike Lees was denied an MC.

In his excellent book, *Mission Accomplished: SOE and Italy 1943-1945*, David Stafford concludes: 'Given Lees' injuries, no disciplinary action was taken against him ... although it was clear he had made himself unpopular with his superiors.' Just how unpopular is evidenced in the above correspondence, penned as Lees languished in a Chester hospital without proper treatment. Arguably, it was Farran's spirited and high-profile support that saved Lees from any greater degree of approbation.

It wasn't until the end of July - well after his MC had been proposed and denied - that Lees was finally moved to the kind of specialist unit that was required to treat his injuries. Through family connections an appeal had been made to Field Marshal Alanbrooke, who was Chief of the Imperial General Staff and a foremost adviser to Winston Churchill. Moved to a hospital near Oxford, Lees finally received the attention and treatment denied to him for approaching four months.

It's perhaps worth pausing at this juncture to revisit some of the extraordinary accusations levelled against Lees. For his service in Italy, he had been accused of being all of the following: insubordinate, unreasonable, tactless, irresponsible, highhanded, biased, reckless and untruthful. Although by the summer of 1945 Lees was yet to learn of most of these allegations - and indeed would not do so during his lifetime - his wartime record had been traduced among his peers.

What on earth had he done to attract such vile approbation and, frankly, distortions of the truth? By his own admission Lees could be tactless and he wasn't always smart and savvy in the handling of his superiors. But does that alone - the fact that he had put some of his superiors' noses out of joint - account for his treatment? Was it all down to a petty quest for revenge; for spite to have its day? If that is the case it seems utterly extraordinary, not to mention unconscionable.

Or was he so vilified simply for his alleged betrayal of orders? The SOE by its own admission sought mavericks, free-thinkers and self-starters, individuals happy to work alone and largely to their own drive and initiative. Lees was absolutely of that ilk and he demonstrated those attributes in his raising of the Secchia partisans and the attack on the Botteghe HQ. In Lees, SOE had got exactly what they had bargained for. If he had, as he was accused, disobeyed orders, what did they expect of such a man in such a position?

More to the point, if you adhere to the belief that the proof is very much in the pudding, the pudding served up at the Botteghe HQ on the night of 26/27 March 1945 proved well worth the eating. The raid, executed to the timing chosen by Lees and Farran, fully delivered. In light of which, and in view of the enormous challenges of mustering such an irregular, multinational force, surely a blind eye should have been turned to a stand-down order that was in any case a little late in reaching the field. At best, those who commanded such a raid should have received fitting recognition and praise.

Instead, Lees – wounded, hospitalised and unable to defend himself – had been utterly denigrated and pilloried. Moreover, there was a foil to his lack of tact with his superiors. The flip side was that Lees was blessed with an instinctive feel for the common man; an extraordinary gift to inspire the warrior spirit in those who were neither trained as regular soldiers, and, in the case of northern Italy in the spring of 1945, might have been forgiven for thinking the risks to themselves and their families too great.

That was an uncommon gift and a remarkable one, yet by war's cnd it went utterly unremarked and unrewarded. Is there perhaps another, deeper and darker explanation for how Lees was treated? Did Michael Lees – like Canadian war reporter Paul Morton – fall victim to those powers who were determined that the actions of the Italian partisans – the dreaded 'reds' – should be sidelined and consigned to the dustbin of history?

Veteran Canadian journalist Don North believes so. In his book *Inappropriate Conduct,* which tells the full story of Paul Morton's wartime career and subsequent betrayal, he argues that Morton and Lees alike were savaged due to their wholehearted support for the partisan cause. 'Lees would suffer the same fate as Paul Morton,' North concluded, 'who was also abandoned by the Canadian Army and the *Toronto Daily Star . . .*'

The darlings of Winston Churchill, the special duty volunteers – the maverick irregulars of the SOE and SAS – never proved popular with the British establishment. By January 1946 the SOE had been officially disbanded, and the SAS itself had ceased to exist three months before (though it would be reformed in the 1950s). With SOE's demise, some eighty-five per cent of the organisation's documents were lost or destroyed, with only fragments being saved for posterity, mostly at the British National Archives, at Kew.

With the case of Mike Lees, the record is patchy. As Lees died before many of the documents cited in this book were released for public perusal, much of the controversy surrounding his treatment at the end of the war comes as something of a shock, even to his immediate family. One thing is for certain: his treatment was unjustified and unwarranted.

Another thing is clear: the history of the Allied treatment of the Italian and Yugoslav partisans remains a controversial subject and is still cloaked in secrecy, more than seventy years after the events. Some British government files on the subject remain closed, even today. I have had one opened, under a Freedom of Information request. It deals with one of the Spanish SAS who served on Operation Tombola and is stamped 'CLOSED UNTIL 2050'. Another I have had opened is entitled 'ITALY: OPER-ATIONS'. The file deals with British government policy towards Italian – and Yugoslav – partisans. Even in the version that I have had opened, large sections of text have been redacted – blacked out.

Part of the file concerns a March 1945 proposal put to the Chief of Staff, to make contact with the Italian nobleman Prince Borghese, 'with the intention of encouraging anti-scorch meas-ures and assisting in the maintenance of law and order'. Don Junio Valerio Borghese – nicknamed 'The Black Prince' – hailed from a titled Italian family with close ties to the Vatican. He'd served as a Naval Commander under Mussolini and was a hard-line Fascist. Upon the Italian surrender to the Allies in September 1943, Borghese had signed a treaty with the *Kriegsmarine* – Nazi Germany's navy – raising an 18,000-strong force that would remain loyal to Hitler until the bitter end.

In the final weeks of the war, Borghese's *Decima Flottiglia* – Tenth Flotilla – as he'd named them, spent much of their time and manpower fighting against the Yugoslav communist par-tisans. At the end of the war Borghese was tried on charges of collaboration with the Nazi invaders of Italy and sentenced to twelve years in prison. He was not perhaps an ideal ally for the British to seek in the closing stages of the war. The March 1945 proposal was ruled out: 'Political considerations . . . make such an attempt to contact this Fascist officer in any way entirely out of the question.' Proposed collaborations with unsavoury individuals plus the freezing out of the Italian partisans and their special forces comrades – certainly, the closing stages of the war in Italy was a time of dark and murky intrigues. Old enmities were being laid aside, in preparation for the new war that was coming – the Cold War.

One intriguing motive for Lees' vilification has been posited – that he was thrown to the dogs due to his spirited support for the Chetniks, the right-wing Yugoslav partisans. There is evidence to suggest that elements of the SOE had been infiltrated by those who have since been revealed to have been spies for the Russians. Their influence, and their misreporting and manipulating of intelligence, are said to have convinced Churchill to drop his support for the Chetniks, and embrace Tito's communist partisans. Was Lees discredited to prevent him from sounding a credible voice in support of Tito's rivals? It seems a distinct possibility.

Whatever the case, in the autumn of 1944 Mike Lees – then seen as a high flier in SOE circles – had been lined up for a post-war role in British intelligence, most likely with the Secret Intelligence Service (MI6). After his vilification at the hands of senior figures in SOE and the Army, Lees' military career was at an end, as were any hopes of a career in the intelligence community. When he finally emerged from hospital, Lees was, according to his family, 'lost'. All that he had lived for had been taken from him.

The exception was family and friends, and of course, Gwendoline, his bride of less than a year. Through Gwen's family connections Lees eventually established a career in the world of business, where he would become the managing director of a multinational company. In later years he took up farming in southern Ireland, while still keeping a home in Dorset. He and Gwen would have two daughters. Typically, he was said to hold few grudges against those who had spoken ill of him during the war, and neither did he ever wish that he had done things differently in Italy. He was proud of what he had achieved.

Lees was dogged by his wartime injuries, being hospitalised repeatedly. He was plagued by debilitating pain – especially in his leg – for the rest of his life. At times it drove him to distraction. He would demand for the leg to be amputated, only to be told by the doctors that it would not necessarily stop the pain, for the nerves had suffered such irreparable damage. At times the pain drove him to the verge of suicide, but as a lifelong Catholic he knew he could not take his own life.

In 1949, Lees was given fitting recognition by the Italian people and nation, being made a Freeman of the City of Reggio Emilia, the conurbation in which he had been hidden by resistance leader Antonio when so badly wounded. He attended ceremonies there and at Villa Rossi, where plaques were unveiled honouring those who had died in the Botteghe assault. In 1989 Lees was also, fittingly, made an honorary member of the SAS Association.

Following a return trip to Italy in 1949, Lees was again hospitalised due to his wartime injuries. It was then that he found the time to pen a book telling the story of his wartime adventures, never intending to publish it. In it he described himself as a 'young adventurer caught up in the world of politics and intrigue'. Decades later Lees was approached by a member of the Special Forces Club, in London, which was set up to honour the memory and preserve the wartime legacy of the SOE and SAS. He asked if Lees might consider publishing his story, which Lees had sent to the Club for their archives.

Lees' book, entitled *Special Operations Executed*, was duly published in 1986. He dedicated it thus: 'To the memory of the late Corporal Bert Farrimond, miner, poacher, entrepreneur and dedicated radio operator . . . Also to those many Italians in the ranks of the Resistance and to those civilians, to whom I owe my escape and my life.'

There seems little better note on which to end the remarkable story of Mike Lees, who died of a heart attack at the age of 72, marching up a steep hill in Milton Abbas, Dorset.

What of the others involved in the battles for northern Italy recounted in these pages? Major Roy Farran went on to forge for himself a successful, colourful and sometimes controversial career, first in the British military, and then in civilian life in Canada, as a newspaperman and politician. His post-war career has been widely written about and requires no further explication here. Notably, he and Lees remained close friends and acquaintances and visited each other often.

Farran fought for decorations to be awarded to any number of the key resistance figures with whom he had soldiered in Italy. One of the many was Barba Nera, the resourceful and tough quartermaster of his Allied Battalion. In most cases, Barba Nera's included, Farran's efforts proved fruitless.

Glauco Monducci – Gordon, the Black Owls commander – was evacuated from the field shortly after Lees. Hospitalised in Florence, he recovered and spent time with the SAS as an informal liaison. After the war he built a fine career in the wine trade and the containerisation business.

Of Modena, the dashing Russian partisan commander, the news was mostly positive. Having married his Italian mistress they emigrated to South America, where they had a long, happy and adventurous life. Any number of Modena's fellow Russians also settled down with local Italian girls, and never once set foot in the mother country again. For those who did return to Russia, as ordered, it proved mostly damaging to health and longevity: Stalin had them sent to the gulags or executed.

Similarly, there had been a brief post-war attempt to hand the 'Spanish SAS' – Raphael Ramos and Francisco Jeronimo included – back to Spain, and into the clutches of Franco's pro-Fascist regime. Thanks to a press outcry in Britain that idea was quietly shelved and most went on to live long and happy lives as British citizens, retaining their anglicised war names.

In the case of Raphael Ramos, Farran played a hand in this. In August 1945 he put forward the Spaniard for a Military Medal in recognition of his actions on the Botteghe HQ raid, stressing the vital role that he'd played saving Mike Lees' life. 'Ramos showed remarkable courage both during and after the attack. His intelligence and initiative in a strange country thirty miles behind the enemy lines showed a devotion to duty worthy of the highest praise and resulted in preserving the life of a valuable British officer.'

In October 1945 Ramos married a Czechoslovakian, Libusa Kodesova, and they settled in the UK. In his naturalisation papers he was described as being 'of no nationality ... DEPOSED BY CIVIL WAR.' He found employment in the newspaper business, working on the *Express & Echo* newspaper in Exeter, in the south west of England. He was a kind man blessed with a warm sense of humour. He died in 1961 aged just forty-two, after a short illness.

Juan Torrents Abadia – John Colman – the father figure of the Spanish SAS, knew Farran well and admired him greatly. A 'gentle man and a gentleman', according to his son, Cliff Colman,

John Colman was with the SAS unit that liberated the Nazi concentration camp at Bergen-Belsen, in April 1945. After the war he married, settled in the UK and raised a family.

Francisco Jeronimo settled in the UK under his war name, Frank Williams. After demobilisation from the Army in 1946, he reportedly met Anthony Eden, then Deputy Leader of the Conservative Party. Williams and other former Spanish SAS asked Eden if the Allies intended to march on Spain, Europe's last bastion of Fascism, to liberate it from General Franco's rule. Eden reportedly said they did. Instead, old enemies rapidly became the newest of friends, as former Fascists and Nazis were recast as the bulwarks against the march of Soviet communism. When Frank Williams realised that Spain was not to be liberated, he reportedly threw away his war medals in disgust.

Williams settled in Carshalton, in Surrey, before moving to Wales in 1948. He married and raised a family in Cardiff, finding work as a pipe-fitter. In Wales he earned the unlikely nickname of 'Blod', short for Blodwin. This was so that in his local pub, whenever a friend shouted out, 'Blod, what're you drinking?' the reply would be issued in a thick Spanish accent. It never failed to bring the house down, as all the locals wondered what valley he might be from. Williams died in 1981 of asbestosis, contracted while fitting asbestos piping.

After the war Karl Nurk likewise became a naturalised British citizen. He went on to serve with the British military in Greece, on peacekeeping operations, attaining the rank of colonel, and he served on various British diplomatic missions overseas. Having retired from the military he had a brief acting career, before heading to South Africa where he lived the last years of his life, being survived by his wife and son.

After the war Canadian reporter Paul Morton – vilified, disgraced, and with his character and credentials in ruins – moved to the far north of Canada and gained employment of sorts in a remote logging camp. There he stayed for several years, drinking heavily. He eventually returned to his native Toronto, married and founded a successful public relations business. It all fell apart in the 1960s when he was accused at the Toronto Press Club by a fellow reporter of fabricating his entire story of behind the lines operations in Italy.

Upon learning the full truth – that he had been branded a fantasist and a liar – Morton spiralled into depression and alcoholism. He spent the final years of his life fixated on trying to clear his name, writing to all and sundry who might vouchsafe for the time he'd spent with Mike Lees and Geoffrey Long on Operation Flap. Towards the end of his life Morton published his story, entitled *The Partisans: Mission Inside*, but only in Italian. Morton's final days were ones of sadness, ruin and regret for what might have been. He died in 1992.

By contrast, the war artist Geoffrey Long – who deployed with Lees and Morton on Operation Flap – continued to serve with Allied forces, recording with pen and brush the devastation of many German cities at the end of the war. Later he returned to South Africa and became a lecturer at Natal University, subsequently moving to London to teach at the Central School of Theatre Design. His war art is still displayed in several museums around the world, including scenes from Operation Flap.

David 'The Mad Piper' Kirkpatrick returned to his native Ayrshire after the war, and chose not to talk about his exploits on Tombola. It wasn't until 2010 when the Italian resistance author and expert Matteo Incerti tracked him down, that

Kirkpatrick finally felt able to break his silence. He did so upon learning that in northern Italy he was viewed as a war hero, his piping the night of the Botteghe raid having saved countless Italians from what would have been savage German reprisals. Kirkpatrick died aged 91 at Girvan Community Hospital in South Ayrshire.

David Eyton-Jones rejoined his parent regiment, the Royal Sussex, after the war, served in the then-Palestine and was demobilised in 1947. He married a former WAAF and they moved to Assam, in India, where Eyton-Jones managed a 1,500-acre tea estate. He oversaw some 750 employees, starting a crèche, school and medical centre for the locals. He and his wife had four children. They returned to the UK, settled in Chidham, a village near Chichester, in a charming riverbank cottage, where his day pipes were arranged on one side of the fireplace and his evening pipes on the other (ten in all). He earned the nickname the 'Baccy Laureate'.

In later years his sight deteriorated, possibly due to the snow blindness that he had suffered on Monte Cusna. After his wife pre-deceased him he was assisted greatly by the then St Dunstan's charity – now Blind Veterans UK (BVUK) – to attend SAS and other military reunions and remembrance parades and to get on with his life generally. He last joined the BVUK contingent on Remembrance Sunday 2010, on London's Horse Guards Parade, along with a handful of fellow surviving Second World War veterans. He died in 2012.

After the war Jock Easton joined the reformed SAS, deploying to Malaya (Malaysia) in 1951, to counter a Chinese-backed communist insurgency. The Malaya missions involved deep jungle penetrations to strike at insurgents' bases and deny them territory. After leaving the military he forged a career as a stuntman of international repute, appearing in such classic films as *The Guns of Navarone* and *Where Eagles Dare*, and working alongside such stars of the screen as Clint Eastwood and Richard Burton. He died aged sixty-eight of cancer after a long illness.

Bob Walker-Brown pursued a post-war career in British special forces, going on to serve as second-in-command of 22 SAS before commanding 23 SAS – the territorial regiment – after which he joined the Defence Intelligence Staff. Married twice, he retired in Wiltshire where he was a keen angler. He had no children. He died in 2009 aged ninety.

Like many of those depicted in this book, Walker-Brown never forgot the Italian partisans with whom he had served. 'I feel an undying sense of gratitude for the very brave assistance of the Italian Partisans and numerous ordinary Italian people,' he would write. 'I think one takes a certain amount of pride in a small operation concluded with a reasonable degree of success and lack of casualties.'

Following the war Bert Farrimond left the military and returned to his home in Lancashire, in the north of England. An accident while riding his motorcycle badly affected his health and led to his early death – hence Lees' posthumous dedication of his book to Farrimond.

For their service with the Secchio partisans, several SAS received decorations (apart from Private Raphael Ramos, mentioned above). Lieutenant Harvey was awarded the DSO for his actions leading the raid on Villa Calvi, and Parachutist Patrick Burke was awarded the Military Medal (MM), for his actions spiriting a wounded Michael Lees to safety on the ladder they'd used as an improvised stretcher. SAS Corporal Ford was also awarded a MM, for his actions leading Farran's Star Column in ambushes on Highway Twelve.

Neither Justo Balerdi – Robert Bruce – nor Sidney Guscott or Stanley Bolden were to receive decorations for their actions in Italy, and despite making the ultimate sacrifice. After the war, Farran wrote to Guscott's family: 'I had great regards for Sergt. Guscott . . . He was a fine, brave boy, and I know he is in good company. One day, when I am considered good enough, I hope to see him in the place to which only the best soldiers go.'

Of those who died on the 14th Army HQ assault, Lieutenant Riccomini's loss deserves special mention. After the war, Bob Walker-Brown wrote to Riccomini's widow that her husband 'died a rare and gallant death at the head of his men during one of the most dangerous and effective attacks ever undertaken by this Regiment against the enemy. Ricci was a very great friend of mine having both been a POW and as an officer was the best in the Squadron. The men would have done anything for him . . .' That was high praise indeed, both for the man himself and for the Botteghe HQ raid.

Riccomini, along with Guscott and Bolden, was buried in Albinea church yard, but they were later moved to Milan Commonwealth War Graves Cemetery, where Riccomini's gravestone bears an extraordinarily poignant inscription in light of the way he distinguished himself during the HQ raid: 'Bitter and brief would I have my end: it were better that way, Lord'.

Flight Lieutenant Furio Lauri became a lawyer after the war. In 1995 he was reunited with the Fieseler Storch in which he had rescued Mike Lees and other wounded Allied servicemen. Sometime after the war it had been purchased by a British air enthusiast, who had begun the work of restoring it to its wartime glory. It is presently on display at the Italian Air Force Museum, in Vigna di Valle, just to the north of Rome.

German General Friedrich-Wilhelm Hauk survived the attack on the Botteghe HQ, but by 2 May 1945 he had in any case been captured by the Allies. He spent three years in a POW camp, before retiring to his home city of Stuttgart. He died of old age at eighty-two.

Field Marshal Albert Kesselring – author of so many of the atrocities against civilians in Italy – was captured on 15 May 1945. Subsequently tried for war crimes committed in Italy, he was sentenced to death. That was commuted to life, and a media and publicity campaign led to his release in 1952, supposedly on the grounds of ill-health. He remained resolutely unrepentant until his death, describing the Marzabotto massacre – the worst in Italy during the war – as a 'normal military operation', suggesting that he had 'saved Italy' and that the Italian people should accordingly build for him 'a monument'.

He died in 1960 following a massive heart attack at the age of seventy-four.

End Note

After the publication of this book and subsequent publicity concerning her late father's wartime career, Christine Bueno, the daughter of SOE Captain Michael Lees, was prompted to revisit her father's papers. As so often is the case, these were stored away in trunks and war chests in the family attic. When Christine sifted through the various maps, pictures and documents, it became clear from all the reunion photos how close her late father remained with Major Roy Farran and other SAS and SOE luminaries. There had been many reunions after the war, both formal and informal.

But it was then she stumbled upon a most extraordinary document, something she certainly had never seen before. It was a fax – yes, this was 1992, and the fax machine was still the fastest means of sending documents internationally back then – from "Major Roy Farran, DSO, MC" to Christine's mother, Gwendoline Lees. So revelatory were the contents of that fax, in terms of the story related in these pages, that I feel it should be included in this new edition of the book, to better set the record straight.

It is reproduced in full over the page:

IN MEMORY OF MICHAEL LEES
A GREAT WARRIOR

I had just finished reading the tributes to David Stirling by Sir Fitzroy Maclean in the Ampleforth magazine, when I heard that Michael Lees, my old comrade-in-arms, had passed away. Now that famous school can add the story of another colourful soldier to its records.

Michael was always something of a hero to me, even when he was technically under my command. He was the typical British public schoolboy, brought up on Kipling and Henty in the tradition of service ... He was fearless and had even less tolerance for pettifogging bureaucrats than I have, which is saying a lot.

In his eyes, he had a simple mission – to do his best to win the war against Hitler, even if that also meant another kind of battle against staff officers, safe in their headquarters, who for abstruse reasons sought to apply the brakes on his efforts.

Built like a Viking, he was a born fighting soldier. He had no time for the labyrinth of byzantine intrigue which surrounded operations in Yugoslavia. His sole objective was to defeat the Germans. He was intensely loyal to the Serbs under General Mihailovitch, who shared his objectives and he wasted little sympathy on those who waged a civil war concurrently: to him they merely confused the battle against the German invaders, his sole target.

He was a brilliant liaison officer behind the lines with Italian partisans and was admired equally by the Communist and Christian Democrat factions. Again, he was frustrated by the policy for partisans to refrain from attacks on the German rear until the grand offensive. Like me, he believed that guerrillas should hit as often as they were able and that inactivity in hiding would destroy their morale.

He insisted on accompanying us in the celebrated attack on the German Army headquarters at Albinea, even though he was very sick with malaria. And he gallantly took part in the assault on Villa Rossi, until he was severely wounded on the spiral staircase. Two of my men carried him to sanctuary on a ladder and he was eventually flown to hospital in Florence in a captured Fieseler Storch short-landing aircraft.

His superiors punished him for allegedly ignoring a signal to delay the attack by ten days. He thus received no award for his gallantry.

In reality, only I received and chose to ignore the signal for the delay. My attack had already begun when it was received. And Mike Lees was under my command and could not in any event have stopped us. My reasoning was that we had already been astonishingly lucky in getting one hundred men into a state of readiness to attack, infiltrating through a German sweep against partisans. I would never have been able to work them up to such a pitch again if they had been ordered to retreat and disperse in the face of the German drive.

Bureaucrats in army command at Florence would never appreciate the subtleties of morale and *esprit-de-corps*. But Mike did when I told him at Casa del Lupo, half-way to the target.

I have met many great and distinguished people in my life, but none greater than Mike Lees. In a sense, he was, in the words of the poet, unwept, unhonoured and unsung. However, not unhonoured by me or by any of the SAS men who served under him.

On behalf of 3rd Squadron, 2nd Special Air Service Regiment, I send my condolences to Gwen and his family.

He was one of us. That is why we made him an honorary member of the SAS.

Major Roy Farran's message – rediscovered by Captain Mike Lees' daughter in December 2018 – requires no further comment from myself. Farran states it all, in simple, eloquent, impassioned prose.

Afterword

Although only briefly mentioned in this book, Major William McKenna requires a special note on behalf of his surviving relatives. In 1950 McKenna became a policeman in Tingewick, Bucks, having served four years in Germany immediately after the war and he remained a regular visitor to the Special Forces Club in London. After his death, his son, Ian, sought to find out more about his wartime record, as his father had rarely if ever talked about the war years. Despite making extensive inquiries, he was unable to discover any record of his father serving with the SAS, although a thin file of papers concerning his SOE service is held in the National Archives. If any reader has any information or recollections concerning Major William McKenna's wartime career, please do contact me and I will ensure the information reaches Ian McKenna.

It would be nice to clear up what is something of a mystery.

Nikki Cartlidge, the granddaughter of SAS Private Robert 'Bob' Sharpe, is likewise involved in trying to trace the records and recollections of any who may be able to shed light on her grandfather's operations during the war years. A veteran of Operation Cold Comfort, little is known about Private Sharpe's service apart from that one ill-fated mission. Nikki Cartlidge is determined that the bravery of those who served in the SAS should be documented and never forgotten. If any reader has any information or recollections concerning Private Sharpe's wartime career, please do contact me and I will ensure the information reaches Nikki Cartlidge, or email her direct on: wwiisasresearch@gmail.com.

Likewise, of course, if any reader is able to shed any further light on the treatment of Mike Lees at the end of the war, or other aspects of his wartime career that are germane, please do get in contact. His surviving family members would be keen to learn of any insights.

In particular, the denial to Mike Lees of his Military Cross stands out as a signal injustice in this story. As an author I've taken the unusual step of starting a campaign calling for Captain Michael Lees to be awarded the Military Cross that was, I believe, wrongly denied him at war's end, or for an equivalent civilian honour to be granted posthumously, and I am grateful for the assistance of surviving family members in furthering this.

To remind you of the story behind the denial of Lees wartime decoration, here it is again in summary:

Captain Michael Lees of SOE commanded the spring '45 mission to destroy the key German Army HQ in Italy, with the aim of shortening the war and saving countless Allied lives. Leading from the front he was shot five times but miraculously escaped and survived, though he was plagued for the rest of his life by his injuries. Written up for a Military Cross at war's end, it was denied.

Fellow commander on the raid, SAS Major Roy Farran, wrote the MC citation for Michael Lees, hailing his "gallantry, initiative and unequalled courage." While both commanders may have disobeyed orders in proceeding with the raid, they did so – Nelson-like turning a blind eye to orders - believing it was the right decision on the ground. Farran was duly awarded the Legion of Merit for the raid and foremost SAS commander Bob Walker-Brown hailed it as, "One of the most dangerous and effective ever undertaken by this Regiment."

You can find out more about this, or contact me with information about Mike Lees (or indeed any of the other heroes of this book) on my Facebook page (facebook.com/damienlewisauthor); my website (damienlewis.com); plus follow me on twitter for updates (@authordlewis).

Acknowledgements

In researching this book I was able to meet, speak to and receive assistance from many individuals who were exceptionally generous with their time. My special thanks and gratitude are extended to all, and my apologies to those that I may have inadvertently forgotten to mention.

First and foremost I'd like to thank the family members of those depicted in these pages, who helped me to tell their stories: Christine and Tony Bueno, for inviting me into your Dorset home and for sharing with me your memories and stories of the late Michael and Gwendoline Lees; James Selby Bennet, for inviting me into your Dorset home and for sharing your recollections and memorabilia of your late uncle, Michael Lees; Mrs J. M. Brian, for corresponding with me over your cousin, Michael Lees; Sir Christopher Lees, for corresponding with me over your second cousin, Michael Lees; Gerald & Nichola Eyton-Jones, for inviting me into your home and for sharing your recollections of the late David Eyton-Jones; Nikki Cartlidge, for sharing with me recollections of your late grandfather, Robert 'Bob' Sharpe's war years; David Farran, for corresponding with me and finding the time to talk about your late father, Major Roy Farran DSO, MC and two bars; Phil Williams, for inviting me into your home and sharing with me your grandfather, Frank Williams's (Francisco Jeronimo) story of the war years; Cliff Colman, for sharing with me your father, John Colman's (Juan Torrents Abadia) story from the war years; Ian McKenna, for inviting me into your home and sharing with me your father, Major William McKenna's story from the war years; Christopher George, for sharing with me the story of your grandfather, Lt. Col. John Douglas George, from the war years; Steven Furneaux, for meeting up and corresponding with me over your grandfather, SAS Trooper Louis Baker's, war years; and Luke Griffiths, for corresponding with me about your grandfather, Major Barton's, war years.

My very special thanks are extended to Jack Mann, Second World War veteran of the SBS, SAS and LRDG, for reading an early draft of this book and for your invaluable insights and recollections from the war years, plus the documents and photographs you were able to share with me. My gratitude is also extended to Ted Ross, wartime radio operator, for sharing with me your recollections of serving with the partisans in Yuogoslavia and your photographs of those extraordinary operations.

In no particular order I also wish to thank the following, who assisted in many ways: research, proofreading and subject matter expertise. Tean Roberts, for your hard work and diligence, as always. Simon Fowler, for your expertise and inspiration, gleaned from the various archives. Paul and Anne Sherratt, for your perceptive comments and guidance. Thanks also to Ben Doyle-Cox, CEO of Platatac, for the very useful introductions you made: they were hugely appreciated. Thanks to Will Ward, Auxiliary Units researcher, for your excellent contacts, and to John Pidgeon, for same. Thanks in particular to Catherine Goodier, archivist at Blind Veterans UK, for all your help and assistance. Thanks also to Sally Allcard, for your expert advice and your translations from Italian and German.

Thanks also to Matteo Incerti, author, journalist and expert on the Italian partisans of the Second World War and the SAS and SOE operators who served alongside them (his books are referenced in the Bibliography). A very special thanks to Don North, the veteran Canadian journalist, who helped in my research of the wartime story and subsequent fate of Canadian journalist Paul Morton (told at great length in his book, *Inappropriate Conduct*). Many thanks also to Rob Hann for the correspondence, advice and for the insight provided in his book, *SAS Operation Galia*, which alerted me to the importance of that mission.

The staff at several archives and museums also deserve special mention, including those at the British National Archives; the Imperial War Museum; and the Churchill Archive Centre at Churchill College, Cambridge. Some files from the National Archives were made available to me as a result of Freedom of Information requests, and I am grateful to the individuals at the Archives who made the decision that those files should be opened.

My gratitude also to my literary agent, Gordon Wise, and film agent, Luke Speed, both of Curtis Brown, for helping bring this project to fruition, and to all at my publishers, Quercus, for same, including, but not limited to: Charlotte Fry, Ben Brock and Fiona Murphy. My editor, Richard Milner, deserves very special mention, as does John English, for his excellent copyediting.

I am also indebted to those authors who have previously written about some of the topics dealt with in this book and whose work has helped inform my writing. I have included a full bibliography.

Thanks are due also to Eva and the ever-patient David, Damien Jr and Sianna, for not resenting Dad spending too much of his time locked away . . . again . . . writing . . . again.

APPENDIX ONE

Roll of Personnel Engaged on Operation Tombola (taken from the SAS post-operational report)

Drop One: 4 March
Major R. A. Farran
Lieutenant J. Easton
Corporal K. Fitzgerald
Lance Corporal R. Bruce (Balerdi)
Parachutist P. Green
Parachutist F. Williams (Jeronimo)
Parachutist T. Kershaw

Drop Two: 7 March
Captain J. Milne
Lieutenant D. Eyton-Jones
Lieutenant T. G. Stephens
Lieutenant A. R. Tysoe
Corporal Larley

Drop Three: 9 March
Lieutenant M. F. N. Eld
Lieutenant K. G. Harvey
Sergeant R. Godwin
Sergeant F. Hughes
Corporal S. Bolden
Lance Corporal R. Ford

Lance Corporal K. Bjorklund
Lance Corporal J. Longburn
Lance Corporal J. Meager
Parachutist J. Brosnahan
Parachutist P. Burke
Parachutist W. J. Gallier
Parachutist W. H. Giles
Parachutist A. Harman
Parachutist C. Manners
Parachutist F. Mulvey
Parachutist C. McConnell
Parachutist J. Morbin
Parachutist J. Murphy
Parachutist E. Pernell
Parachutist A. Tate
Parachutist F. Taylor
Parachutist W. Whittaker
Parachutist G. Wooding

Drop Four: 10 March
Lieutenant J. Riccomini
Corporal W. Cunningham
Parachutist S. Carlisle

Drop 5: 24 March
Trooper D. Kirkpatrick

By Foot: 17 March
Serjeant S. Guscott
Parachutist R. Ramos

APPENDIX TWO

Casualties (SAS) on Operation Tombola (taken from the SAS post-operational report)

2nd SAS Regiment
Killed
Serjeant S. Guscott
Lance Corporal R. Bruce (Balerdi)

Missing – believed killed
Lieutenant J. Riccomini
Corporal S. Bolden

Wounded
Sergeant F. Hughes
Lance Corporal J. Layburn
Parachutist F. Mulvey
Parachutist S. Carlisle

Injured in parachute drop
Lieutenant J. Easton

Russians
Killed: 3
Wounded: 3
Missing: 6

Italians
Wounded: 3

Bibliography

J. G. Beever, *SOE Recollections and Reflections 1940–45*, The Bodley Head, 1981

Rudolf Bohmler, *Monte Cassino A German View*, Pen & Sword, 1965

Basil Davidson, *Special Operations Europe*, Victor Gollancz, 1980

Roy Farran, *Operation Tombola* (1960), Arms and Armour Press, 1986

Roy Farran, *Winged Dagger: Adventures on Special Service* (1950), Cassell, 1998

Tony Geraghty, *This is the SAS*, Arms and Armour Press, 1982

Matteo Incerti, *Il bracciale di sterline*, Aliberti editore, 2012

Matteo Incerti, *Il paradiso dei folli*, Imprimatur srl, 2017

Matteo Incerti, *Il suonatore matto*, Imprimatur srl, 2014

Michael Lees, *Special Operations Executed*, William Kimber & Co., 1986

Brian Lett, *SAS in Tuscany 1943–1945*, Pen & Sword, 2011

Brian Lett, *SOE's Mastermind*, Pen & Sword, 2016

Gordon Lett, *Rossano: An Adventure of the Italian Resistance*, Hodder and Stoughton, 1955

Laurence Lewis, *Echoes of Resistance: British Involvement with the Italian Partisans*, D. J. Costello, 1985

Charles Macintosh, *From Cloak to Dagger*, William Kimber & Co., 1982

Mike Morgan, *Daggers Drawn*, Sutton Publishing, 2000

Don North, *Inappropriate Conduct*, iUniverse, 2013

Patrick K. O'Donnell, *The Brenner Assignment*, Da Capo Press, 2008

David Stafford, *Mission Accomplished: SOE and Italy 1943–45*, The Bodley Head, 2011

Maurizio Di Terlizzi, *Fieseler Fi-156 Storch in Italian Service* (Aviolibri Special 12), IBN, 2009

Ex-Lance Corporal X, *The SAS and LRDG Roll of Honour 1941–47*, SAS-LRDG-RoH.com, 2016

Maurice Yacowar, *Roy & Me*, AU Press, 2010

Index

BLIND VETERANS UK

Blind Veterans UK is the national charity for blind and vision-impaired ex-Service men and women. They believe that no one who has served our country should have to battle blindness alone.

Founded in 1915, the charity's initial purpose was to help and support soldiers blinded in the First World War. But the organisation has gone on to support more than 35,000 blind veterans and their families, spanning the Second World War to recent conflicts including Iraq and Afghanistan.

The charity was established by Sir Arthur Pearson, founder of the Daily Express and President of the Royal National Institute of Blind People, in response to blinded soldiers returning from the Front during the First World War.

Pearson had lost his own sight through glaucoma, but was determined to continue his life actively. He was determined to ensure that the blind veterans of the First World War would receive the training and support they needed to live fulfilling, independent lives.

This same work continues today and while they initially cared for veterans blinded in active Service, today they will help veterans no matter what caused their sight loss.

No matter how long they served or how they lost their sight, Blind Veterans UK are here to support ex-Service men and women experiencing severe sight loss. The veterans range from those suffering from macular degeneration and age-related conditions, to veterans injured in Iraq, Afghanistan and other military conflicts.

The charity has two training and rehabilitation centres, in Brighton and Llandudno, which provide training, respite and residential care as well as recreational facilities. They also provide services and support across the UK via a network of nineteen community teams.

Services offered by Blind Veterans UK include rehabilitation programs, art and craft classes, sports and recreation, clubs and societies, information technology and independent living training, care and welfare.

Blind Veterans UK currently supports over 4,700 veterans, more than ever before in the charity's history. Visit blindveterans.org.uk/support to learn more about the charity and how you can support its vital work today.